VIOLENCE IN THE WORK OF COMPOSITION

VIOLENCE IN THE WORK OF COMPOSITION

Recognizing, Intervening, Ameliorating

EDITED BY
SCOTT GAGE
AND KRISTIE S. FLECKENSTEIN

UTAH STATE UNIVERSITY PRESS
Logan

© 2022 by University Press of Colorado

Published by Utah State University Press
An imprint of University Press of Colorado
245 Century Circle, Suite 202
Louisville, Colorado 80027

 The University Press of Colorado is a proud member of
the Association of University Presses.

The University Press of Colorado is a cooperative publishing enterprise supported, in part, by Adams State University, Colorado State University, Fort Lewis College, Metropolitan State University of Denver, University of Alaska Fairbanks, University of Colorado, University of Denver, University of Northern Colorado, University of Wyoming, Utah State University, and Western Colorado University.

∞ This paper meets the requirements of the ANSI/NISO Z39.48–1992 (Permanence of Paper).

ISBN: 978-1-64642-279-1 (paperback)
ISBN: 978-1-64642-280-7 (ebook)
https://doi.org/10.7330/9781646422807

Library of Congress Cataloging-in-Publication Data

Names: Gage, Scott, 1980– editor. | Fleckenstein, Kristie S., editor.
Title: Violence in the work of composition : recognizing, intervening, ameliorating / edited by Scott Gage and Kristie S. Fleckenstein.
Description: Logan : Utah State University Press, [2022] | Includes bibliographical references and index.
Identifiers: LCCN 2022019664 (print) | LCCN 2022019665 (ebook) | ISBN 9781646422791 (paperback) | ISBN 9781646422807 (ebook)
Subjects: LCSH: English language—Rhetoric—Study and teaching (Higher)—Social aspects. | Violence in language.
Classification: LCC PE1404 .V56 2022 (print) | LCC PE1404 (ebook) | DDC 808/.042071173—dc23/eng/20220520
LC record available at https://lccn.loc.gov/2022019664
LC ebook record available at https://lccn.loc.gov/2022019665

The University Press of Colorado gratefully acknowledges the support of the Texas A&M University–San Antonio toward this publication.

Cover illustration © pathdoc/Shutterstock.

To those who battle every day, with body, mind, and spirit, against the violences of white supremacy, and to those whose battles seek a world made anew in justice.
SG

To my students, who delight me, inspire me, and always, always teach me.
KSF

CONTENTS

ACKNOWLEDGMENTS

Although we title this book *Violence in the Work of Composition*, we might have as appropriately titled it *Hope in the Work of Composition*. For though the ensuing chapters look unflinchingly at evidence of violence within classrooms and programs, they are equally unflinching in their embrace of hope. Individually and collectively, they embody what Martin Luther King Jr. calls acceptance of "finite disappointment" while remaining steadfast to "infinite hope." In the spirit of that infinite hope, we thank the many people who supported this project.

To begin, we thank our contributors. We are grateful for your patience and compassion as we tried, and all too frequently failed, to offer feedback without inflicting editorial violence. We are grateful, as well, for your commitment to this project and for all you have done to provide us with a more profound understanding of the stakes that accompany our work as compositionists. You helped us to recognize the dismaying breadth of violence's reach across our discipline, offered strategies for contending with that violence, and deepened our hope in violence's cessation. We like to think that this collection is but a first step.

Just as we learned from our contributors, so have we learned from the students who so generously shared their voices and experiences across the chapters of this book. Without their courage in speaking, this collection would have been sadly impoverished. In the same spirit, we thank our own students—past and present—who always ignite hope in our hearts and who always instruct us in the humanity (and humility) required to teach in an age of violence. We are more fully caring, more fully committed to kindness in and out of the classroom because of you, and, thus, we acknowledge your gifts to us.

Because no book of this kind can exist without the support of colleagues, we thank those whose influence weaves invisibly in and out of these pages. In particular, Scott thanks his colleagues in the Department of Language, Literature, and Arts, whose dedication to the difficult, and often uneven, work of antiracism and decolonization emboldens him with hope and purpose. Scott also thanks the colleagues who work with him in the First-Year Composition program: Lizbett Tinoco, Sonya Eddy, Sarah Dwyer, Lisa Jennings, Curt Meyer, Christen Barron, Petra Baruca, Aravis Thomas, Sam Garcia, Amarilis Castillo, Robert Cavazos, Robert Talbert, Yvette Torres, and April Poissant. You inspire him, you encourage him, and you teach him. Similarly, Kris thanks the Department of English for its steadfast commitment to diversity and antiracism in hiring practices, in classroom practices, and in support of each other. In addition, Kris thanks Sue Hum, Nancy Myers, Kathi Yancey, and Michael Neal for their support and, especially, for their patient encouragement as they listened to evolving ideas, read drafts, and provided generous and invaluable feedback.

Next, we thank Utah State University Press for finding value in this book, and we extend our deepest gratitude to Rachael Levay, both for her ongoing support of the project and for her kindness as we completed it. As important, we thank our reviewers, who, while praising our vision, also provided valuable and transformative insight on where we fell short. Scott specifically thanks those reviewers who provided insightful comments that informed his revision of the introduction. As a result of their feedback, he has grown not only as a writer but also, and more importantly, as a human being struggling to see and respond ethically to violence in its myriad forms. The collection as a whole has benefitted immeasurably from your thorough and honest responses, and we thank you. In addition, we also offer our sincerest thanks to the production crew at University Press of Colorado, led by the inestimable Daniel Pratt, who possesses the gift of listening care-fully.

Thank you to Texas A&M University–San Antonio, and thank you specifically Dean Debra Feakes; Dr. Katherine Gillen; and the Language, Literature, and Art Department's Advisory Council, for the subvention funding provided in support of this book.

Finally, we thank our families. Scott thanks Katie and Vera for their love, for their belief, and for their forgiveness. Kris thanks her family— Anna, Mark, Ian, Lukas, and Morgan—for solving computer glitches, listening as she repeatedly rehashed ideas, and reminding her that risks, especially emotional ones, are always worth taking. The best way to learn to love is to love.

So many people, named and unnamed, helped with this collection, and we thank them all. Together, we are jointly committed to mitigating violence, even if only in small ways, so that our students, our children, and our children's children will live less with finite disappointment and more with infinite hope.

VIOLENCE IN THE WORK OF COMPOSITION

Introduction

RECOGNIZING, INTERVENING, AMELIORATING

Responding to Violence in the Work of Composition

Scott Gage

The ensuing chapters of this collection introduce students grappling with violence in its myriad, pernicious forms. A Black undergraduate student compelled to suppress their voice, identity, and lived experiences by the dictates of a writing program's Eurocentric learning outcomes. Students entering the composition classroom classified, differentiated, and (de)valued by longitudinal assessments of their emotional and behavioral characteristics. Students required to engage with and through digital interfaces that both reify the white normative body and jeopardize student subjectivity. A white undergraduate student from a rural and impoverished background subtly coerced to conform to middle-class narrative expectations by editing and tempering their lived experiences. Graduate student tutors risking multiple forms of retraumatization—their own and others'—as they work with writing center clients struggling with disclosures of sexual violence.

The chapters here also introduce faculty, tenured and nontenured, contingent and graduate, grappling with ways to alleviate or mitigate the violence that infiltrates their students' academic lives. The composition instructor on Indigenous land listening to, learning from, and establishing relationships with local elders. The writing center director preparing tutors to resist linguistic imperialism. The writing program administrator (WPA) collaborating with faculty and graduate teaching assistants (GTAs) to develop nonviolent means to respond to violent student writing. Individually and collectively, these teachers and administrators identify instances and spaces of violence or the threat of violence in their own work. They, then, strive to avert it entirely, or to divert it in part.

Nor are these faculty safe from violence. Just as students are entangled in the coils of institutional and disciplinary violence, so too are

https://doi.org/10.7330/9781646422807.c000

faculty, even if not always equitably. The instructor of an online composition course whose university's free speech policies silence their ability to respond to a student's anti-LGBTQ+ hate speech. The female WPA subject to a faculty member's increasingly overt and hostile misogyny. And, just as faculty are vulnerable to violence, we are equally at risk of perpetrating violence. As institutional agents, faculty are positioned (more so than students) to walk a razor's edge between suffering the ravages of violence and inflicting those ravages, unintentionally or not. The WPA whose disciplinary arguments about the value of multimodal composing ignore and negate students' access to and relationships with technology. The composition instructor who performs argumentative violence despite their pedagogical investment in nonviolent forms of argument.

These brief snapshots describe just a few of the students and teachers contending with violence in their lived experiences across our discipline. The snapshots also demonstrate the troubling extent to which violence both circulates through and structures our discipline and the labor that defines it. *Violence in the Work of Composition* takes such violence as its focus. The collection's many voices arise from spaces that contend with violence as it inflects and, perhaps, infects the work we perform across our most common disciplinary sites, namely our classrooms, writing programs, and writing centers. Understood across this collection as any influence limiting a living being's capacity to achieve full realization (Galtung 1969), violence is interwoven with our discipline in ways both overt and covert. Overt violence is Slavoj Žižek's (2008) "subjective violence" (1), Johan Galtung's (1969) "personal or direct" violence (170). It is violence involving "a clear subject-object relation" (Galtung 1969, 171) through which harm is exacted on flesh and/or psyche by "a clearly identifiable agent" (Žižek 2008, 1) who apparently intends to wound or, at worst, kill. It is visible as an "event" (Galtung 1990, 294), a seemingly "irrational explosion," a "perturbation of the 'normal,' peaceful state of things" (Žižek 2008, 2). Visible to "barefoot empiricism" (Galtung 1990, 294–95), overt violence appears quantifiable, subject to representation through the number, the percentage, the statistic.

Covert violent, in contrast, escapes and resists quantification; it escapes and resists visibility. It is Žižek's (2008) "objective violence" (1), Galtung's (1969) "structural violence" (171). It is the system that engenders "unequal power . . . and unequal life chances" (171) as well as the "subtle forms of coercion that sustain relations of domination and exploitation" (Žižek 2008, 9). It is the "invisible background" (10), the "tranquil waters" (Galtung 1969, 173), the "air . . . one learns how to breathe" (Lawrence and Karim 2007, 5). A product of the institutionalization and normalization of unequal power distributions, covert violence provides a breeding ground for social injustice. That injustice, in turn, erupts into overt violence, binding both overt and covert violence in an insidious and often deadly feedback loop.

This book is a collection about both students and the faculty committed to their flourishing, despite our complicated relationship to violence, overt and covert. It is a book about the violence that circulates through our work as compositionists; the violence with which we are complicit without knowing; the violence to which we, as well as our students, are subject; and the violence which we individually and collectively seek to redress. But it is also a collection about the quotidian nature of violence within and across our disciplinary landscape. It is a book that understands violence as always already present both in our lives and in the lives of our students, always already cloaking itself in familiarity, in invisibility, in silence. *Violence in the Work of Composition* represents one effort to break through that silence and reclaim voices, selves, and worlds in the wake of their undoing.

Although a long view of history may suggest a decrease in violence, specifically overt violence (Pinker 2011), a more immediate view suggests the opposite; we are increasingly harming one another overtly through word, fist, and gun, covertly through hierarchy, policy, and law. By addressing these forms of violence in composition studies, this book builds on and extends previous disciplinary work that pierces the silence of and on violence. For example, teacher-scholars such as Michael Blitz and C. Mark Hurlbert (Blitz and Hurlbert 1998) have wrestled with the burdens overt violence introduces into the classroom, while J. Elspeth Stuckey (1991) has interrogated the teaching of literacy as a covert violence regulating socioeconomic access. More recently, Paul Heilker (2015) has asked, "In how many ways, and to how great a degree, is writing instruction . . . violent?" (49–50). Asao Inoue (2019) provides one answer to Heilker's question, arguing that the imposition of a single standard in writing classrooms "lead[s], if one pushes the logic far enough, to killing" (307). *Violence in the Work of Composition* is indebted to these teacher-scholars, who, among many others cited across the collection, have raised concerned voices demanding we pay attention to the interrelationship between violence and composition studies. Despite their efforts, their warnings and concerns, attention to violence in our discipline has not been focal, stable, or systematic. Rather, that attention tends to treat violence indirectly, frequently naming and addressing specific iterations of violence instead of also naming and addressing violence itself. Centering violence as its focus, this collection contributes to three goals: first, recognizing and acknowledging the threads of overt and covert violence that weave through our work as teachers and administrators; second, devising strategies that intervene in violence to curtail its emergence, limit its scope, and diminish its effects; and third, considering new ways of thinking about violence that offer hope for mitigating it beyond the immediate classroom or programmatic initiative. In addressing these goals, *Violence in the Work of Composition* invites systematic scrutiny of violence, maps violence as event and process, and envisions concrete ways to redress the harmful material consequences of violence for our discipline, our programs, our students, and ourselves.

VIOLENCE: ITS MEANINGS AND COMPLEXITIES

What is "violence?" As academics, we have been disciplined to answer such questions by defining, examining, and/or critiquing a key term. This disciplining shapes us in profound ways, so I find it difficult to pursue other methods even though I know and *feel* that approaching a term like violence as I have been taught to is both a fraught and troubling process. Brad Evans and Terrell Carver (Evans and Carver 2017) go further, labeling such efforts "perilous and intellectually damaging." "Violence is all about the violation of bodies and the destruction of human lives," they write (5). As such, any effort to intellectualize violence, reducing the lived experience of pain and trauma to a definition, theory, or object of analysis, risks enacting its own violence by diminishing, and perhaps exploiting, the visceral reality of violence's impact on people and communities. As Mark Vorobej (2016) writes, "violence hurts" (1), and examining violence jeopardizes perpetuating that hurt even as such examinations strive to lessen its severity. How, for example, might someone directly impacted by overt violence respond to an effort to fulfill genre convention by defining this collection's key term? Might any effort—and by extension, the genre convention guiding it—exacerbate their grief and anguish, especially given the certainty that any definition of violence offered will fail to honor their experience of it? Fraught and troubling, indeed. Despite their warnings, Evans and Carver (2017) do not argue that we should not define or examine violence, only that violence should "never be studied in an objective or unimpassioned way" (5).

Adding to the challenges of defining violence is that violence is complicated, "a multilayered, complex phenomenon that is difficult to conceptualize" (Engels 2015, 145). Vorobej (2016) offers similar insight, writing that "violence remains a complex, unwieldy, and highly contested concept" (1). Several factors contribute. For example, violence can "take ever new forms" (Bernstein 2013, 177), or as Han Byung-Chul (2018) asserts, "violence is simply protean" (vii). Additionally, violence is deeply paradoxical, encompassing both destruction and creation (Rae and Ingala 2019). Perhaps the most important factor contributing to the complexity of violence, and with it, the difficulty of wrangling it into an academic definition, is the range of actions and consequences that may be recognized as violent or nonviolent as well as those for which such labels are at best ambiguous: " 'Violence' is a vague term because it has a fuzzy and indeterminate range of application. In other words, many acts . . . clearly qualify as being violent, and many acts are clearly disqualified as not being violent. But in between these two extremes, there exist a large number of borderline . . . cases where it's just not clear . . . as to whether the act in question is violent" (Vorobej 2016, 3). What is clear is the following: limiting violence to physical harm and destruction alone is insufficient, and perhaps itself an act of violence or cruelty. Jon Pahl (2010) argues as much, contending that violence consists of bodily injury and "social and linguistic systems of exclusion and collective coercion, degradation, or destruction of property, persons, and the environment" (15). Gavin Rae and Emma Ingala (Rae and Ingala 2019) extend Pahl's argument, writing that violence's "physical variety is not the fundamental one." Rather, violence is "constitutive of . . . institutions, language, logic, subjectivity" (1).

If the term "violence" only referred to physical harm, then all we could ever say of violence is that it occurs at the moment of wounding and incapacitation. Although clearly instantiations of violence, such moments are always already preceded by, and interwoven with, covert forms of violence. For this reason, and in hopeful respect to those who have suffered, and who are continuing to suffer, from violence in its myriad forms, *Violence in the Work of Composition* embraces a capacious understanding of violence as any influence that decreases a living being's potential to thrive, flourish, and achieve full realization. The definition emerges from Galtung (1969), who writes, "*Violence is present when human beings are being influenced so that their actual somatic and mental realizations are below their potential realizations*" (168, emphasis original). Violence, he continues, is "*the cause of the difference between the potential and the actual,* between what could have been and what is" (168, emphasis original). In a later work, defining violence as "avoidable insults to basic human needs" (Galtung 1990, 292), or more simply as "needs-deprivation" (295), Galtung has, across his career, offered definitions of violence that, first, neither diminish nor exclude the range of experiences people and communities have had with violence and that, second, create definitional space for violence's complexity, including its mutability, paradoxes, and ambiguities. Of course, each definition of violence "brings with it certain costs and benefits" (Vorobej 2016, 2), including areas of unawareness such as Galtung's failure to account for gender (Confortini 2006). Acknowledging Galtung's limitations, this collection sees in his definitions an important benefit: a framework through which to speak about violence in spaces where violence may not always be readily apparent, namely the composition classroom, the writing program, and the writing center, and to do so in ways sensitive to violence's multifaceted impact on living beings.

Central to Galtung's work on violence is a three-part taxonomy including direct, structural, and cultural violence. Direct violence is the most overt form in Galtung's triad. This form of violence occurs interpersonally between people and communities and frequently involves physical injury, with killing its most extreme expression. Direct violence is, therefore, largely understood as a decidedly visible form of violence. It is violence in which the perpetrators may be seen, named, or observed; it is violence that "has an author" (Galtung and Höivik 1971, 73). Žižek (2008) concurs, writing that subjective violence, Žižek's term for violence that may be attributable to specific individuals or groups, is "the most visible" enactment of human violence (1). Although direct violence and its consequences may be readily observable as a wound upon a body, it may also result in harm that is less easily seen, marked, or recorded, such as psychological abuse or injury. As Galtung (1969) himself explains, the "borderline between physical and psychological personal violence is not very clear" (175). Nor does direct violence have to assume expression through fist or weapon; it can manifest through speech, including threats, which, Galtung (1990) argues, are "also violence" (292). No matter the form direct violence assumes, the impacts are similar: destruction, degradation, dehumanization. Those impacts resonate with Elaine Scarry's (1985) argument that physical pain erodes the world-making potential of the individual subjected to it. As Scarry contends, pain, whether inflicted through torture or some other means of direct violence, is "language-destroying" (20); it strangles the language potential of the body experiencing pain, frequently reducing that body "to the sounds and cries a human being makes before language is learned" (4). In stripping the body's capacity for language, pain—and the direct violence producing it—undermines the body's capacity to assert subjectivity and to participate in world-creation. At stake in direct violence, then, whether realized through a gun or through a grade, is "the making and unmaking of the world" (23).

If direct violence is the most overt form of violence in Galtung's triad, then structural violence is the most covert. This form of violence emerges from systemic inequalities, "above all in the distribution of power" (Galtung 1969, 175). It involves granting and denying access, privilege, and opportunities to lead fully realized lives. Accruing over time, structural violence kills "slowly, and undramatically," whereas direct violence kills "quickly" (Galtung and Höivik 1971, 73). And because structural violence emanates from systems, hierarchies, and laws, identifying a single human agent, or even multiple human agents, responsible for the violence proves difficult if not impossible. As Galtung and Höivik (1971) argue, structural violence is "anonymous" (73). These aspects of structural violence render it a covert and largely invisible form of human violence. Put starkly in comparison to the physical wounding caused by direct violence, structural violence "does not show" (Galtung 1969, 173). Again, Žižek (2008) agrees, arguing that objective violence, his term for systemic forms of violence, is "invisible," a repercussion of "the smooth functioning of our economic and political systems" (2). For Žižek, then, structural, or objective, violence forms "the background which generates . . . outbursts" (1) of direct, or subjective, violence. This framing, therefore, presents explosions of direct violence not as anomalies in an otherwise peaceful world but as a violence engendered by larger systems and structures. Thus, structural violence appears to do more than distribute power and resources inequitably; it sets the material and political conditions in which some bodies are accepted while other bodies are rejected, some bodies are able to succeed while other bodies are more likely to fail, and some bodies live while others are killed or allowed to die.

The third form of violence in Galtung's taxonomy, cultural violence, stalks the boundary between overt and covert violence. This violence also lurks at the intersection of direct and structural violence, providing legitimacy and justification to both. As Hannah Arendt (1970) explains, violence, by its instrumental nature, "always stands in need of guidance and justification" (51). Cultural violence fulfills this need. Through internationalization (Galtung 1990), cultural violence renders direct and structural violence "acceptable in society" (292). Encompassing "the symbolic sphere of our existence" (291), including language, ideology, art, and so on, it "preaches, teaches, admonishes, eggs on, and dulls us into seeing exploitation and/or repression as normal and natural, or into not seeing them . . . at all" (295). Because cultural violence can manifest through rhetoric, it functions overtly as an act of violence we may read or hear and attribute to an identifiable actor at the same time that it functions covertly since rhetoric itself does not produce visible injury. Rhetoric can, however, "encourage us to see the world in ways that lead to violence" (Engels 2015, 15). It can also "create an environment in which violence can seem logical, necessary, justifiable, and even righteous" (16). By generating such contexts, cultural violence inhibits the ability to recognize "the everyday forces that produce and promote violence" (3). If people cannot register those forces, then they may "no longer see[k] to eliminate [violence], nor even understand it" (Lawrence and Karim 2007, 5). We may, in fact, overlook or disregard violence, accepting it as normal, as "routine" (5). In cultural violence, then, is the possibility of forgetting violence both as it ravages communities and as it emerges from the ideologies, assumptions, and rhetorics informing our work as compositionists.

The voices in and across the chapters comprising *Violence in the Work of Composition* speak to each form of violence in Galtung's triad as it both emerges from and circulates through the work we perform across our most common disciplinary sites, namely our classrooms, writing programs, and writing centers. In doing so, the chapters call us to treat violence as a central concern for compositionists teaching in a millennium marked heavily by violence (Lawrence and Karim 2007, 3). That call is even more exigent in a politically, economically, and culturally divisive moment where the efforts to dismantle structural and cultural violences are met with not only structural and cultural resistance but with direct violence. That is, the chapters, and the voices speaking through them, call us to hold steady and vigilant attention on violence as we perform the labor of our discipline, for, as the chapters remind us, violence is a presence and influence always already shaping and emerging from our work as compositionists; it is always already inevitable. However, although violence is inevitable, "it is not inexorable as an evil force" (13). The voices comprising and echoing across this book call us to remember that as well. Specifically, they call us to remember that we are "better served by limiting the harmful effects of violence" (13). The chapters here offer three responses that limit these effects.

RESPONDING TO VIOLENCE: RECOGNIZING, INTERVENING, AMELIORATING

The first response, recognizing, limits violence's capacity to conceal itself and exact harm covertly. Although overt violence seems most prevalent because of its stark visibility, violence more often inflicts pain and suffering in ways both subtle and obscure. As Richard Bernstein (2013) explains,

"Violence does not appear in the world 'marked' as violence. Violence disguises itself. It presents itself as something innocent, necessary, justified, legitimate" (178). Presenting itself in these ways, violence fades into the backgrounds of our everyday lived experiences; it becomes part of our normal, and so becomes difficult to see. Engels (2015) confirms the challenges of perceiving violence in everyday life, writing, "It is hard to see the violence inherent in what we take to be normal" (142). When we cannot clearly see violence, when we cannot clearly detail its presence and impact in our lives, then its damage persists, steady, without notice, and often without resistance. Thus, the effects of covert violence accumulate, killing gently over the course of our lives. Recognizing responds to these effects by revealing and illuminating covert violence, by exposing it as violence, bare and unmistakable. It does so through systematic critique and analysis, bringing violence to "public self-consciousness" (Bernstein 2013, 177). Exposing violence through recognizing is crucial, because "[w]e can only seriously consider a proper response to violence when we analyze and understand it" (177). Recognizing supports our understanding of violence; it helps us to see the myriad complex and ambiguous ways violence exists in our lives. In doing so, recognizing prepares us to answer, to take action, to intervene.

If recognizing supports our ability to see and understand the presence and influence of violence in our lives, then intervening supports our ability to disrupt the material consequences of violence. More specifically, intervening supports our ability to decrease or eliminate the distance Galtung (1969) argues that violence generates between a living being's potential well-being and their actual well-being. Intervening is, therefore, a form of social action, which Kristie S. Fleckenstein (2010) defines as "behavior designed to increase individual and collective human dignity, value, and quality of life" (1). It is action "motivated by the desire to improve aspects of reality that harm individuals and communities" (5). Importantly, intervening as a form of social action is not separate from recognizing. Rather, it is a partner to recognizing. As Fleckenstein (2010) explains, social action "includes the recognition of oppression, deprivation, cruelty, and violence as well as the desire to change those ills" (5). Such desire is an essential counterpart to recognizing, since by itself recognizing offers no recourse for mitigating violence's capacity to harm, raising challenging questions about the value and ethics of studying and critiquing violence. As Evans and Carver (2017) ask, "Why study violence, after all, unless more peaceful relations among people are to be imagined?" (3). Intervening supports our ability to imagine those more peaceful relations. Moreover, intervening supports our ability to act so as to bring both those relations and the conditions fostering them into existence.

Although intervening helps us to limit or alleviate the harm violence inflicts, it is insufficient in and of itself to wholly remedy violence, necessitating a third form of response: ameliorating. Intervening is insufficient because the actions we take to redress violence are frequently limited to a specific instantiation of violence; they are frequently guided by the shape violence takes in a particular context. Thus, while intervening may redress that specific form of violence, it does not account for the ways that form is likely to morph and evolve. As Bernstein (2013) writes, "We cannot anticipate the ways in which violence will manifest itself in the course of history" (177). Because we cannot predict the forms violence will assume, including the harm that could emerge from our very efforts to intervene in violence, responding fully to violence requires constant engagement, including ongoing recognition of violence's new forms as well as ongoing intervention in those forms. Ameliorating supports such persistence. Acknowledging that "there is no escape from violence" (Lawrence and Karim 2007, 13), this form of response treats violence as a permanence constantly unfolding into the future in new iterations. Thus, ameliorating prepares us to engage with violence in a sustained way; it asks us to consistently attend to violence as we move through the world, especially the world of our institutions, programs, and classrooms.

VIOLENCE IN THE WORK OF COMPOSITION: CHAPTER OVERVIEW

As the chapters here seek to recognize, intervene, and ameliorate, they also reveal four key patterns important to violence in our work as compositionists. First, the chapters show that violence in composition can be especially insidious, as it functions covertly, inflicting harm, for example, through disciplinary standards and programmatic or institutional policies. And even in moments when composition's violence is more overt, the chapters remind us that its impact registers primarily at the level of emotion, psychology, or epistemology; it is violence that marks "the mind and the spirit" (Galtung 1990, 294).

Second, whether covert or overt, violence in the work of composition appears across the chapters to set limits on available forms of being and becoming. For students, these limits narrow the range of what is possible for them as humans developing perspective, self, and agency, in part through their composing practices. For compositionists, these limits constrain our potential to be nonviolent—or at least, less violent—in our work, to listen deeply to our students and be present as teachers (O'Reilly 1998), for example, or to attend to our students with compassion (Inoue 2019). In fact, such constraints frequently cast us into roles that produce and promote violence, making us agents of harm despite our best intentions and desires. As Evans and Carver (2017) caution, "Violence is not carried out only by irrational monsters" (6). The chapters of this book confirm their warning, offering various examples of how compositionists can, however unintentionally, become complicit in violence at best, instruments of violence at worst.

Third, the chapters included in this collection ask us to remember that violence in the work of composition is complex. For example, the forms of violence addressed in the chapters occur across various disciplinary sites, with reverberating consequences across time. Violence in composition is, therefore, complex, in part because it is fluid and distributed, circulating through and across both disciplinary and institutional contexts. This dispersal impedes any effort to localize violence in our work, to attempt to contain it and, in so doing, limit the damage and suffering it effects. A counterpart to this aspect of violence is its dependence on context. As Bruce Lawrence and Aisha Karim (Lawrence and Karim 2007) assert, "[Violence] is always contingent on specific structures and human agents situated in temporal-spatial contexts" (14). At the same moment in which the collection's chapters call us to perceive violence's capacity to move, to disperse, to circulate, they also invite us to understand that violence is always bound by the local, always shaping and shaped by the place and conditions in which it appears, as well as by the individuals acting upon and in response to one another in a given situation. Thus, composition's violence is a complexity not only because it is distributed across contexts but also because it is simultaneously situated within a given place and time. As a result, both what violence is and how violence functions in one context will not necessarily resemble what it is and how it functions in another. Violence's complexity introduces difficulty in naming consistent patterns both in the forms violence manifests and in the pain violence inflicts through the work of composition, contributing to equal difficulty preparing for future enactments of violence as well as difficulty developing sustained disciplinary responses. A final aspect of violence's complexity the chapters invite us to grapple with is the interrelation of its forms. The chapters together speak to "the porous boundaries of each violent act" (Lawrence and Karim 2007, 12), illustrating how no form of violence is ever singular, how no form ever operates in isolation. Indeed, the chapters show that violence "always spills over" (12) in the work of composition, with direct forms in the classroom emerging from and reifying structural forms in the writing program, with cultural forms in the discipline legitimizing and perpetuating those structural forms, and so on. Such porosity necessarily complicates how compositionists might respond to the presence and influence of violence in our work, leading to a fourth realization.

Specifically, the chapters here invite awareness that any response to violence, whether in the form of recognizing, intervening, or ameliorating, is as complex as violence itself. To begin with, the responses to violence each chapter addresses often contain within them the potential both to generate new violences and to sustain or support existing violences. Substantiating Galtung's (1990) warning that "one type of violence may be reduced or controlled at the expense or increase or maintenance of another" (293), the chapters demonstrate that any response is always already fraught, always already capable of triggering additional, though unintended, harm. The latent potential of recognizing, intervening, and ameliorating themselves to enact violence signals the difficulty of redressing violence in the work of composition. Next, the chapters show that responding to violence in composition is complicated because any effort to respond presents a nearly insurmountable challenge. For example, structural forms of violence present a "certain stability," so they "may not very often be changed that quickly" (Galtung 1969, 173). As such, responding to structural violence in composition may require years of steadfast, patient, and emotionally taxing labor with sometimes disappointing results. Additionally, direct and structural violence "*seem* often to be coupled in such a way that it is very difficult to get rid of both evils" (185, emphasis original). As one example, a teacher-scholar attempting to address a form of direct violence they identify may be prevented from doing so because of the violence's entanglement with institutionally sanctioned power differentials between teachers and students. Lastly, the chapters reveal that response, like violence, is always multifaceted and intersecting; its forms never occur singularly or in isolation. Thus, recognizing always functions as a facet of intervening, which always entails new ways of recognizing, which can, however fleetingly, open possibilities for ameliorating, and so on. As evidence, the collection's chapters frequently enact multiple forms of response in conjunction with one another, most often moving back and forth between acts of recognition and acts of intervention.

Although recognizing, intervening, and ameliorating cannot be so easily demarcated and disentangled, we have arranged the chapters of *Violence in the Work of Composition* into three parts that emphasize the work specific to each response. This arrangement is not intended to suggest that each response functions separately from the others. Rather, it is intended to help illuminate important characteristics about the ways each response functions, however messily, as an individual disruption in composition's continually unfolding violence. For example, the chapters in part 1, "Recognizing," emphasize that this particular response to violence requires (1) examining contexts beyond a given classroom, writing program, or writing center and (2) auditing the commonplace assumptions and practices informing the work that occurs in those spaces.

This work begins in part 1, "Recognizing," with Jamila Kareem's "Covert Racial Violence in National High-School-to-College Writing Transition Outcomes," in which the author addresses a critical moment in students' lives as writers: the transition from writing in high school to writing in college. Kareem argues that the disciplinary guidelines informing this transition, specifically the WPA Outcomes Statement for First-Year Composition, enact covert racial violence through their privileging of Eurocentric epistemological perspectives. These perspectives inhibit minoritized students from successfully transitioning into the composition classroom. Thus, Kareem demonstrates the need to extend recognizing beyond the context of a single composition classroom. By examining the moment of transition from high school to college, Kareem invites recognition of this moment as a temporal space marked by a racialized violence in which composition is directly implicated.

While Kareem asks us to consider the violence impacting students as they transition into the composition classroom, Kerry Banazek and Kellie Sharp-Hoskins invite consideration of the violence that occurs as disciplinary arguments traverse institutional levels, traveling both upward toward university administration and downward toward the composition classroom. In "Scalar Violence in Composition," Banazek and Sharp-Hoskins contend that violence in composition is always a function of scale, arising, in particular, as arguments travel across institutional levels without sensitivity to the values, subjectivities, and lived experiences of the people occupying each level. Demonstrating their argument through a hypothetical scenario in which a writing program administrator ushers arguments for digital composition up and down levels of scale, the authors emphasize the complexities involved with recognizing violence in the work of composition, especially as that violence emerges from various institutional locations. In this way, Banazek and Sharp-Hoskins exemplify the necessity of interrogating multiple contexts simultaneously when recognizing violence in composition.

Pushing the work of recognizing further, Lisa Dooley extends composition's relationship with violence beyond a single pedagogical experience to the assessment practices students are subjected to as early as grade school. Focusing both on ACT's WorkKeys Suite and on ACT Engage, Dooley argues that these forms of neoliberal assessment, which measure and seek to remediate students' social and emotional behaviors, enact the violence of colonization as they wedge students into categories defining their potential for future workplace success. Such violence acts slowly, both accruing over time and shaping students in the years preceding their presence in our classrooms. Compositionists, Dooley argues, are responsible for addressing such violence not only because it impacts the students with whom we will one day work but also because it intersects with our disciplinary expertise on assessment. "Recognizing Slow Violences and Decolonizing Neoliberal Assessment Practices," therefore, presents an urgent call for compositionists to expand the work of recognizing violence by perceiving its presence across students' educational lives. Recognizing violence in composition, Dooley ultimately shows, requires an examination of students' lives to identify moments where the violence students experience long before entering our classrooms is surreptitiously interrelated with the very work we perform in those classrooms.

If the three chapters that open part 1 address contexts beyond but related to the composition classroom, the three chapters that close part 1 address readily familiar classroom practices. Addressing violence's dependence on specific contexts, rather than its movement across contexts, these chapters suggest that recognizing composition's violence involves deep and honest auditing of common assumptions and practices. Katherine Bridgman's chapter "By Design: Violence and Digital Interfaces" begins this work. In the chapter, Bridgman examines the inclusion of digital technologies in the composition classroom, specifically elucidating the cultural violence introduced through digital interfaces. Focusing on Blackboard, Bridgman reveals that such platforms, under the guise of transparency, privilege the normate body and, in doing so, both erase students' embodied subjectivities within the classroom and legitimate such erasures beyond the classroom. In the commonplace practice of teaching writing with digital technology, then, Bridgman helps us recognize the risk of introducing an insidious violence that, in eliding students' embodied subjectivities within the classroom, ripples outward from the classroom and justifies increasingly lethal forms of violence.

Just as Bridgman recognizes violence in a common pedagogical practice among compositionists—the teaching of writing with digital technology—Trevor C. Meyer recognizes violence in a common pedagogical focus: the teaching of argument. In "The Productive Violence of Pedagogy: Argumentation and Change in the Writing Course," Meyer reviews major theories of argumentation across our discipline's history to reveal that our approaches to teaching argument have trapped us in a zero-sum game in which any orientation to argument results in pedagogical violence, even those most explicitly striving for nonviolence. Thus, Meyer argues for a new orientation to argument that embraces its inevitable partnership with violence as pedagogically productive. Such an orientation treats violence as generative, supporting students in their rhetorical ability to disagree effectively and to engage discursively with difference. Meyer's chapter reveals the paradoxes involved in any effort to teach nonviolent forms of argument to achieve nonviolent ends. In doing so, it highlights the deep interrogations necessary for recognizing violence in our everyday classrooms practices.

Part 1 concludes with Cathryn Molloy and Jim Zimmerman's chapter, " 'I've Gotten a Lot of Sympathy and That's Not What I'm Looking For': Epistemic and Ontological Violence in Writing as Healing Pedagogies." This chapter, like the two that precede it, suggests a disconcerting potential for compositionists to inflict harm on students by asking them to engage in the most fundamental practice of our discipline: writing. Specifically, Molloy and Zimmerman expose the violence that can be enacted on students through one of the most common features of any composition classroom: the writing prompt. Focusing on classrooms that employ writing as healing pedagogical approaches, the authors argue that the prompts circulated in such classrooms risk enacting violence on students, especially when they include compulsory disclosures of pain. Drawing from a mixed-methods study, Molloy and Zimmerman invite recognition of two forms of violence resulting from such prompts: epistemic and ontological violence. Offering a third example of recognizing's potential to uncover the violence lurking in routine classroom practices, Molloy and Zimmerman invite examination of even the most seemingly benign aspects of our work.

Whereas the chapters included in part 1 emphasize recognizing as a response to composition's violence, presenting myriad forms of interrogation through which we may reveal this violence, the chapters included in part 2 emphasize intervening and present myriad disruptions in the violences that recognizing helps us to see. Despite the different forms of action and disruption they describe, the chapters included in part 2, "Intervening," demonstrate striking consistency in their representation of what intervening is and how it functions as a response to composition's violence. Specifically, all of the chapters affirm three important features of intervening. First, the chapters suggest that intervening both emerges from and responds to local contexts. Thus, intervening in composition's violence necessitates intimate engagement with the locations in which we perform the work of our discipline. Second, the chapters show that intervening is itself subject to violence, specifically the structural violences emerging from institutions. Across part 2, the authors encounter institutional constraints, their efforts to intervene in composition's violence often frustrated by institutional culture and policy. Such moments show that intervening, always already set in opposition to a local status quo, is subversive and revolutionary (and by extension, that composition's violence persists through the maintenance of the status quo). Third, part 2's chapters highlight actions critical to, and constitutive of, intervening: collaboration, reflection, and narration.

Part 2 begins with Allison Hargreaves's "kn k'ək'niyaʔ / *I'm listening*: Rhetorical Sovereignty and the Composition Classroom." Hargreaves's chapter offers a compelling portrait of a scholar-practitioner responding to local context. Specifically, Hargreaves demonstrates the power of listening in her effort to teach, as a non-Indigenous woman, in ways that honor and heal on land wounded by settler colonialism. Listening, Hargreaves shows, entails making students of ourselves so that we may learn from the land on which we teach, including its knowledges, languages, histories, and people. Hargreaves shares what she has learned about intervening: composition's ongoing involvement in the violence of settler colonialism cannot be redressed simply by adding Indigenous writers to a course reading list or by fostering more inclusive classrooms; it must involve positioning ourselves as guests on native lands and localizing writing instruction in collaboration with Indigenous stakeholders.

While Hargreaves shows how intervening can emerge from the local contexts in which we work, provided we both listen to and learn from those contexts, Joshua L. Daniel and Lynn Lewis show how broader national contexts can infuse the local with violence and set limits on intervention. Noting an alarming uptick in the circulation of hate speech and incidents of violence on our campuses since the 2016 US presidential election, the authors present a local context marred by national politics, fear and anger, and, most significantly, a felt sense of acceleration, leaving them always hurried, always harried, and barely able to keep up with the work of administrating a composition program. Across "In the Weeds," Daniel and Lewis share their experiences through four anecdotes narrating their efforts to perform the day-to-day work of writing program administration in the midst of increasingly explicit expressions of misogyny and unsettling suggestions of direct violence on campus.

Importantly, the authors accompany their narratives with moments of individual and collective reflection. These moments offer Daniel and Lewis opportunities to stop, breathe, and process their experiences. The moments, then, offer us insight into reflection's potential to support intervening by supporting deceleration.

"In the Weeds" emphasizes reflection's capacity to help us slow down and process the experience of violence in our work, offering compositionists a moment, however fleeting, to re-center and to carry ourselves forward. The next chapter in part 2, "Antiracism is Antiviolence: Utilizing Antiracist Writing Assessment Theory to Mitigate Violence in Writing Centers," emphasizes reflection's capacity to support intervening through self-interrogation. In this chapter, Eric Camarillo recognizes academia's emphasis on correcting student writing as a form of imperialist violence reifying white language supremacy. Concerned that the writing center he directs at a Hispanic-Serving Institution may be participating in this violence, Camarillo draws on Asao Inoue and Nancy Grimm to argue for an antiracist ecological model of assessment through which the writing center may make imperialism's violence explicit and through which both tutor and student may confront dominant academic discourses.

If the chapters comprising part 2 show that intervening always occurs within specific contexts shaped by institutional cultures and policies, then Elizabeth Powers's chapter, "Cultivating Response to Hate Speech in the Digital Classroom," shows the structural violence such policies can inflict on intervening itself. Specifically, her chapter addresses the severe limitations that one institution's student free speech policy set on Powers's ability to intervene in the circulation of anti-LGBTQ+ hate speech in an online classroom. Powers's chapter presents a troubling narrative in which a student was able to continue trolling their class, posting anti-trans messaging to the class's discussion board, not in spite of institutional policy but because of it. Powers's chapter highlights the structural violence that can arise from the tense dance between on-the-ground needs in the classroom and institutional policies that are often far removed from such spaces. The chapter also shows how Powers adapts "rhetorical looking" to develop a set of protocols for communication and community-building in the online classroom.

Powers reminds us that institutions can inflict structural violence on compositionists seeking interventions against violence within their classrooms. In contrast, Thomas Sura and Ellen Skirvin show what interventions may be possible when administrators at the programmatic level take violence seriously, both in student writing and in teacher response, and actively pursue tactics for mitigating such violence. In "Rhetorical In(ter)vention: Teacher Guides for Responding to Covert Violence in Student Writing," Sura and Skirvin address the covert violence that emerges when students argue in ways that deny the immanent value of others. Sura specifically highlights the ways invitational rhetoric may support compositionists, especially new and developing teachers, both in identifying covert violence in student argumentation and in cultivating responses that neither replicate nor exacerbate that violence. As the author contends, compositionists have a responsibility to respond to covert violence when it appears in students' arguments, but, if we fail to employ nonviolent means in our response, we risk perpetuating the very violence in which we hope to intervene. Importantly, Sura and Skirvin extend this responsibility to writing programs, showing that programs, like the teachers laboring within them, bear a responsibility to demonstrate alternatives to covert violence in student argumentation.

The final chapter of part 2, Krista Sarraf's "Training Tutors to Respond: The Potential Violence of Addressing Sexual Violence Disclosures in the Writing Center," takes up Sura and Skirvin's concerns about response to student writing and extends them to students' disclosures of sexual violence during writing center consultations. Sarraf examines the various forms of violence entangled with such disclosures, from policies that strip survivors of control over the terms and locations of disclosure, to writing center sessions that risk retraumatizing both student and tutor alike, and from reporting mandates that cast students as plaintiffs instead of survivors, to the limits those same mandates set on how tutors are able to respond to students who disclose. Sarraf reveals the complex violences involved with sexual violence disclosures in the writing center and argues for a trauma-informed approach to tutor training. This approach seeks a twofold intervention in the violences interwoven with disclosure: the violences tutors risk inflicting on students through their responses to disclosure and the violences writing centers risk inflicting on tutors through training and preparation.

Like many of the contributions to part 2, Sarraf's chapter details the complicated ways intervening can itself become subject to violence. Importantly, Sarraf's chapter also details the complicated ways intervening can itself become a *form* of violence. This blurred differentiation between violence and intervening—between violence and nonviolence—becomes focal in part 3, "Ameliorating." Consisting of a single culminating chapter, part 3 explores violence and nonviolence not as clearly delineated and opposing realms of human action but as two paradoxically aligned human experiences, each always already distinct from the other, each always already contained within the other. Thus, the third and final part of *Violence in the Work of Composition* emphasizes what may be ameliorating's most troubling but important feature: its embodiment as a necessarily incomplete and imperfect process rife with ambiguity.

Kristie S. Fleckenstein shares one pathway through this ambiguity in her chapter, "Vigilant Amelioration through Critical Love: Lessons My Students Taught Me." Fleckenstein begins with the distressing recognition that education, an enterprise she once envisioned as an ideal means for peacefully mitigating violence, is frequently a source of violence. Despite this recognition, and the easy despair and cynicism to which it could give rise, Fleckenstein persists in the hope of education's potential as a corrective to violence. Acknowledging that, alone, our good intentions are inadequate for redressing violence, Fleckenstein offers "critical love" as a means not only to navigate the ambiguous dynamic between violence and nonviolence but also to secure education's capacity to ameliorate violence. As Fleckenstein explains, critical love is an orientation toward others that combines love's openness and care with reason's caution and rationality. Such a stance leads to "vigilant amelioration," a response to violence requiring persistent scrutiny and revision. Examining an experience in which an icebreaker activity produced radically different outcomes, Fleckenstein presents two dynamics in critical love facilitating the emergence of vigilant amelioration: vulnerability and calculability. Together, these dynamics reveal ameliorating to be an emergent practice and offer hope that continually becoming nonviolent in our work as compositionists may be possible even if achieving a stable state of nonviolence is not.

Again, the three parts organizing *Violence in the Work of Composition* are not intended to suggest that recognizing, intervening, and ameliorating function separately from one another. Similarly, the three parts are also not intended to suggest that responding to composition's violence is a linear process that may be pursued in step-by-step fashion. Rather, the arrangement of chapters is intended to offer readers pathways through a charged and complicated conversation about a charged and complicated reality. These pathways invite inter- and intra-organizational relationships among the collection's contents. For example, proceeding in a linear way from beginning to end presents an *inter*relationship among the chapters, especially those within parts I and II. Following this path through those sections of the book invites readers to track violence in composition as it moves from the level of discipline and program down to the level of the classroom, the writing center, and the writing assignment. As readers track composition's violence downward, they may also track a movement within parts I and II from covert expressions of violence in composition to moments when the covert risks becoming overt. For example, Kareem's chapter addresses the disciplinary racialized violence latent within the WPA Outcomes Statement 3.0 while Molloy and Zimmerman focus on the violent constraints writing assignments can set on students' ways of knowing and being.

If reading from beginning to end introduces an interrelationship among the collection's chapters, then reading back and forth across the collection presents an *intra*relationship. Indeed, all chapters comprising *Violence in the Work of Composition* echo one another as they address violence across similar locations and contexts. More specifically, though, the collection generates pairings between the chapters that resonate with one another most loudly across the collection's individual parts, amplifying the voices speaking about similar forms of violence and response. One example of this dialogue occurs when reading Banazek and Sharp-Hoskins's chapter together with Daniel and Lewis's. Both chapters offer perspectives on the violences that emerge and circulate when writing program administrators traverse institutional and programmatic contexts. If Banazek and Sharp-Hoskins ask us to recognize scalar violence as constitutive of the violence shaping and operating through the work of composition, then Daniel and Lewis offer a lived account of what such violence can look like in everyday practice, including the steady emotional exhaustion scalar violence can wring from writing program administrators engaged in fulfilling basic responsibilities. Together, these chapters illustrate the subtle and ever-present impact violence exerts on compositionists generally, and on writing program administrators specifically, as it accrues daily in our professional lives.

Collectively, the chapters included in *Violence in the Work of Composition* offer hope that violence, however deeply embedded in our lives, may be lessened, its harms reduced or at least stayed. As in all work on violence, the "questions proliferate, and the answers provided are provisional" (Lawrence and Karim 2007, 10). Indeed, like Evans and Carver's (2017) collection, *Violence in the Work of Composition* does not "ai[m] to offer definitive conclusions to the problem of violence." At the same time, the chapters here do not "blink at violence" (Lawrence and Karim 2007, 11). Rather, they do the urgent, challenging, and brave work of confronting violence, an act of hope that invites us "to wrestle with [violence's] force and to find ways to transform its potential for destruction into options for growth, if not peace" (14). To be sure, the chapters here are a "provocation to thought" (Evans and Carver 2017, 12), but they are also an instantiation of hope, for it is through hope that this book's voices—students and faculty—can both speak about the myriad violences interwoven with our work and reaffirm our capacity to respond, whether by recognizing, intervening, or ameliorating. It is through hope that we can even assert this capacity. Importantly, *Violence in the Work of Composition* shows that we not only have the capacity to respond to violence but also the obligation to respond, that we have a duty to ease the severity of violence's pain, to dull the sharp edge of its cut. Lives depend on our doing so.

REFERENCES

Arendt, Hannah. 1970. *On Violence.* New York: Houghton Mifflin Harcourt.

Bernstein, Richard J. 2013. *Violence: Thinking without Banisters.* Cambridge: Polity Press.

Blitz, Michael, and C. Mark Hurlbert. 1998. *Letters for the Living: Teaching Writing in a Violent Age.* Urbana: National Council of Teachers of English.

Confortini, Catia C. 2006. "Galtung, Violence, and Gender: The Case for a Peace Studies / Feminism Alliance." *PEACE & CHANGE* 31, no. 3: 333–67.

Engels, Jeremy. 2015. *The Politics of Resentment: A Genealogy.* University Park: Pennsylvania State University Press.

Evans, Brad, and Terrell Carver. 2017. "The Subject of Violence." In *Histories of Violence: Post-War Critical Thought,* edited by Brad Evans and Terrell Carver, 1–13. London: Zed Books.

Fleckenstein, Kristie S. 2010. *Vision, Rhetoric, and Social Action in the Composition Classroom.* Carbondale: Southern Illinois University Press.

Galtung, Johan. 1969. "Violence, Peace, and Peace Research." *Journal of Peace Research* 6, no. 3: 169–91. JSTOR.

Galtung, Johan. "Cultural Violence." 1990. *Journal of Peace Research* 27, no. 3: 291–305. JSTOR.

Galtung, Johan, and Tord Höivik. 1971. "Structural and Direct Violence: A Note on Operationalization." *Journal of Peace Research,* 8, no. 1: 73–76. JSTOR.

Han Byung-Chul. 2018. *Topology of Violence.* Cambridge, MA: MIT Press.

Heilker, Paul. 2015. "Coming to Nonviolence." *The Journal of the Assembly for Expanded Perspectives on Learning* 20: 44–51. https://trace.tennessee.edu/cgi/viewcontent.cgi?article=1263&context=jaepl.

Inoue, Asao B. 2019. *Labor-Based Grading Contracts: Building Equity and Inclusion in the Compassionate Writing Classroom.* Fort Collins: WAC Clearinghouse.

Lawrence, Bruce B., and Aisha Karim. 2007. "General Introduction: Theorizing Violence in the Twenty-First Century." In *On Violence: A Reader,* edited by Bruce B. Lawrence and Aisha Karim, 1–15. Durham: Duke University Press.

O'Reilly, Mary Rose. 1998. *Radical Presence: Teaching as Contemplative Practice.* Portsmouth: Boynton/Cook.

Pahl, Jon. 2010. *Empire of Sacrifice: The Religious Origins of American Violence.* New York: New York University Press.

Pinker, Steven. 2011. *The Better Angels of Our Nature: Why Violence Has Declined.* New York: Penguin Books.

Rae, Gavin, and Emma Ingala. 2019. "Introduction: The Meanings of Violence." In *The Meanings of Violence: From Critical Theory to Biopolitics,* edited by Gavin Rae and Emma Ingala, 1–9. New York: Routledge.

Scarry, Elaine. 1985. *The Body in Pain: The Making and Unmaking of the World.* New York: Oxford University Press.
Stuckey, J. Elspeth. 1991. *The Violence of Literacy.* Portsmouth: Boynton/Cook.
Vorobej, Mark. 2016. *The Concept of Violence.* New York: Routledge.
Žižek, Slavoj. 2008. *Violence: Six Sideways Reflections.* New York: Picador.

PART 1

Recognizing

1

COVERT RACIAL VIOLENCE IN NATIONAL HIGH-SCHOOL-TO-COLLEGE WRITING TRANSITION OUTCOMES

Jamila M. Kareem

The passage from high school to college academic writing is not race-less. In an Institutional Review Board–approved research study I conducted from 2015 to 2016, I attempted to capture some of the stories of Black American students transitioning from writing in high school to writing in college courses.[1] One key finding concluded that most of the students in the study had become accustomed to suppressing racial experiences and histories when they write for school contexts (Kareem 2018). One participant stated that in writing for school, "sometimes I feel like when I write in my academic voice, it's not me . . . I feel like if the university was more productive, they'd let me be myself while also getting work done in providing the information in the way that I feel would be more beneficial to me to write." Another participant emphasized perceived control of the writing process by teachers: "I like to use stream of consciousness a lot. Which they told me not to do that in high school, but it seems to work the best, pretty much. Even though it was open, there pretty much was a right answer, so it was a little hard to be creative." Even though practices such as stream of consciousness and rhetorical application of conversational tone and style are common to nonacademic discourses and non-Euro-Western rhetorical traditions, such epistemological perspectives about writing are not supported by most learning outcomes of college writing programs or individual courses. Learning outcomes explicitly and implicitly drive the teaching and learning activities in higher education.

College writing programs often adopt the recommendations of the WPA Outcomes Statement for First-Year Composition to complement their institution-approved outcomes. Although the recommendations are voluntary, the context and content of the Outcomes Statement

https://doi.org/10.7330/9781646422807.c001

presumes that every student is starting from the disposition of valuing Eurocentric language practices and a desire to represent Eurocentric epistemological perspectives (EEP)—defined as the view that any knowledge worth pursuing is based in Eurocentric customs, traditions, and behaviors—in their academic writing practices. In this chapter, I argue that the Outcomes Statement enacts EEP, which inflict covert racial violence by marginalizing the linguistic epistemologies of raciolinguistically minoritized students at a particularly vulnerable moment: the transition from high school to college writing. As a result, new college students who value institutionally marginalized raciolinguistic practices in their writing might find that their mother tongues bleed as they "grat[e] against the linguistic barbed wire of the institution" (Naynaha 2016, 197). Specifically, the Outcomes Statement seems to disregard the presence of racialized ideologies in discipline-supported writing expectations. As representative measures, these suggestions carry the values of the discipline—values entrenched with racist ideologies (Martinez 2014; Kynard 2008; Prendergast 1998) about language.

As authors in this collection illustrate, formal schools have long been sites of racial culture-pillaging, often under the guise of literacy education. As a discipline that increasingly claims to support inclusive and equitable education opportunities, these guidelines should reflect values for college-level writing education that sustain rather than eradicate raciolinguistic cultural values and plurality. This chapter closely examines the covert racial violence undergirding these national recommendations for transitioning high school academic writers to college-level writing. The chapter first describes EEP, detailing how they function in writing curricula in particular. It then demonstrates the influence of EEP in the Outcomes Statement, detailing the consequences of such an influence on raciolinguistically minoritized students. Finally, the chapter offers suggestions for antiracist revisions to the document.

EUROCENTRIC EPISTEMOLOGICAL PERSPECTIVES AND COVERT RACIAL VIOLENCE

Denying the value of racialized experiences comes in part as a result of standardizing Eurocentric epistemologies about literacy and writing. Scholars have defined EEP in a variety of similar ways (Leonardo 2009; Collins 2008; Kincheloe 2008; Bernal and Villalpando 2002). For the purposes of this rhetorical analysis, I position EEP as theories of knowledge that value decontextualization, universalism, positivism, and hyperindividualism.

These attributes represent the key aspects of Eurocentrism that are most encouraged by college academic discourses. Within composition studies, they have become a part of the powerful knowledge, or "knowledge [that] offers an objectively better basis for understanding the world than others," about the ways to write effectively for college academic situations (Rudolph, Sriprakash, and Gerrard 2018, 24). These epistemologies of academic writing nullify language behaviors that do not conform to Eurocentric ways of knowing. For example, these epistemologies situate other knowledge bases, such as Afrocentric, Latinx, or Indigenous experiences, as specialized rather than systemic.

Decontextualization is the preference for facts and data without social, cultural, or political contexts. Asao B. Inoue (2016) describes this as part of whiteness as a discourse. He details one assumption about the relationship between writers and their subject matter as "little emphasis on connectedness, relatedness, feeling, interconnection with others" (147). Because of this desire for isolation of research and writing from writers, "socially-oriented values and questions are less important and often political (bad) by their nature" (147). Both formalism and decontextualized constructs embody this notion.

Compounding decontextualization, EEP embody ideas of universalism as well. Universalism, as it relates to knowledge-making and validation, purports that scientifically deduced knowledge is always true, in every circumstance across time and place (Kincheloe 2008). In other words, the processes used to determine truths about the physical world are applied to determining so-called truths about social, political, and cultural sectors. According to Inoue (2016), discourses of whiteness situate "thinking/rationality and knowledge [as] non-political, unraced, and . . . objective," and, therefore, "deductive logics are preferred" (147) in every situation. EEP endorse universalism, as a product of and support for the predominant racial, linguistic, and social culture of power.

Similar to universalism and aligning with decontextualization, positivism is a belief in the indisputable power of objectivity, a belief with implications for hyperindividualism. It furthers universalism and relies on decontextualization by enforcing objectivity in all knowledge-validation processes. Of course, this appearance of neutrality is tied to the social and political racial culture of power and expression. According to EEP, positivist approaches come primarily from the individual, and the individual is revered in EEP above all else as the primary source to draw out meaningful inquiries and present meaningful solutions. Inoue (2016) refers to this concept as "hyperindividualism," or the notion that "self-determination and autonomy [are] most important or most valued" and that "social and cultural factors are external constraints to the individual" (147). Thus, any knowledge-affirmation ideology that values context, culture, and social activity over or alongside individual development is seen as inferior.

Over the last few decades, scholars in composition studies and literacy studies have advanced acceptance of so-called inferior epistemological perspectives and challenged the place of EEP and their ideologies in the teaching and administrating of college writing (Ruiz and Sánchez 2016; Kynard 2013; Perryman-Clark 2013; Kells 2007; Kells, Balester, and Villanueva 2004; Smitherman 2000). Many of these scholars have offered examples of perspectives shaped by Latinx and Afrocentric worldviews. For comparison's sake, I will take a look at an Afrocentric epistemological perspective based in what Geneva Smitherman (2000) calls an African worldview and what Staci M. Perryman-Clark (2013) calls an African American worldview. Both Smitherman and Perryman-Clark classify this worldview as emphasizing a distinct link between the material and the spiritual—the street and the church. Bidirectional, the link privileges the spiritual, or the power of God and the like. The connection between these elements is a foreign concept to EEP, because those epistemologies place little to no importance on the interconnection between the self, others, space, time, and ideas.

EEP see the properties of cultural and social constructs as a constraint to the development of knowledge, but an Afrocentric epistemology situates these properties as necessary to create interdependence across the different domains of reality. Interdependence in all things is also present in the rhetorical conception of "Nommo, the magic power of the word" (Smitherman 2000, 203). With this notion, the interdependence between the spiritual (the word) and the material (the action) results in "synergic interaction" that shapes "a given reality" (201). Nommo and the link between secular and spiritual practices also encompass ideas of liberation, or "the freedom to define one's own identity" (Perryman-Clark 2013, 12). Whereas EEP focus on the self as the primary source of important questions and solutions to problems, an Afrocentric perspective emphasizes the self as the sole source of establishing one's own identity.

Used as a part of writing instruction, EEP, and their unquestioned place, result in covert racial violence because they subtly demean other ways of understanding the world. Any analysis or interpretation reflecting, for example, Afrocentric worldviews cannot function in a space that values Eurocentric worldviews above all others. Students who adhere to Afrocentric epistemological perspectives, thus, may experience covert racial violence when they apply these knowledge-making processes to their coursework. Covert racial violence is race-driven brutality done surreptitiously. It includes any systemic and epistemic efforts that erase racial histories and culture (Rudolph, Sriprakash, and Gerrard 2018; Peters 2015). Such efforts often go unnoticed or are seen as the norm of everyday social life, and, frequently, perpetrators are unaware of their covert racial violence. EEP exhibit this kind of violence in the teaching of writing as they establish specific ways that students should discourse, and those ways are directly tied to a Euro-Western outlook, the most socially dominant racial cultural outlook. Not only are students affected by this epistemological stance, but composition studies as a discipline is also limited by the ways that it understands how to compose, teach, learn, and research writing. Although we may be subconsciously ignorant, we can consciously work to recognize EEP and their accompanying values in our pedagogies and writing programs. For example, we might look for ways that our programmatic and course-based student learning outcomes encourage decontextualization. This value of EEP often takes the form of generalized conceptions of critical thinking or writing skills. In any setting in which we forgo the writer's social, cultural, and racio- or ethnolinguistic contexts when assessing writing, we perpetuate EEP and enact covert racism.

Further, we endorse universalism when our outcomes and resultant pedagogies indicate but one tactic for demonstrating or incorporating a particular practice. Teaching students responsible and effective ways to use narrativizing as a citation practice, for example, can prove just as cogent as teaching documentation practices such as MLA, APA, or *Chicago Manual of Style*. We can see our preference for objectivity without cultural or social context whenever we discuss language and rhetorical practices without recognition of social or cultural forces. While we may acknowledge these in many emerging theories and methodologies in our field's research, the overwhelming majority of our daily praxes and practices in working with students and our institutions do not invoke such theories often due to multidimensional constraints.

While scholars may not have looked closely at racial violence in the transition-level practices of a document such as the Outcomes Statement, a small segment of the field has made efforts to combat, challenge, or simply call out these tendencies. The turn of the twenty-first century brought with it a heightened focus on the color line in composition studies. In 1998, Catherine Prendergast suggested that composition studies fails to adequately examine how the history of race and racism in our culture connects to writing as an activity and a product as well as in the teaching of these elements in writing. Prendergast argues that "if race has been an absent presence, racism has been an absent absence. Even when the subject of a study is identified by race or ethnicity, the legacy of racism in this country which participates in sculpting all identities—white included—is more often than not absent from the analysis of that writer's linguistic capabilities or strategies" (36). The failure to examine race is due to the norm of racism in society, but Prendergast attributes the failure more specifically to Victor Villanueva's (1997) notion of "colonial sensibility" (quoted in Prendergast 1998, 37). Following Villanueva in suggesting that this sensibility most frequently and most intensely affects people of color, Prendergast urges composition teachers to scrutinize the absent presence of race (37). This colonial sensibility is what allows both those oppressing others and those being oppressed by institution-sanctioned literacy practices to see that oppression as the norm. If we wholeheartedly believe that the recommended outcomes in the Outcomes Statement are designed to "articulat[e] what composition teachers nationwide have learned from practice, research, and theory" (Council of Writing Program Administrators 2014, 1) and these recommendations continue to occlude race- and ethnicity-consciousness in practice, research, and theory, then we will continue to preserve a colonial sensibility in FYW (First-Year Writing) programs and courses. These gaps in studying writing prevent us, as a field, from taking action against the racialization of both disciplinary and institutional writing curriculum goals and redressing their impact on teaching and learning in the writing classroom. Investigating such racialization proves difficult in any case, because they are so ingrained in cultural conceptions of whiteness and Eurocentrism that they have become "unconscious" in the academy and especially in writing curriculum (Prendergast 1998; Brandt 1992).

Following the publication of Prendergast's article, Jacqueline Jones Royster and Jean C. Williams brought to our attention the specific absent presence of racial diversity in our imagined students, researchers, and teachers. In "History in the Spaces Left: African American Presence and Narratives of Composition Studies," the authors describe the representation of the generic student in writing studies scholarship. For these authors, "while this seemingly neutral approach could be thought of as placing all students on an equal level, the neutrality often erases the presence of students of color with the resultant assumption that, in not being marked as present, they in fact were not there" (Royster and Williams 1999, 568). If the perspectives a discipline chooses to include as part of its histories represent what it privileges, the "spaces left" by perspectives of Black, Latinx, and other peoples of color in composition studies' histories point to the disenfranchisement of these viewpoints about writing and teaching writing. These disciplinary absences manifest first in the theories that inform practices and then in the ways administrators create programmatic goals and the ways instructors engage with student writing.

Complementing Royster and Williams's work (1999) is the edited collection *Race, Rhetoric, and Composition,* by Keith Gilyard (1999). This primarily theory-centric collection presents readers with extensive and expansive efforts to theorize race as it relates to rhetorical and composition studies. Just a couple years following this, Andrea Greenbaum (2001) produced the collection *Insurrections: Approaches to Resistance in Composition Studies,* which included several contributions concerned with race-consciousness and antiracism in theory-development and pedagogical practices. Part two of that anthology is titled "Race and the Politics of Literacy" and comprises chapters on the often unspoken relationship between racial identity and literacy practices in composition classrooms. These examples are just some of the scholarship that has recognized the importance of withstanding and speaking to EEP through our theory, research, teaching, and administration.

Coincidentally, perhaps, the first version of the Outcomes Statement was published during the same era, in 1999. That factor adds an additional layer to the social-cultural-historical context of the outcomes' development. These aspects are discussed further in the next section, which delves into the covert racism of the Outcomes Statement. However, the emergence of the outcomes does introduce a critical question: with so much theoretical and practical scholarly material at that time drawing connections among race, language, literacy, writing, teaching, and learning, why did it have little to no influence on the evolution of the outcomes document? Further, with two other versions of the statement and even more scholarship published following the 1999 statement, where were the influences of that scholarship in the realm of racist ideologies and WPA work? These questions point to ways in which covert racism operates.

Jennifer Clary-Lemon's (2009) article, "The Racialization of Composition Studies: Scholarly Rhetoric of Race since 1990," reiterates that, even though the concept of race is commonplace, it may remain ambiguous, further arguing that the discipline must work to collectively interpret and define our racial ideologies. Enacting a similar agenda of consciousness-raising, in "Outside the Text: Retheorizing Empiricism and Identity" Raúl Sánchez (2012) exposes and disrupts decontextualizing practices

in disciplinary theory development by interrogating the field's historical practice of separating writer from subject and by foregrounding "a
terminology that can walk both sides of the simultaneously disappear-
ing yet irreducible line between the materiality of the writer and the
discursivity of the subject [which situates] identity . . . [as] an aspect
of the idea of traffic between textuality and the 'outside' of textuality,
the aspect with which composition studies historically is most concerned: agency" (236). In the same year, the compilation *Race and
Writing Assessment* (Inoue and Poe 2012) was published to address the
still unresolved race hurdle in writing instruction and assessment.
Soon after, the intersectional work in critical race theory, literacy, and
composition studies by scholars such as Kynard (2013), Aja Y. Martinez
(2014), and Perryman-Clark (2013) and in linguistics, writing pedagogy, and race by Suresh Canagarajah (2013), Malea Powell (2014),
Vershawn Ashanti Young et al. (2014), Michelle Hall Kells (2016), and
others emerged in our disciplinary spaces. Recognizing these critical
contributions to our collective intelligence as a discipline reveals the
limitations exhibited in the disciplinary recommendations for learning
and teaching first-year composition, the WPA Outcomes Statement for
First-Year Composition.

COVERT RACIAL VIOLENCE IN THE OUTCOMES STATEMENT

As stated, the Outcomes Statement comprises the learning outcomes
that the discipline recommends for the completion of first-year composition. More specifically, the architects of the Outcomes Statement, the
Council of Writing Program Administrators (CWPA) (2014), explain
that it "describes the writing knowledge, practices, and attitudes that
undergraduate students develop in first-year composition, which at
most schools is a required general education course or sequence of
courses" and that the "Statement therefore attempts to both represent
and regularize writing programs' priorities for first-year composition,
which often takes the form of one or more required general education
courses" (1). Before digging into the covert racism and racial violence
of the Outcomes Statement, I want to provide a bit of history about and
context for the document, its creation, and its trajectory.

The original edition of the Outcomes Statement was released in the
Fall/Winter 1999 issue of *WPA: Writing Program Administration* and first
reprinted in *College English* in 2001 (Harrington et al. 2001) by composition and WPA scholars who had formed what was initially deemed
the Outcomes Group and who later adopted the designation of the

Outcomes Collective (Dryer et al. 2014). The steering committee of the original Outcomes Collective included Susanmarie Harrington (rhetoric and composition and literacy), Rita Malencyzk (rhetoric and politics of writing program and center administration), Irv Peckham (writing program administration), Keith Rhodes (writing pedagogy), and Kathleen Blake Yancey (writing knowledge and practice transfer and portfolio assessment) (Harrington et al. 2001).[2] According to the steering committee (Harrington et al. 2001) in a brief article introducing the Outcomes Statement to *College English* readers, the research and development of the outcomes were partially in response to a WPA-L (Writing Program Administration listserv) discussion. It revolved around the question: "Given sufficient commonality, would it be possible to articulate a general curricular framework for first-year composition, regardless of institutional home, student demographics, and instructor characteristics? Could we do this in a way that doesn't prescribe or infringe?" (Harrington et al. 2001, 321). These goals are neither lofty nor noble; they are practical and even well-intentioned.

As shown by the inductive inquiry, the Outcomes Statement aims to formulate a framework that suggests outcomes for learning irrespective of students' identity constructs. This well-intentioned objective is covertly racially violent in that it evades acknowledgment of the role that our society and education system's racialized ideology plays in the practice of and theorization about writing and writers. Previously, I stated that the Outcomes Statement disregards social and cultural forces in all versions of the document released thus far, and the statement's goal of decontextualization makes it clear why. Dylan B. Dryer et al. (2014) explain that the "statement's language was designed to encourage local adaptability in order to combine guidance and freedom while also striving to be applicable to the widest possible range of postsecondary institutions" (130). Yet the document also represents ideologies about writing instruction and assessment in FYW as well as across the curriculum, so the race evasive diction exemplifies that our discipline has no appreciation of the systemic place of racial constructions in the lived and learning experiences of writers, regardless of their racial culture, college or university, or chosen career fields. The 2008 version of the document added the "Composing in Electronic Environments" area, "given the increasing ubiquity of digital composing" (130); therefore, given the increasing racial representation of writing programs and courses and the still pervasive racist ideologies in how writing is taught, a revision that reflects critical analysis of racial difference, raciolinguistic literacies, and racialized social structures, is overdue. The Outcomes

Statement commits covert racial violence through its application of and de facto recommendation of EEP.

Decontextualization in particular comes out in the "Knowledge of Conventions" section of the document. This section provides suggestions for the teaching and learning of practices that "govern such things as mechanics, usage, spelling, and citation practices" in writing, "but [that] also influence content, style, organization, graphics, and document design" (Council of Writing Program Administrators 2014, 3). One outcome, for instance, suggests that students leaving first-year composition should "[l]earn common formats and/or design features for different kinds of texts" (3), which demonstrates a preference for the application of conventions without consideration for social or cultural context. Yes, the outcome specifies "for different texts," but it also focuses on common formats and features without knowledge of the social context of these aspects. Similarly, another proposed outcome from this section states that students should "develop knowledge of linguistic structures, including grammar, punctuation, and spelling, through practice in composing and revising" (3), and this recommendation isolates conventions "from the diverse contexts of which it is a part and that grant [them] meaning" (Kincheloe 2008, 22). Certainly, students should learn to navigate the linguistic conventions of these territories in order to speak truth to power. However, as a student participant in a study by Valerie Kinloch (2010) suggests of assimilating into the linguistic conventions of college writing, "fixing" Black English to dominant American English "would mean something's wrong" with him, even as he recognizes that he "want[s] to be successful in life" (Kinloch 2010, 11). Within the Outcomes Statement, such a conception of good college-level writing ignores the impact of sociocultural identities and racialized social systems on engagement with academic literacy practices.

Researchers within composition and literacy studies have argued that, in fact, these conceptions aim to erase any sign of Blackness, Brownness, Indigeneity, and determined anti-whiteness from students whom mainstream K–16 education practices have racially marginalized (Perryman-Clark 2013; Kynard 2013, 2008; Villanueva and Smitherman 2003; Delpit 1995; Smitherman 1993). The methodical aims of universalism make similar moves in the "Critical Thinking, Reading, and Composing Outcome" section, which recommends that first-year composition students "locate and evaluate (for credibility, sufficiency, accuracy, timeliness, bias and so on) primary and secondary research materials, including journal articles and essays, books, scholarly and professionally established and maintained databases or archives, and informal electronic networks and internet sources" (Council of Writing Program Administrators 2014, 2). Although worthwhile research practices to habituate, these recommendations place a strong importance on officially validated, primarily print-based forms, even as writing is a highly contextualized act. Whiteness-centric knowledge validation and discursive practices, such as the ones suggested by this outcome, maintain the literacy experiences of students who easily align with Eurocentric perspectives, and exclude the literacy experiences of those who value Indigenous, Afrocentric, and other non-Eurocentric epistemological perspectives.

The outcome illustrates a hyperindividualist ideology as well, because the inquiry process is initiated and executed by the individual. The social contexts of knowledge validation are not considered. As Patricia Hill Collins (2008) explains about Eurocentric masculinist epistemology, "knowledge claims are evaluated by a community of experts whose members represent the standpoints of the groups from which they originate," and, therefore, "within the Eurocentric masculinist process this means that a scholar making a knowledge claim must convince a scholarly community controlled by white men that a given claim is justified" (202). The ranking of epistemological approaches here exemplifies a racialized social system, or a social hierarchy that structures all systemic elements of social life in relation to racial categories (Bonilla-Silva 1997, 469). EEP indicate critical thinking results from universal, rational approaches to a topic, but racialized positions make universal approaches limited and rational perspectives varied rather than static. Racialized positions cause teachers to perceive some students' application of community consciousness to interpret new information as weak or insignificant (Gilyard and Richardson 2001, 42). When faculty are limited in their evaluations and critiques of material, they cannot sustain the culturally based critical thinking practices of different kinds of student writers.

The critical thinking, reading, and composing outcomes value an understanding of prevailing racial culture perspectives on the relationship between assertion and evidence, no matter how diverse the range of texts that students consult. The "Rhetorical Knowledge" outcomes likewise denote observance of EEP, as they imply a somewhat objective, hyperindividualist approach to rhetorical considerations. If "rhetorical knowledge is the ability to analyze contexts and audiences and then to act on that analysis in comprehending and creating texts," it is based in objective, positivist interpretations of audiences and contexts, because to "[l]earn and use key rhetorical concepts through analyzing and composing a variety of texts" assumes that some rhetorical concepts objectively function across contexts and cultures (Council of Writing Program Administrators 2014, 1). Furthermore, when the Outcomes Statement suggests that teachers help students "gain experience reading and composing in several genres to understand how genre conventions shape and are shaped by readers' and writers' practices and purposes" (1), it does so with the caveat that these analyses and understandings will be tied to the social and material conditions of Euro-Westernism.

Such unquestioned assumptions exemplify how EEP lead to covert racial violence in the transition from high school to college writing as represented in the discipline-backed document. One way it does so is by establishing proposed assessment measures that evaluate all students against EEP. Carmen Kynard (2008) alludes to the impact of this covert racial violence in an example from "Writing While Black: The Colour Line, Black Discourses and Assessment in the Institutionalization of Writing Instruction," in which "[t]hose students who most overtly manipulated Black discourses and personal essays to construct the ethos and rhetorical styles of their writing were penalized and received a failing score (8 students)" (10). Kynard notes that "in these failing essays, students expressed, to varying degrees, a mistrust of Orwell and cast his criticism of imperialism as important but absolutely locked in whiteness. Those who expressed this sentiment most forthrightly (2 students) received the lowest grades on the exam" (10). The point here is not that the lower-scoring students did not "separate assertion from evidence, evaluate sources and evidence, recognize and evaluate underlying assumptions" (Council of Writing Program Administrators 2014, 2), but that they were only rewarded for these practices when the outcomes matched the prevailing interpretations and assumptions of Orwell's work.

Illustrating how asking students to become better academic writers and members of academic discourse communities may mean asking them to disparage their cultural discourses, Kinloch (2010) shows the need for more student perspectives in order to understand "effective ways to locate students' literacies and languages within the context of schools" (2). One participant of Kinloch's study asserted, "Taking away how students talk is taking away the students' culture [*sic*], it's saying that the students' [*sic*] language is not correct, is inferior to the dominant culture, and incorrect in comparison to others" (12). The frustration this student expresses suggests a desire for college writing curriculum and pedagogy that sustains diverse raciolinguistic cultures.

As shown here, the Outcomes Statement enacts covert racial violence by keeping the ideals of EEP in circulation. It is violent, because the outcome areas intellectually brutalize writers by institutionally ostracizing the writing knowledge and writing practices of raciolinguistic and ethnolinguistic communities. Even in its objective to reflect a flexible, adaptable, and descriptive rather than prescriptive document, the Outcomes Statement demonstrates universalism: these outcome areas and suggested practices objectively apply to all student writers. However, collective knowledge from the field over the last decade demonstrates that raciolinguistic traditions often influence the ways that writers make sense of their worlds. The racist ideologies of the statement are covert because they are intertwined with accepted beliefs about what makes objectively good writing according to EEP. With collegiate academic communities leading the charge for this type of disciplinary knowledge about writing, secondary schools will continue to follow suit. Through pinpointing the rhetorical act of covert racial violence in these guidelines, I hope that our discipline can begin to create top-down antiracist and culturally sustaining guidelines for writing across the transition.

COMBATING COVERT RACIAL VIOLENCE IN THE HIGH-SCHOOL-TO-COLLEGE WRITING TRANSITION

As the field stands, there is not enough in-depth research about race in the high-school-to-college writing transition. The goal of this collection is to advocate for recognizing, intervening in, and ameliorating violence in the work we do as compositionists, so we have a responsibility to recognize and respond to the racialized experiences that students bring with their literacy histories into composition programs and classrooms. Antiracist outcomes resist the foundational concept of universal, decontextualized objectivist ideologies, even in academic contexts. They reflect that academic researchers and writers should not "remov[e] a phenomenon from the diverse contexts of which it is a part and that grant it meaning" because doing so weakens understanding of writing practices (Kincheloe 2008, 22). Antiracist outcomes, thus, actively work to oppose racist interpretations of college writing standards, interpretations that "substitute words like 'professional' for white so that any racism that might be revealed is semantically concealed" (Condon and Young 2017, 7). The field has also failed to give any substantial examination into what aspects of societal racial hierarchies, or the racialized social system (Bonilla-Silva 1997, 469), bleed into constructions of successful college writing.

The goal of the Outcomes Statement is to be applicable to a variety of writing programs with a variety of constituencies. However, in its attempt "to both represent and regularize writing programs' priorities for first-year composition" (Council of Writing Program Administrators 2014, 1), the Outcomes Statement represents the EEP of whiteness as a discourse and of white supremacist literacy. The "Rhetorical Knowledge" section of the Outcomes Statement suggests that students should become versed in what Elaine Richardson (2003) calls "capitalistic-based literacy" (Kindle Ch. 1). This kind of literacy is fragmented, fixed to consumption and positivism, and situated as "needed to succeed in the corporate educational system" (Kindle Ch. 1). Antiracist revisions to the Outcomes Statement combat writing curriculum invested in neoliberal, up-from-oppression ideologies that result in covert racial violence. Rather than relying on rhetorical knowledge that stresses the universalism and positivism of "learn[ing] and us[ing] key rhetorical concepts through analyzing and composing a variety of texts," I suggest revising this area to include the following outcomes: "utilizes form and content at an appropriate level for true audiences" and "incorporates figurative language appropriate to the situation and audience knowledge, or uses prose to clarify idioms, proverbs, and other forms of figurative language." With these revisions, the "contractual relationship" between writers and readers found in discourses of whiteness (Inoue 2016) is called into question, moving towards more call-response and community-influenced relationships valued by many Latinx-centric, Afrocentric, autochthonous, and "world majority" (Fox 1995) communities.

To the "Critical Thinking, Reading, and Composing" area of the document, I propose adding the outcome "complements lived experience with primary research and secondary research." Rather than the fragmented and obedience-driven (Richardson 2003) expectations of the current outcomes for critical thinking (see "Use composing and reading for inquiry" and "Locate and evaluate . . . primary and secondary research materials"), the antiracist revision works to sustain cultures and teach students responsible ways to use lived experience as a source in context with broader knowledge. A revision to the "Processes" section includes the additional outcome of: "include input from community members, family, or mentors in their writing process." Community consciousness is key to the important processes of many communities of color; it ensures that their traditions and cultural perspectives remain in the social world the same way that the prevailing EEP has remained. Finally, to the "Knowledge of Conventions" area, I suggest the outcome "describe or demonstrate the cultural basis for grammar and style conventions." For composition students of color in particular, this outcome expresses antiracist ideologies because it invites them (and all students) to apply culturally developed knowledge about language and writing practices to institutional standards.

The irony of writing this chapter in the covertly racist dominant Euro-American academic English does not escape me. Like my interview participants described in the chapter opening, I am one of the many Black Americans indoctrinated in what Jeff Zorn (2010) calls the "Formal Written Standard." I and some of the high-achieving—by current traditional standards—interviewees may have been indoctrinated to the point of no return. Like Aja Y. Martinez (2009), "I [have been] the 'exceptional minority' . . . who believed the ideological myth that access and retention in higher education are achieved primarily through an individual's effort," and "although I do not claim to be free from or outside of the . . . ideology concerning structural and systemic inequality, I am becoming aware of how not to respect it" (585). Additionally, I recognize that the document discussed here can be applied in antiracist ways.

Composition is a field built out of social inequities in higher education, and recent developments related to implicit racial bias in the field as a whole, and in WPA work more specifically, call for a deep and critical analysis of the racial violence of every institutional and public representation of the work we do. Antiracist outcomes resist the foundational concept of universal, decontextualized, objectivist outlooks, even in academic contexts. They reflect that academic researchers and writers should not "remov[e] a phenomenon from the diverse contexts of which it is a part and that grant it meaning," because doing so weakens understanding of the full dimension of the topic rather than create an intractable claim (Kincheloe 2008, 22). These outcomes actively work to oppose racist interpretations of college writing standards. So, for example, students might write for various sociocultural contexts and socioculturally diverse readers. Perhaps they develop the habits of mind to question, critique, and create inquiry from the worldviews shaping the development of a scholarly text, its methodology, and its evidence. This approach gives students of color, in particular, the capability to engage the many worldviews of their identities without exchanging one for the other because they are transitioning to college writing.

NOTES

1.   Study approved by IRB with anonymized participants.
2.   In parenthetical notations, I have provided the committee members' areas of research or practice according to either their faculty web pages (Harrington, Malencyzk, Rhodes, and Yancey) or ResearchGate web page in lieu of a faculty page (Peckham).

REFERENCES

Bernal, Dolores Delgado, and Octavio Villalpando. 2002. "An Apartheid of Knowledge in Academia: The Struggle over the 'Legitimate' Knowledge of Faculty of Color." *Equity and Excellence in Education* 35, no. 2: 169–80. doi: 10.1080/713845282.

Bonilla-Silva, Eduardo. 1997. "Rethinking Racism: Toward a Structural Interpretation." *American Sociological Review* 62, no. 3: 465–80. https://www.jstor.org/stable/2657316.

Brandt, Deborah. 1992. "The Cognitive as the Social: An Ethnomethodological Approach to Writing Process Research." *Written Communication* 9, no. 3: 315–55. doi: 10.1177/0741088392009003001.

Canagarajah, A. Suresh. 2013. *Translingual Practice: Global Englishes and Cosmopolitan Relations.* New York: Routledge.

Clary-Lemon, Jennifer. 2009. "The Racialization of Composition Studies: Scholarly Rhetoric of Race Since 1990." *College Composition and Communication* 61, no. 2: W1–W17. http://www.ncte.org/library/NCTEFiles/Resources/Journals/CCC/0612-dec09/CCC 0612Racialization.pdf.

Collins, Patricia Hill. 2008. *Black Feminist Thought.* 2nd ed. New York: Routledge.

Condon, Frankie, and Vershawn Ashanti Young. 2017. "Introduction." In *Performing Anti-racist Pedagogy in Rhetoric, Writing, and Communication*, edited by Frankie Condon and Vershawn Ashanti Young, 3–16. Boulder: University Press of Colorado.

Council of Writing Program Administrators. 2014. *WPA Outcomes Statement for First-Year Composition (v3.0).* http://wpacouncil.org/positions/outcomes.html.

Delpit, Lisa. 1995. *Other People's Children: Cultural Conflict in the Classroom.* New York: W. W. Norton.

Dryer, Dylan B., Darsie Bowden, Beth Brunk-Chavez, Susanmarie Harrington, Bump Halbritter, and Kathleen Blake Yancey. 2014. "Revising FYC Outcomes for a Multimodal, Digitally Composed World: The WPA Outcomes Statement for First-Year Composition (Version 3.0)." *WPA: Writing Program Administration* 38, no. 1: 129–43. http://www.wpa council.org/archives/38n1/38n1dryer-bowden.pdf.

Fox, Helen. 1995. *Listening to the World: Cultural Issues in Academic Writing.* Urbana: National Council of Teachers of English.

Gilyard, Keith, ed. 1999. *Race, Rhetoric, and Composition.* Portsmouth: Boynton/Cook.

Gilyard, Keith, and Elaine Richardson. 2001. "Students' Right to Possibility: Basic Writing and African American Rhetoric." In *Insurrections: Approaches to Resistance in Composition Studies*, edited by Andrea Greenbaum, 37–51. New York: SUNY Press.

Greenbaum, Andrea, ed. 2001. *Insurrections: Approaches to Resistance in Composition Studies.* New York: SUNY Press.

Harrington, Susanmarie, Rita Malencyzk, Irv Peckham, Keith Rhodes, and Kathleen Blake Yancey. 2001. "WPA Outcomes Statement for First-Year Composition." *College English* 63, no. 3: 321–25. JSTOR.

Inoue, Asao B. 2016. "Discourse of Whiteness." Published July 15, 2016. https://docs .google.com/document/d/1k-m31a9NELQ4q1ZnB6Z_EbLhuu53YOIjxOR-8_pbOks /edit.

Inoue, Asao, and Mya Poe, eds. 2012. *Race and Writing Assessment.* New York: Peter Lang.

Kareem, Jamila M. 2018. "Transitioning Counter-Stories: Black Student Accounts of Transitioning to College-Level Writing." *Journal of College Literacy and Learning* 44: 15–35. https://storage.googleapis.com/wzukusers/user-20714678/documents/18c7c7c b77a144579ae489703ebc2ba1/Kareem%20Galley_Final%20for%20PRINT.pdf.

Kells, Michelle H. 2007. "Writing across Communities: Deliberation and the Discursive Possibilities of WAC." *Reflections: A Journal of Writing, Service-Learning, and Community Literacy* 6, no. 1: 87–108.

Kells, Michelle Hall. 2016. "Writing across the Communities and the Writing Center as Cultural Ecotone: Language Diversity, Civic Engagement, and Graduate Student Leadership." *Praxis* 14, no. 1: 27–33. https://search-ebscohost-com.ezproxy.net.ucf.edu/log in.aspx?direct=true&db=eue&AN=125957416&site=eds-live&scope=site.

Kells, Michelle H., Valerie Balester, and Victor Villanueva. 2004. *Latino/Latina Discourses: On Language, Identity, and Literacy Education.* Portsmouth, NH: Boynton/Cook/ Heinemann.

Kincheloe, Joe L. 2008. *Knowledge and Critical Pedagogy: An Introduction.* New York: Springer.

Kinloch, Valerie. 2010. " 'To Not Be a Traitor of Black English': Youth Perceptions of Language Rights in an Urban Context." *Teachers College Record* 112, no. 1. http://www .tcrecord.org/Content.asp?ContentId=15798.

Kynard, Carmen. 2013. *Vernacular Insurrections: Race, Black Protest, and the New Century in Composition-Literacies Studies.* New York: SUNY Press.

Kynard, Carmen. 2008. "Writing While Black: The Colour Line, Black Discourses and Assessment in the Institutionalization of Writing Instruction." *English Teaching: Practice and Critique* 7, no. 2: 4–34. https://eric.ed.gov/?id=EJ832206.

Leonardo, Zeus, ed. 2009. *Race, Whiteness, and Education.* New York: Routledge.

Martinez, Aja Y. 2014. "A Plea for Critical Race Theory Counterstory: Stock Story versus Counterstory Dialogues Concerning Alejandra's 'Fit' in the Academy." *Composition Studies* 42, no. 2: 33–55. https://www.uc.edu/content/dam/uc/journals/composition -studies/docs/backissues/42-2/Martinez%2042.2.pdf.

Martinez, Aja Y. 2009. " 'The American Way': Resisting the Empire of Force and Color-Blind Racism." *College English* 71, no. 6: 584–95. JSTOR.

Naynaha, Siskanna. 2016. "Assessment, Social Justice, and Latinxs in the US Community College." *College English* 79, no. 2: 196–201. http://www.ncte.org.ezproxy.net.ucf.edu /library/NCTEFiles/Resources/Journals/CE/0792nov2016/CE0782Assessmentpword .pdf.

Perryman-Clark, Staci. 2013. *Afrocentric Teacher-Research: Rethinking Appropriateness and Inclusion.* New York: Peter Lang.

Peters, Michael A. 2015. "Why Is My Curriculum White?" *Educational Philosophy and Theory* 47, no. 7: 641–46. doi: 10.1080/00131857.2015.1037227.

Powell, Malea. 2014. "A Basket Is a Basket Because . . . : Telling a Native Rhetorics Story." In *The Oxford Handbook of Indigenous American Literature,* edited by James H. Cox and Daniel Heath Justice, 471–88. New York: Oxford University Press.

Prendergast, Catherine. 1998. "Race: The Absent Presence in Composition Studies." *College Composition and Communication* 50, no. 1: 36–53. doi: 10.2307/358351.

Richardson, Elaine. 2003. *African American Literacies.* New York: Routledge. Kindle.

Royster, Jacqueline Jones, and Jean C. Williams. 1999. "History in the Spaces Left: African American Presence and Narratives of Composition Studies." *College Composition and Communication* 50, no. 4: 563–84.

Rudolph, Sophie, Arathi Sriprakash, and Jessica Gerrard. 2018. "Knowledge and Racial Violence: The Shine and Shadow of 'Powerful Knowledge.' " *Ethics and Education* 13, no. 1, 22–38. doi: 10.1080/17449642.2018.1428719.

Ruiz, Iris, and Raúl Sánchez. 2016. *Decolonizing Rhetoric and Composition Studies: New Latinx Keywords for Theory and Pedagogy.* New York: Palgrave Macmillan.

Sánchez, Raúl. 2012. "Outside the Text: Retheorizing Empiricism and Identity." *College English* 74, no. 3: 234–46. JSTOR.

Smitherman, Geneva. 2000. *Talkin' That Talk: Language, Culture, Education in African America.* Abingdon: Routledge.

Smitherman, Geneva. 1993. "The Blacker the Berry, the Sweeter the Juice: African American Student Writers and the National Assessment of Educational Progress." Paper presented at the Annual Meeting of the National Council of Teachers of English, Pittsburgh, PA.

Villanueva, Victor. 1997. "Maybe a Colony: And Still Another Critique of the Comp Community." *JAC* 17, no. 2: 183–90. http://www.jstor.org/stable/20866125.

Villanueva, Victor, and Geneva Smitherman. 2003. *Language Diversity in the Classroom: From Intention to Practice.* Carbondale: Southern Illinois University Press.

Young, Vershawn Ashanti, et al. 2014. *Other People's English: Code-Meshing, Code-Switching, and African American Literacy.* New York: Teachers College Press.

Zorn, Jeff. 2010. "'Students' Right to Their Own Language': A Counter-Argument." *Academic Questions* 23, no. 3: 311–26. doi: 10.1007/s12129-010-9175-x.

2

SCALAR VIOLENCE IN COMPOSITION

Kerry Banazek and Kellie Sharp-Hoskins

To understand the phenomenon of violence in composition and inter-vene in the reproduction of related violence, we must pay attention to its scales. Scale, in this chapter, refers to the size, scope, or level of complex-ity associated with a defined area or phenomena. It articulates boundaries by which can we identify, measure, quantify, or otherwise delineate mean-ing and recognize violent actions and effects. This definition resonates with the term's vernacular uses in the field—scholars often refer to large- or small-scale studies—and with the attention that scalar issues receive as sites of and resources for study. Indeed, in the last decade scholars in rhetoric and composition have embraced the concept of scale to grapple with new materialisms and complexity theory (Mays 2015; Jung 2014; Yood 2013) as well as the colonial and transnational reach of composition (Dingo 2012; Hesford 2011; Canagarajah 2002). Importantly, such schol-arship not only identifies scale (singular) but insists on scales (plural) as integral to understanding composition because scales exist *in relation* to each other: small scale is defined in relation to large scale, national levels of scales in relation to transnational, and so forth. Moreover, because composition scholarship ranges from experiential narratives to pedagogi-cal paradigms, program profiles to national policy advocacy, and propos-ing best practices to critiquing colonial assumptions about writing in transnational contexts, the field itself is always already operating at—and across—multiple levels of scale. These operations invite foregrounding of *scalar violences* within the field of composition—studies of how violence is marked, measured, and matters both within and across defined and interrelated scales. One form of scalar violence occurs when arguments and their attendant values traverse scales without sensitivity to differ-ences in scale and, thus, to differences in values, functions, agendas, and lived experiences. While violence that attends specific levels of scale (within classrooms, within institutions, within the field) is addressed, though often tacitly, in composition studies, the violence that results

https://doi.org/10.7330/9781646422807.c002

from arguments and values *crossing* scales has not yet become an explicit, regular locus of inquiry. Because scalar shifts involve complex transformations, they often indicate a shift in *kind* and not just a shift in size or quantity. Understanding and responding to the violence of composition thus demands direct attention to how violence functions as arguments traverse scales of composition.

To that end, the pages that follow begin by articulating a relationship between scales and violence that foregrounds their cooperation and current treatment in composition studies. Building on this work, we then investigate the violence that emerges when arguments "jump" scales—that is, when they cross levels of scales but remain partially indifferent to the effects of that crossing on the bodies and values that comprise those different scales. Arguments that justify curricular innovation cross multiple levels of scale, jumping from the meso-level of program, which encompasses many classrooms, students, and teachers, up to broader levels of institution and discipline, as well as down to narrower levels of the individual classroom, encompassing one teacher and group of students subject to a single syllabus. We identify possible violent effects of such scalar jumps through examination of a specific case, tracking how promotion of digital composition work intersects with both pro- and anti-instrumentalist arguments at various levels of scale. This case demonstrates how a lack of sensitivity to how arguments jump scales can create, corroborate, or exacerbate violence, preying on vulnerabilities associated with subjectivity and embodiment. The chapter concludes with a call for individual and infrastructural reorientations attuned to the potential violence of arguments' scalar jumps and equipped to intervene in the reproduction of such violence.

SCALES AND VIOLENCE: APPROACHING COMPLEX DYNAMICS

To understand the relationship between scale and violence broadly, James Gilligan's (1996) study of violence as a social, cultural, and national epidemic is instructive, revealing how "the microcosm of any one family's violence can only be understood fully when it is seen as part of the macrocosm, the culture and history of violence, in which it occurs." He explicitly links daily domestic violence to "cycle[s] of generational violence" within families and "the very land on which we [are] living, a land purchased with the blood of the natives whom we displaced" (15). Writing in what seems a markedly different context than the academic discipline of composition, Gilligan nonetheless introduces the importance of naming relationships between violence and scale without conflating differences in scale or their differential effects; "one family's violence" is shown to exist in complex, rather than merely causal, relations to a larger "culture and history of violence" (15). Work that describes composition as a complex system consequently also sets the stage for our observations about scalar violence. For Margaret Syverson (1999), writers, readers, and texts form a complex system, "but even beyond this level of complexity, they are actually situated in an ecology, a larger system that includes environmental structures, such as pens, paper, computers, books . . . and other natural and human-constructed features, as well as other complex systems operating at various levels of scale, such as families, global economies, publishing systems, theoretical frames, academic disciplines, and language itself" (5). Importantly for our work, the differences in scale she describes cannot be reduced to differences in size or site, insofar as levels of scale interact and interanimate. Indeed, the complexity of systems means attempting to study a scale in isolation necessarily begets functional misunderstandings; Julie Jung's (2014) articulation of a *systems rhetoric* is built on recognition that

> "descriptions of complex systems at one level of scale are insufficient: a complex system cannot be understood by reducing it to its component parts, since it's the *interaction* among parts and not the sum of their individual properties that produces macrolevel behaviors attributable to the system as a whole. To begin to understand a complex system, then, one needs to generate descriptions of localized interaction occurring at different levels within the system."

Jung draws our attention to two critical points that can sponsor a reorientation to scale in composition studies that is more attuned to potential violences: first, to understand their nature, we must look beyond the idea that scales have or include discrete elements or parts, and, second, to understand their function we must look across scales to their transactions and emergent effects.

Below we pursue this reorientation using the language of scalar transactions to study how arguments travel, drawing on systems rhetoric explicitly to "generate descriptions of localized interactions occurring at different levels within the system" (Jung 2014). This work of identifying scalar violence has additional precedents in composition scholarship which signify under a variety of names, motivated by disparate theoretical commitments. Projects framed in terms of trauma, for example, link individual to community or collective violence and to transgenerational trauma (Worsham 2006; Borrowman 2005; Wolters 2004; Bernard-Donals 2002). Literacy scholars, too, emphasize the impact of transacting scales when they identify the violent work of institutions, norms, and socialization to discipline individuals (Wan 2014; Donehower, Hogg, and Schell 2007; Prendergast 2003). And in relation to the teaching of writing, composition scholars investigate how violence functions across scale as systemic inequities emerge within institutions and classrooms. Writing about the racial violence of teaching writing as a Black woman, for example, Carmen Kynard (2015) shares stories of the everyday violence that "serve not as micro-instances of campus racism but as macro-pictures of political life in American universities" (1).

The relationships between "micro-instances" of violence and "macro-pictures of political life" can be understood with respect to Lynn Worsham's (1998) landmark articulation of pedagogic violence, defined as "violence [which] addresses and educates emotion and inculcates an affective relation to the world" (216). Here, the violence that emerges across transacting scales is again fundamental to the function of violence itself; in her words, violence has an "objective or structural role in the constitution of subjectivities and in the justification of subjection" (215). In effect, this is seen when students, teachers, administrators, researchers, and others in composition are affectively interpellated as subjects as, for example, basic writers or underprepared (Rose 1989; Shaughnessy 1977), EAL (English as an Additional Language) or multilingual (Casanave 2008; Costino and Hyon 2007), digital natives (Thomas 2011), good teachers (Sharp-Hoskins and Robillard 2012), low-wage workers (Bousquet, Scott, and Parascondola 2004), and so forth.

For Worsham (1998) as for Gilligan (1996), the violence of subject-making and managing "the forms and effects through which violence is lived and experienced" (Worsham 1998, 215) cannot be disarticulated from violence's structural work at scalar crossings. This is corroborated, too, by Veena Das and Arthur Kleinman (2000), who argue that to understand violence—and especially how violence accrues geographically or geopolitically—"it becomes necessary to consider how subjectivity . . . is produced through the experience of violence and the manner in which global flows, involving images, capital, and people become entangled with local logics in identity formation" (1). Scalar violence is further affirmed across rhetoric and composition studies as scholars turn to networks and systems (Hesford, Licona, and Teston 2018; Mueller et al. 2017; Hesford and Schell 2008) as well as borders and decolonial thinking (Cisneros 2013; DeChaine 2013) to account for the asymmetrical distribution of violence, precariousness, and livability that follows the movement of description, language, and arguments across contexts and levels of scale.

This latter focus on the movement of *arguments* across scales most explicitly sponsors our own study of scalar violence, which considers how arguments within composition studies can produce violent affects. We follow Rebecca Dingo (2012), for example, who argues that "rhetoricians must look not only at static rhetorical occasions . . . but they must examine how rhetorics travel—how rhetorics might be picked up, how rhetorics might become networked with different arguments, and then how rhetorical meaning might shift and change as a result of these movements" (2). As Dingo shows through her study of gendered rhetorics, the effects of arguments radically shift across scales, moving from affirmation and empowerment of women at a policy conference through "local and global structures that exacerbate inequalities, such as international trade agreements, (neo)colonial power relationships, changing cultural practices, political unrest, and environmental degradation" (3). Our own study likewise identifies how arguments that travel across scales of composition do so with differential effects.

Importantly, investigating the potential violence of curricular innovation requires us not only to track arguments but to account for how the capacity for violence emerges in relation to their movement. Our analysis further aims to name false equivalences—which is to say, equivalences that misrecognize differences between levels of scale—and instances in which compositionists deploy the technique media theorist Zach Horton (2017) calls "scalar collapse," which consists "of conjoining two or more different scales within a single medium, enabling access from the first to the second by homogenizing their differential dynamics and subordinating the second to the first" (36). Throughout our case, "scalar jumps" flag arguments developed in one scalar context traveling to other levels of scale without fully acknowledging consequential, differential effects; these identifications encompass taking note of when and where a kind of scalar collapse has occurred and marking potential for consequent harm (which *may* be realized). In other words, delineating how arguments are made at particular levels of scale can reveal how boundaries are crossed and with what effects, which helps us name and understand the particularity of some violences endemic to composition. It is by further focusing on *who* is likely to be disproportionately impacted by related experiences that we expose latent violence inherent in specific scalar jumps associated with the mobilization of rhetorics that justify curricular innovation.

ORIENTING TO SCALE IN COMPOSITION STUDIES: USING DIGITAL COMPOSITION AS A GUIDE

Because complexity is best addressed in the contexts where it is found, the remainder of this chapter is dedicated to a hypothetical case that examines arguments for digital composition and design assignments and models acts of tracking, articulation, examination, and scalar reorientation. Our hypothetical case reflects patterns and trends in the field and from our experiences without (re)attaching violence to particular bodies already differentially exposed to scalar violence. Like reading or writing, digital composition is not a singular neutral activity but rather a suite of culturally situated practices and values that can be rationalized and mobilized toward diverse ideological and practical ends. The descriptive choices we make as authors foreground just a few of the many violences that have potential to emerge as arguments about digital composition jump from one scale to another to another, which include naming the harm such movement can inflict on different bodies and subjects. Many of the dynamics explored below could be articulated in relation to arguments for any kind of literacy activity, yet focusing on digital composition lends specificity to our discussion and mirrors the degree to which related conversations are currently "live" at many institutions. Despite having reached a point in the history of composition where such work is buoyed up by more than thirty years of scholarship, digital compositionists are still frequently required to defend its value.

Our scenario begins with arguments about digital composition that may be made by a writing program administrator (WPA) frequently called upon to perform actions at middle scales and to marshal arguments across scales using their bodies as well as their expertise. We imagine this decision-maker as a specialist committed to making ethical, disciplinarily responsible arguments for inclusion of digital assignments across a writing program and whose arguments are informed by dynamic, ongoing debates in the field. Whether they use the term *design* explicitly or not, our administrator's arguments align at least loosely with James Purdy's (2014) observation that, as a field, "what we mean to do" when we invoke design is "to account for multimodal and digital texts, avow the materiality of composing, and wrestle with questions of disciplinarity" and with his linked assertion that such "intentions are both a way to establish a broader conception of composing and a way to prepare for the composing possibilities of the future" (620). Although not all administrators will have this specific expertise (the violence of contingent administration is a separate, worthy topic), focusing on the disciplinarily prepared administrator demonstrates how the violence of scalar jumps is not one that can be solved through disciplinary training alone (i.e., at one level or scale). Moreover, good intentions—that sponsor arguments about using digital composition to benefit a wide cross section of students—travel with differential effects, and translation of goals into experiences is a scalar transaction, a messy, ongoing process that has potential to cause complex material effects and do (unwitting) harm.

MESO-SCALE ARGUMENTS: DISPARATE VALUES AND ADMINISTRATOR BODIES

Imagining the administrator described above, one "upward" scalar jump required of them is to make program-level arguments about digital composition by asking for resources. Because digital classroom work requires infrastructural support (access to tools, spaces, and training), even a WPA steering a program that has significant curricular autonomy must usually travel—arguments in hand—to the office of a dean or provost before expanding digital or design-centered program offerings. Beyond requesting resources, arguments at this scalar boundary are freighted with the potential to help our administrator intervene in institution-level narratives about what composition is, where its value lies, and when compositionists should be consulted by upper administration in the future. Whatever curricular change is on the table in a particular moment, rhetoric deployed in support of it is subject to the reality that naming, as Wendy Sharer, Tracey Anne Morse, Michelle F. Eble, and William P. Banks argue, is not arbitrary: "those who teach writing and those who administer writing programs," they contend, "need to be involved in defining the terms and setting the parameters" (Sharer et al. 2016, 3). While arguments for digital composition described at a programmatic level of scale will often be articulated in disciplinary terms—our administrator may, at various moments, promote digital assignments for their ability to disrupt current-traditional teaching and assessment (Shipka 2011), support multilingual writers (Gonzales 2018), and pose questions of access and accessibility (Dolmage 2018; Butler 2016)—an experienced WPA will likely deploy different warrants when negotiating with an upper administrator or a funding body. Like composition skills more broadly, digital composition skills can easily be framed as stepping stones to industry jobs and in relation to their support of STEM majors, business colleges, or global citizenship initiatives. Multiple expediencies ensure use of these framings: a dean may be unable to hear an overly disciplinary argument, institutional initiatives may invite specific reasoning, and questions of exchange value may be paramount to the argument's success. Concessions made (regarding how arguments must be framed) when negotiating this scalar boundary are relatively easy to pass off as temporally limited "necessary evils" or even as unlikely to travel back to a program's home department. As such, they are prone to erasing linguistic evidence of their own existence: arguments made in a dean's office stay in the dean's office. Yet it is in the context of this kind of scalar jump that we see most clearly how such deeply instrumentalist (tool- and finance-centric) arguments for digital composition are just as readily available as anti-instrumentalist (socially situated, student-centered, sometimes explicitly anti-capitalist) arguments for digital design work, and we begin to see how values from institutional mission statements and fiscal agendas "leak" into large- and meso-scale initiatives that support digital composition work.

One potential for everyday violence that exists in these situations is lodged there because of social macrocosms that operate both at the level of the institution and beyond. Women, queer and gender nonconforming individuals, disabled scholars, and scholars of color who occupy administrative roles often do so despite having had deep, personal experiences with institutional violence as a result of institution-level policies (including harassment, exclusions, and denials of earned expertise), and they are disproportionately taxed by the emotional pressures this situation creates. These individuals are particularly likely to hold values—emerging from experience as well as expertise—that conflict with visions of the university as a business, service provider, or neoliberal global training center. As the recent collection *Black Perspectives in Writing Program Administration*, edited by Staci Perryman-Clark and Collin Lamont Craig (2019), documents in relation to Black bodies and Black intellectual traditions, WPAs who do not occupy normative embodied positions face repeated pressure either to "cause trouble" by refusing to accept readily available scripts while arguing for their programs *or* to process the cognitive dissonance deploying such scripts produces. And scripts that work for others may still not be enough to prevent their authority from being questioned (4). Because such administrative choices structurally mimic choices people who belong to minority communities make in the face of everyday racisms, sexisms, ableisms, and homophobias, they contribute to decision fatigue and feelings of alienation and so function differently at a bodily level than seemingly similar "difficult" decisions function for individuals whose personal histories are less comprehensively structured by institutional inequities. This is a real violence linked to both mental and physical health outcomes, yet it is often relegated to invisibility precisely because it requires attention to how bodies store experience across time, a scalar phenomena our field tends to address in positive terms (for instance in relation to transfer or development of intuition) rather than through acknowledgment of how bodies suffer from routine, long-term management of microaggressions.

TRANSACTING CLASSROOMS: AMBIGUOUS VALUES
HAVE DIFFERENTIAL IMPACTS ON TEACHER BODIES

Continuing to follow arguments across scales in this section, it becomes evident that the potential need to advance both instrumental and anti-instrumental arguments about digital design within composition may participate in an uneven distribution of negative affects and harm to different kinds of administrator bodies. These effects are only exacerbated as program-level arguments, justified in multiple and sometimes competing ways, jump "down" and reach individual teachers, who are encouraged (sometimes required) to integrate digital composition into their own courses. While the existence of multiple possibilities for justifying design thinking ostensibly supports teachers, they can cause confusion and put pressure on new teachers and veteran teachers new to digital and design-oriented assignments, which may require these teachers to marshal individualized justifications that serve as pseudo-contracts with students and to negotiate conflicts that arise around unclear expectations for design-centered pedagogy.

Justificatory tensions can cause issues in any classroom, but their latent dangers multiply when contextualized by the large number of teachers who were not necessarily trained formally to perform the design work our field increasingly asks of them. Being skilled as a digital composer does not automatically translate into having good intuition about what kind of setup will help a video-, audio-, or social media–based assignment meet the needs of a specific class or student. In fact, sometimes those instructors most adept at picking up digital composing skills struggle to provide architecture to help students who are uncomfortable with digital or design-based assignments. The myth that young faculty and graduate students do not need specialist training in order to teach well with technology sets them up for undue scrutiny and overly critical self-evaluation. Because surveillance histories are violent, gendered, and racialized, experiences of even seemingly benign or "helpful" scrutiny are received and lived differently by different bodies.

Advocates for design-focused composition classes and units focused on digital projects, like the administrator introduced above, often speak or write into this situation by foregrounding an Aristotelian notion of "available means" or process pedagogies. Such framings have the benefit of being able to transcend media specificity, centering concepts composition instructors *are* trained to work with. Advocates also, whether implicitly or explicitly, frequently argue for pedagogies that promote student adoption of digital DIY (do-it-yourself) ethics. The next sections address conceptual particulars of DIY ethics in more detail, but they bear introduction here because, even though building them into curricula may aim to take pressure off teachers, it doesn't take equal pressure off all instructors. When they jump scales downward, policies that encourage promotion of DIY ethics in the classroom limit the appeals to expertise available to instructors as well as their ability to conceptualize and honor extracurricular dynamics implicated in learning to do design work in a classroom setting. Both are more challenging issues for teachers whose embodiment or positionality invites students to question their authority; this again includes women, queer and gender nonconforming individuals, scholars of color, and instructors with visible and invisible disabilities, as well as new instructors, individuals who appear particularly young or old, and contingent faculty. These challenges are intensified by the entangled, contradictory institutional and disciplinary pressures that have jumped down from multiple levels of scale to promote DIY ethics without acknowledging their complexities. This jump thus sets certain kinds of bodies up to experience disproportionate classroom resistance and, in an affective cascade, to perform additional emotional labor as they parse the causes of that resistance and manage it across time. As noted above, this differential distribution of affective labor is a form of structured violence, given the physical and psychological costs such labor exacts.

IN THE DIY CLASSROOM: STUDENTS' HISTORIES AND AESTHETICS INTERACT WITH STRUCTURAL VALUES

As indicated thus far, travelling arguments about digital composition participate in a complex array of conditions, and articulations that seem straightforward and progressive at the level of field-wide or curriculum-level discussions can produce wildly different effects at other levels. When arguments about DIY ethics jump down to the level of the classroom, they not only impact teacher bodies but the range of student bodies there.

In relation to digital composition, the phrase *do-it-yourself* can serve as a catch-all name for pedagogical approaches that also value learning with and from one's peers; it can be shorthand for an instructor's attempts to craft a decentralized learning environment that promises (and sometimes delivers) feelings of empowerment to students; it may tap histories that surround remix cultures (Palmeri 2012) or punk and situationist aesthetics (Sirc 2002). Or it may drift into an instructor's lexicon through exposure to Digital Humanities lab culture (Sayers

2011) or makerspace discourse (Shivers-McNair 2016). Initiatives that draw on related histories and use promotion of DIY ethics to signal anti-instrumentalist or anti-capitalist commitments are, on the surface, difficult to disparage. Scholarship in composition and technical communication reminds us, however, that inflexible anti-instrumentalist positions are disproportionately hostile to low-income, nontraditional, and first-generation college students whose lived experiences and culturally situated expectations structure their ideas about the value of labor, expertise, and money in complicated ways, and that values inherited across scales run a higher risk of becoming inflexible.

DIY pedagogies rely on students' problem-solving skills and ability to leverage extracurricular knowledge (and have thus been compared to students' right to their own language), but they also rely on students' previous experiences with specific technologies, previous training in research and technical skills, willingness to ask for help (a skill that often codes differently for first-generation and multilingual students), and ability to put in hours troubleshooting outside class. These reliances advantage students from affluent or STEM high schools and homes or communities where mentors are college-educated and fluent in some computational literacies, even if those literacies are not the exact literacies a student is working to develop. Even the last "requirement," time for troubleshooting, can be a hostile expectation. Not only does it disadvantage students with jobs, caring responsibilities, and disabilities who have less flexible schedules, it isolates students reluctant to admit that their access to computers is intermittent (e.g., who commute but rely on campus computer labs) or whose primary device—which may be a phone or tablet rather than a computer—lacks the memory and processing power to run design software smoothly. It also disadvantages students with limited or intermittent access to the internet: a good connection that can be accessed wherever they are working becomes more essential as soon as students are tasked with teaching themselves a new technical skill (by Googling how to solve code or software problems, following tutorials on YouTube, or asking questions on message boards). Since lower-income students are more likely to use a phone rather than a computer to access the internet (Rideout and Katz 2016) and broadband is less available in rural areas (Lohr 2018), these disadvantages impact individual student bodies in decidedly differential ways. Such impacts, of course, are not bound by classroom walls or semester calendars but affectively and violently structure long-term relations to composition (digital or otherwise), technology, confidence, expertise, and education.

REVERBERATIONS AND INTERANIMATIONS:
REFOCUSING ATTENTION ON COMPLEXITY

The "answer" to this situation is not as simple as turning away from digital assignments or removing references to DIY ethics from curricula. Looking to an alternative way of framing related work, arguments for the introduction of skills that lead to jobs (out of respect for students' whose lived experiences make them particularly worried about employability) can also cause trouble when they jump into classrooms as an inflexible focus. This move simultaneously encourages student buy-in *and* prompts instructors to overvalue aesthetics that are appealing (nonthreatening) for white, middle-class audiences. Rhetorics of professionalization—as arguments that travel—always contain a potential for violence that takes the form of erasure. Undervaluing the contributions of underrepresented students can in turn drive students who have affective, identity-laden relationships to nondominant aesthetics out of composition courses and the larger field of composition. For student bodies, then, related experiences of violence include weathering individual classroom situations that are abusive as well as enduring the forced affective labor and material uncertainty that attend reimagining which (if any) major fields have potential to be more welcoming.

Moreover, scalar violences recur and undergo functional transformations as arguments about digital composition jump, in turn, upward from the level of the student to the level of the teacher, the WPA, the college or university, and the field. For instance, insights and sample projects collected in finish-oriented classrooms make for strong "evidence" of the effectiveness of these classrooms; the things they do best are easier to carry across scales and show off via Powerpoint than process-oriented or metacognitive outcomes. But the same sublimated assumptions that hurt individual students by encouraging instructors to uphold culturally dominant notions that assign differential economic, intellectual, and moral value to design features associated with minority and majority aesthetics cause trouble when translated back up to the level of program design and research: there, they undermine the field's ability to interrupt dominant forms of representation and expression. This scenario exposes one way in which "micro"-exercises of aesthetic judgment can have cascading effects, participating in forms of pedagogic violence that capitalize on students' "affective relation to the world" (Worsham 1998, 216). That this violence is only clearly discernable when we look at relations in context suggests that intervening at the level of individual action—at one level of scale—is insufficient for ameliorating related micro- and macroaggressions and exclusions (Jung 2014). In other words, scalar jumps and their effects are never discrete; neither do the exemplary dynamics isolated above come close to describing—let alone exhausting—the scenario posed. Jumps can be vertical or lateral, asynchronous or simultaneous, and they take on distinct textures based on local situations. For instance, what it looks like to support subjectivity-affirming digital aesthetics at a land grant, Hispanic-Serving Institution in southeastern New Mexico may differ in significant ways from similarly affirmative work on another campus.

NAMING SCALAR CROSSINGS AND HONORING VULNERABILITIES

This exploration of how some arguments surrounding digital design hypothetically traverse scales of composition begins to delineate the complex, necessary work of tracking scalar violence in the field. In this formulation, simple answers rarely exist, because situations are differently risky for different bodies. Operating under the premise that even the best practices available to us as compositionists are structured by existing vulnerabilities, we see this not as a flaw in our field but as a realistic description that applies to all fields and as necessary incitement for ongoing reassessment of how emergent properties impact bodies variously. Imagining how, why, and where harm is made possible is what sets us up to recognize and then to intervene. In our conclusion, then, we respond to this setup (made possible by identifying scales of composition and by tracking arguments that move across them) with suggestions for intervention that apply to both the specific hypothetical case described and other cases implicated in our broader argument that violence in composition *is* scalar, that bodies and experiences and lives are moralized, managed, and misrecognized as arguments and composition's values move across scales. Neither exhaustive nor absolvent, we advocate flexible heuristics that proceed knowingly across scales in order to intervene in the reproduction of vulnerability exacerbated by unexamined scalar crossings and suggest a need for infrastructures that support and sustain use of such heuristics.

Given our examples as well as their overdetermined role in composition writ large, we encourage administrators—already required to work at multiple levels of scale—to map the scales of their workflow, identifying where and how arguments travel disciplinarily, institutionally, and programmatically. With potential to be an overwhelming task (for those already overworked), it can begin by simply marking the interfaces of labor: where, when, how, and to whom do these administrators talk about their work? With whom do they communicate in person? With department chairs, general education committees? With program assistants, graduate assistants, adjunct instructors, faculty? With collaborators, conference attendees, editors? With whom do they communicate through intermediaries—deans, provosts, chancellors? Writing students, faculty across campus, scholars, and other WPAs in the field? Identifying these groups points to the scope and scales of WPA work, and intervention becomes easier through following accounts of how, when, and which arguments travel differently to each group. A WPA who has marked the interfaces of their work (load) is better prepared to consider, for example, how an argument they make to colleagues in favor of using departmental funds to update a computer lab might travel to and land with writing instructors who feel alienated by digital technologies. This could invite formulation of arguments for the other kinds of resources required to make the lab live up to its potential (food that draws instructors to an open-house event that demystifies the space, consultants to staff open lab-hours for students, speakers who are experts in digital culture, and so forth). It might further help them prioritize development of trainings to help teachers meaningfully incorporate technologies into their curriculum and anticipate how the range of students who will be in their classes may assign "meaningfulness" in different ways (and, ideally, to argue for stipends to support teachers interested in learning more about the possibilities and limits of teaching in related contexts).

Importantly, it is not only administrators who are imbricated in the scalar violence of composition. Marking interfaces and tracking arguments across them can be practiced by anyone seeking to interrupt how composition reproduces violence. Teachers of writing can mark the interfaces that structure their classes, revealing not only teacher/student relations but teacher/program relations, teacher/teacher relations, and teacher/field relations. Considering how arguments come into and move out of the individual classroom both respects and rejects its clear boundaries so that descriptions at one level of scale (within the classroom) can be contextualized by their entanglements with others. For instance, an instructor who has marked the fact that the strong, anti-instrumentalist argument for humanistic knowledge that they value comes from their engagement in institution- and field-level conversations *might also* mark the fact that students who experience scarcity in their daily lives are, rightfully, more skeptical of arguments that value knowledge for knowledge's sake or that promote artistry *at the expense* of employability. This might help the instructor engage students in more dynamic ways without feeling like their own core values have been compromised—an outcome that diffuses the need for excess emotional labor rather than forcing them to choose between bearing an affective burden or translocating it onto students. Students, too, can gain new perspectives on how to navigate composition by tracking how arguments traverse scalar relations. For instance, naming the expectations they carry laterally from one class to another might help them resist sexist evaluation of teachers, while naming a classroom practice that puts undo pressure on them as functionally different from an institutional policy might help them better advocate for their needs. Training students to ask themselves where their ideas have come from, how they land with other students and instructors, and why these landings have certain functional characteristics might further become an explicit goal in some composition classrooms.

Ultimately, our goal is not to stop making arguments that fall in the categories referenced throughout this chapter but rather to commit to tracking how their rhetoric circulates at multiple scales, paying special attention to places where material conditions and embodied experiences exert transformative pressure on disciplinary possibilities. The urgency of this call depends on the reality that circulation of our rhetorics across scales and the emergent properties that accompany those crossings influence students', instructors', and administrators' ability to engage day-to-day classroom experiences in safe, meaningful ways.

REFERENCES

Bernard-Donals, Michael. 2002. Review of *Between Hope and Despair: Pedagogy and the Remembrance of Historical Trauma. JAC: A Journal of Composition Theory* 22, no. 3: 705–13. JSTOR.

Borrowman, Shane, ed. 2005. *Trauma and the Teaching of Writing.* Albany: SUNY Press.

Bousquet, Marc, Tony Scott, and Leo Parascondola, eds. 2004. *Tenured Bosses and Disposable Teachers: Writing Instruction in the Managed University.* Carbondale: Southern Illinois University Press.

Butler, Janine. 2016. "Where Access Meets Multimodality: The Case of ASL Music Videos." *Kairos* 21, no. 1. http://kairos.technorhetoric.net/21.1/topoi/butler/index.html.

Canagarajah, Suresh. 2002. *A Geopolitics of Academic Writing.* Pittsburgh: University of Pittsburgh Press.

Casanave, Christine Pearson. 2008. "The Stigmatizing Effect of Goffman's Stigma Label: A Response to John Flowerdew." *Journal of English for Academic Purposes* 7, no. 4: 264–67. doi: 10.1016/j.jeap.2008.10.013.

Cisneros, Josue David. 2013. *The Border Crossed Us: Rhetorics of Borders, Citizenship, and Latina/o Identity.* Tuscaloosa: University of Alabama Press.

Costino, Kimberly A., and Sunny Hyon. 2007. "'Class for Students like Me': Reconsidering Relationships among Identity Labels, Residency Status, and Students' Preferences for Mainstream or Multilingual Composition." *Journal of Second Language Writing* 16, no. 2: 63–81. doi: 10.1016/j.jslw.2007.04.001.

Das, Veena, and Arthur Kleinman. 2000. "Introduction." In *Violence and Subjectivity*, edited by Veena Das, Arthur Kleinman, Mamphela Pamphele, and Pamela Reynolds, 1–18. Los Angeles: University of California Press.

DeChaine, D. Robert. 2013. *Border Rhetorics: Citizenship and Identity on the US-Mexico Border*. Tuscaloosa: University of Alabama Press.

Dingo, Rebecca. 2012. *Networking Arguments: Rhetoric, Transnational Feminism, and Public Policy Writing*. Pittsburgh: University of Pittsburgh Press.

Dolmage, Jay. 2018. "Open Access(ibility?)." In *Circulation, Rhetoric, and Writing*, edited by Laurie E. Gries and Collin Gifford Brooke, 262–80. Logan: Utah State University Press.

Donehower, Kim, Charlotte Hogg, and Eileen E. Schell, eds. 2007. *Rural Literacies*. Carbondale: Southern Illinois University Press.

Gilligan, James. 1996. *Violence: Reflections on a National Epidemic*. New York: Vintage.

Gonzales, Laura. 2018. *Sites of Translation: What Multilinguals Can Teach Us about Digital Writing and Rhetoric*. Ann Arbor: University of Michigan Press.

Hesford, Wendy S. 2011. *Spectacular Rhetorics: Human Rights Visions, Recognitions, Feminisms*. Durham: Duke University Press.

Hesford, Wendy S., Adela C. Licona, and Christa Teston, eds. 2018. *Precarious Rhetorics*. Columbus: Ohio State University Press.

Hesford, Wendy S., and Eileen E. Schell. 2008. "Configurations of Transnationality: Locating Feminist Rhetorics." *College English* 70, no. 5: 461–70. JSTOR.

Horton, Zach. 2017. "Composing a Cosmic View: Three Alternatives for Thinking Scale in the Anthropocene." In *Size and Scale in Literature and Culture*, edited by Michael Travel Clarke and David Wittenberg, 35–60. New York: Palgrave Macmillan.

Jung, Julie. 2014. "Systems Rhetoric: A Dynamic Coupling of Explanation and Description." *Enculturation* 17. http://enculturation.net/systems-rhetoric.

Kynard, Carmen. 2015. "Teaching while Black: Witnessing and Countering Disciplinary Whiteness, Racial Violence, and University Race-Management." *Literacy in Composition Studies (LiCS)* 3, no. 1: 1–20. doi: 10.21623%2F1.3.1.2.

Lohr, Steve. 2018. "Digital Divide Is Wider than We Think, Study Says." *New York Times*, Dec. 4, 2018. https://www.nytimes.com/2018/12/04/technology/digital-divide-us-fcc-microsoft.html.

Mays, Chris. 2015. "From 'Flows' to 'Excess': On Stability, Stubbornness, and Blockage in Rhetorical Ecologies." *Enculturation* 19. http://enculturation.net/from-flows-to-excess.

Mueller, Derek N., Jennifer Clary-Lemon, Louise Wetherbee Phelps, and Andrea Williams. 2017. *Cross-Border Networks in Writing Studies*. Anderson: Parlor Press.

Palmeri, Jason. 2012. *Remixing Composition: A History of Multimodal Writing Pedagogy*. Carbondale: Southern Illinois University Press.

Perryman-Clark, Staci, and Colin Lamont Craig, eds. 2019. *Black Perspectives in Writing Program Administration*. Urbana: NCTE.

Prendergast, Catherine. 2003. *Literacy and Racial Justice: The Politics of Learning after Brown v. Board of Education*. Carbondale: Southern Illinois University Press.

Purdy, James P. 2014. "What Can Design Thinking Offer Writing Studies?" *College Composition and Communication* 65, no. 4, 612–41. JSTOR.

Rideout, Victoria, and Vikki S. Katz. 2016. "Opportunity for All? Technology and Learning in Lower-Income Families." The Joan Ganz Cooney Center at Sesame Workshop. Winter 2016. https://www.joanganzcooneycenter.org/wp-content/uploads/2016/01/jgcc_opportunityforall.pdf.

Rose, Mike. 1989. *Lives on the Boundary: The Struggles and Achievements of America's Underprepared*. New York: Free Press.

Sayers, Jentery. 2011. "Tinker-Centric Pedagogy in Literature and Language Classrooms." In *Collaborative Approaches to the Digital in English Studies*, edited by Laura McGrath. Logan: Computers and Composition Digital Press/Utah State University Press.

Sharer, Wendy, Tracey Anne Morse, Michelle F. Eble, and William P. Banks. 2016. *Reclaiming Accountability: Improving Writing Programs through Accreditation and Large-Scale Assessment*. Logan: Utah State University Press.

Sharp-Hoskins, Kellie, and Amy E. Robillard. 2012. "Narrating the Good Teacher in Rhetoric and Composition: Ideology, Affect, Complicity." *JAC: A Journal of Composition Theory* 32, no. 1: 305–36. JSTOR.

Shaughnessy, Mina. 1977. *Errors and Expectations: A Guide for the Teacher of Basic Writing.* New York: Oxford University Press.

Shipka, Jody. 2011. *Toward a Composition Made Whole.* Pittsburgh: University of Pittsburgh Press.

Shivers-McNair, Ann. 2016. "What Can We Learn about Writing and Rhetoric from a Makerspace?" Sweetland Digital Rhetoric Collaborative, Gayle Morris Sweetland Center for Writing, University of Michigan. Mar. 17, 2016. http://www.digitalrhetoriccollaborative .org/2016/03/17/what-can-we-learn-about-writing-and-rhetoric-from-a-makerspace/.

Sirc, Geoffrey. 2002. *English Composition as a Happening.* Logan: Utah State University Press.

Syverson, Margaret. 1999. *The Wealth of Reality: An Ecology of Composition.* Carbondale: Southern Illinois University Press.

Thomas, Michael, ed. 2011. *Deconstructing Digital Natives: Young People, Technology and the New Literacies.* New York: Routledge.

Yood, Jessica. 2013. "A History of Pedagogy in Complexity: Reality Checks for Writing Studies." *Enculturation* 16. http://enculturation.net/history-of-pedagogy.

Wan, Amy. 2014. *Producing Good Citizens: Literacy Training in Anxious Times.* Pittsburgh: University of Pittsburgh Press.

Wolters, Wendy. 2004. "Without Sanctuary: Bearing Witness, Bearing Whiteness." *JAC: A Journal of Composition Theory* 24, no. 1: 399–424. JSTOR.

Worsham, Lynn. 2006. "*Composing (Identity) in a Posttraumatic Age.*" In *Identity Papers: Literacy and Power in Higher Education,* edited by Bronwyn Williams, 170–81. Logan: Utah State University Press.

Worsham, Lynn. 1998. "Going Postal: Pedagogical Violence and the Schooling of Emotion." *JAC: A Journal of Composition Theory* 18, no. 1: 213–45. JSTOR.

3

RECOGNIZING SLOW VIOLENCES AND DECOLONIZING NEOLIBERAL ASSESSMENT PRACTICES

Lisa Dooley

I have a question: How *careful* and *cooperative, creative* and *disciplined* are you? Here's another one: To what extent do you exude *goodwill, optimism,* and *savvy*? Without knowing you—or anything about you and your lived embodied reality and experiences—would a complete stranger evaluate you the same way that you evaluated yourself? Or, instead, would that stranger have to know more about you in order to evaluate the degree to which you exhibit these behaviors? Now, what if the data gathered about you was aggregated over a continuum of kindergarten through your career and you were marked and tracked over this period of time as normative or nonnormative, prepared or unprepared, likely or unlikely to be successful? Here's a final set of questions: If, through a series of assessments, you are evaluated as "unready" and "unprepared"— marked as having either little potential for success or less potential than "normal"—and then this data affixed to your embodied identity is made available to educators and prospective employers, what sort of damage could it do? Does there exist the possibility, even the probability, that your career prospects could be diminished, thus affecting your quality of life? What about the impact to your psyche if you begin to believe results indicating that you have decreased potential for success? What violences happen when assessments of worth and potential have material and psychological consequences?

The social/emotional characteristics that I mentioned above (carefulness, cooperation, creativity, discipline, goodwill, optimism, and savvy) are just a few of the behavioral characteristics that are evaluated by the assessments that comprise the Expanded Framework for Readiness of ACT (American College Testing).[1] Decontextualized and disembodied social/emotional behavioral assessments—which pose threats of violence through the misalignment between one's personal

https://doi.org/10.7330/9781646422807.c003

potential for success and a stranger's assessment of this potential—are exactly what ACT is marketing to parents, educators, and employers as predictive of normativity and success in students' future careers. With far-reaching and harmful consequences for embodied identities being assessed as "unready" and potentially "unsuccessful,"[2] I understand these assessments as performances of violence in which a body assessed as lacking potential is marked for failure in the neoliberal market-driven economy.[3] It is my argument, then, that assessments such as those included in ACT's Framework commit acts of slow violence, effected by the growing neoliberal mindset that "manages bodies" to the detriment of those bodies.

Contemporary assessments impact people in profound and violent ways. Scholars in the field of composition studies have both the skills and the responsibility to recognize and reimagine assessment methodologies and methods that better address violent, colonizing assessment practices. Chris Gallagher (2011) contends that as compositionists we "are well aware that assessment is, to invoke Edward White's apt phrase, a 'site of contention'" and recognize that "assessment is about power and politics not only in terms of who is assessed and how, but also who assesses and how" (458). Acknowledging that our field is not exempt from the impact of assessments has encouraged and sustained fruitful ongoing conversations. Scholars like Bob Broad (2003), Norbert Elliot (2005), Peggy O'Neil et al. (2009), Asao Inoue and Mya Poe (2012), Cruz Medina and Kenny Walker (2018), William P. Banks et al. (2018), and Nicole I. Caswell and Stephanie West-Puckett (2019) have for years been talking, writing, and presenting at conferences about contextualized, localized, student-centered, process-focused assessments and socially just assessment pedagogy. In spite of these important discussions taking place in the field, we still encounter colonizing assessment practices (like ACT's Framework) that perform violences and do harm. It is my argument that assessments such as those included in ACT's Framework commit acts of slow violence effected by the growing neoliberal mindset that seeks to control and thereby harm young bodies. Such neoliberal practices effectively colonize the embodied identities of those subjected to the Framework. Before they enter our classrooms, the students that we teach have already been assessed in unfair, inequitable, and harmful ways. So, when problematic assessment practices like the large-scale longitudinal assessments housed within ACT's Framework act upon our students, we as scholars, teachers, and compositionists should be concerned about the tests being given and the impact of the appraisals rendered. Our expertise holds us responsible for recognizing and intervening in all forms of assessment, especially those that perform violence, no matter the level of education at which the assessment/violence occurs.

In response to violent assessment practices, I proceed in the following manner. First, I articulate my understanding of assessment, colonization, and slow violences. Then, before analyzing the Framework as an enactment of slow violence, I discuss a key culprit: neoliberalism and neoliberal assessment practices. Next, I demonstrate those practices and describe the harm they cause. Finally, I make a call to recognize and intervene in violent neoliberal assessment practices and to utilize nonviolent assessment methods.

COLONIZATION, ASSESSMENT, AND SLOW VIOLENCE

Broadly speaking, I understand assessment as classification through evaluation with the objective of assigning value. When evaluations mark deficit and deviation from an assumed "norm," bodies are classified as average/normal or the inverse, atypical/abnormal. Then, average/normal bodies are upheld as standard and the nonnormative bodies are othered and discounted (Dolmage 2014, 2012; Gould 1996). The field of composition studies traditionally defined assessment as an evaluative tool to determine adherence to a universalized, "correct," teacher-articulated final product (Elbow 1973) that was discussed through a framework of validity and normativity (Cushman 2016). Then, a transformation took place. As foci in the field changed from a product orientation to process pedagogy and then from process to postprocess, space emerged for scholarship that engaged with antiracist (Inoue 2009; Villanueva 1999), anti-ableist (Dolmage 2012), contextualized and localized (Gallagher 2011; Broad 2003), student-centered assessments, as well as nonviolent (Lederman and Warwick 2018), socially-just assessment pedagogy (Caswell and West-Puckett 2019). These conversations engage assessment as socially situated and negotiated, maintaining a focus on students that considers assessment's impacts and damages (i.e., violences) done—particularly to those marginalized and multiply marginalized. Though this transformation marks an important conceptual shift away from assessment-as-method-of-determining-normativity, Nicole I. Caswell and William Banks acknowledge that "unfortunately, as we sit in campus assessment conversations . . . the discourse of normalization (e.g., base lines, norms, agreement, and standards) remains" (Caswell and Banks 2018, 360). Matthew Gomes (2018) echoes this observation and discusses assessment as a colonial project, explaining that "while colonization is historical, it is also ongoing and continual" (205). Even in this enlightened moment in composition studies, when assessments—tasked with indexing and quantifying deficit and deprivation—construct embodied identities, they also create stratification and denote deviations as "problems" by assessing for defect and deficit. Distance from the established norm determines the degree to which the test-taker is "normal." These assessments, then, operate as methods of colonization.

Colonization (Haas 2015, 2012; Anzaldúa 2012; Tuhiwai Smith 2012) takes place when humans are denied the right to govern themselves and are managed by another. The history of colonization is narrated by violent accounts of domination, oppression, and (white) supremacy. From forced migration and enslavement to disenfranchisement and marginalization, colonization has landed with brutal impact on those assessed as "nonnormative" (i.e., nonwhite, noncisgender male, non-Western, nonheterosexual, nonnormatively abled), and it has been weaponized for violent assault. Angela M. Haas (2015) notes that colonization "has a long history of prescribing personal and community identities and the values associated with those identities" (191), and colonized bodies—along with their cultures and identities—were (and still are) appropriated for use by colonizers. Colonization is about managing bodies, in part through identity politics; it's about articulating valued identities and characteristics (emergent from hegemonic norms) and then justifying colonization's work of management and governmentality with those same normative assumptions.

Assessment and colonization make common cause, for, combined, they create the types of assessment that measure bodies against arbitrary norms. Through methods of evaluation and classification, bodies are evaluated and measured against subjective norms, while assessments of normativity act upon these bodies by ascribing meaning to them, shoring up power and privilege through the inclusion of some bodies while justifying exclusion of other bodies through a process of othering. Make no mistake, this "acting upon" bodies *is itself* a performance of violence, one that has impacts on and consequences for those being assessed. Regardless of the form it takes, colonization performs violences. Colonization enacted through assessment (and colonization as assessment) provides just one lens through which to view colonization as violences and, more specifically, as slow violences.

Slow violences are outgrowths of colonization. In taking up this argument, it is important to discuss the term *violences* and to differentiate between types of violences and enactments of violences. To begin, I should make a quick differentiation: it is *not* violence that we are discussing, rather it is violenc*es* that we are considering. Violence is not singular; it is layered with a multiplicity of manifestations, actualizations, impacts, and effects. Violences perform, as Johan Galtung (1990) describes, "avoidable insults to basic human needs, and more generally to life, lowering the real level of needs satisfaction below what is potentially possible" (292), and violences are "that which increases the distance between the potential and the actual, and that which impedes the decrease of this distance" (1969, 168). So violences impede: they impede self-realization, self-actualization, and self-confidence. And, through structural inequality, violences set up systems of exclusion and inequity.

Though multiple violences exist, it is overt violences that are most often acknowledged as violence at all. In *The Violence of Literacy*, J. Elspeth Stuckey (1991) posits, "Too often, people perceive broad change only in terms of violence. They overlook the incremental, daily violence against those who are not favored by the system" (127). The violences that Stuckey describes materialize in the overlooking, disregarding, disenfranchising, marginalizing, and ignoring of less powerful and less privileged bodies by those with more power and privilege. These incremental, repeated, and unrelenting violences are, arguably, most lethal when they are covert.

Persistent, incremental violences are slow violences; as Rob Nixon (2011) explains, they occur "gradually and out of sight" (2). There is an important distinction to be made between singular violent events and accumulative violences. Nixon (2011) parses this differentiation between violence "conceived as an event or action that is immediate in time, explosive and spectacular in space, and as erupting into instant sensational visibility" and "violence that is neither spectacular nor instantaneous, but rather incremental and accretive, its calamitous repercussions playing out across a range of temporal scales" (2). Slow violences—residing in the psyche and imprinting on the flesh of those that they inflict—are accumulative, exponential in impact, and impose long-term damage.

Slow violences permeate assessment practices. As discussed by Josh Lederman and Nicole Warwick, when educators "quantify unquantifiable matters just for the sake of satisfying institutional pressures" (Lederman and Warwick 2018, 230), slow violences are enacted. When a culture of silence—when "the object of structural violence may be persuaded not to perceive [the violence enacted] at all" (Galtung 1969, 173)—is supported and preserved, slow violences are enacted. When erasure occurs or is attempted, slow violences are enacted.[4] My point is that some bodies determine what (and whom) to quantify, what is unsayable, and who is erasable, while others—the quantified ones being treated unjustly and unequally—are the ones being erased. Certain bodies determine who is acknowledged and who is not, whose story is told and whose is ignored, whose bodies are upheld by privilege and whose are discounted and marginalized, who counts as a witness to these violences, and (more importantly) who does not.

Colonization's slow violences occur when a person is evaluated, interpreted, and reduced to the characterization made by another and then acted upon as a result of that decontextualized depiction. These slow violences circulate through countless colonizing assessment practices. While I argue in this chapter that violences permeate assessment practices through the management of bodies, I (even more importantly) also contend that mitigating violent impacts and enactments of violences requires recognizing violences as they permeate assessment. This being said, for the remainder of this chapter I will focus on neoliberalism—as exemplified through ACT's Expanded Framework for Readiness—to discuss one enactment of slow violences.

SLOW VIOLENCES IN ACTION: NEOLIBERALISM AND THE ACT FRAMEWORK

Fundamental to my discussion in this chapter is a clear sense of neoliberalism and how it constitutes a specific problem. To begin, my understanding of neoliberalism draws upon the scholarship of Cathy Chaput (2010) and Rebecca Dingo (2012). Neoliberalism governs bodies and manages everyday activities through specific practices tasked with intervening in lives and impacting bodies. According to Chaput (2010), it "functions through a series of political and cultural interventions designed to implement competition as an economic rationality that counters purportedly irrational social practices" (4). Dingo (2012) clearly articulates the reach of neoliberalism, from capitalist market logic to infiltration into all facets of life, explaining that "the *ideology* of neoliberalism trickles into our everyday lived experiences" (10, emphasis original). This seepage of neoliberal ideology—where significance and value is assigned in relation to one's ability to support the economy—has informed the narrative of what it means to be a "good worker" in the neoliberal economy. Disrupting this narrative is essential and includes identifying neoliberal constructions of "valuable" bodies, witnessing as an act of recognition, and confronting the slow violences of neoliberalism.

Since violence studies examine both "the use of violence and the legitimation of that use" (Galtung 1990, 291), then neoliberalism fits well into this purview of study. It is, in many ways, a self-fulfilling prophecy: neoliberalism enacts a slow structural violence, covertly setting up scenes of inequality that privilege some through the facade of choice while punishing others who have been excluded. These violences can be performed when evaluations of inferiority impact both financial sustainability (like being hired for a job) and access to education and fiscal opportunities (like loans and grants). Through the guise of choice, systems maintain power with exclusionary practices of classification and categorization that materialize through neoliberal assessment.

Neoliberalism is one vivid performance of colonization, a performance that makes visible the slow violences of colonization and assessment. The violences carried out through neoliberal assessment practices are particularly evident in ACT's Framework. This suite of assessments is designed to chart individuals from kindergarten through their time in the workforce, marking bodies from an early age and then following them until retirement in order to aggregate purported behavioral data to predict academic performance, career readiness, and proclivity to become useful (i.e., profitable) employees.[5]

Though the Framework includes a variety of assessments developed to measure and remediate students' social/emotional behaviors and skills, for the purposes of this chapter I would like to focus on ACT WorkKeys Suite and ACT Engage.[6] As explained by Wayne Camara, Ryan O'Connor, Krista Mattern, and Mary Ann Hanson in one of the 2015 ACT Research Reports, ACT's Holistic Framework of Education and Workplace Readiness features "assessments, curriculum, and skill profiles that build and measure essential workplace skills," like ACT WorkKeys Talent, an "assessment to measure behaviors and attitudes related to important workplace outcomes" and ACT Engage,[7] "a measure of a student's level of motivation, social engagement, self-regulation" (Camara et al. 2015, 6). These assessments identify "at-risk" students who may benefit from (profitable) interventions to support them throughout their education and beyond. In an attempt to justify this charting and tracking of bodies, Camara et al., on behalf of ACT, give the following explanation: "The framework describes what individuals need to know and be able to do to be successful. A hierarchical taxonomy within each broad domain organizes the more specific dimensions and the knowledge and skills and provides a common language for describing the precursors of success. The focus is ultimately on knowledge, behaviors, and skills because these are amenable to change" (9). Based on a set of standards developed by

ACT, and enacted through the performance of neoliberalism within a colonial agenda, normativity is evaluated subjectively and prescribed as a precursor to a neoliberal sense of academic and career preparedness and success. As in all colonial endeavors, these standards are both articulated and assessed by those in positions of power and privilege. In this case, the standards being evaluated are explained, if unsatisfyingly, by Camara and his colleagues: "Ideally, we prefer to develop standards through an analysis of actual—not expected—student performance. Unfortunately, such empirical data do not currently exist for many of the constructs of interest; therefore, the approach we have taken is to establish a set of standards linked by hypothesized learning progressions that can then be validated empirically" (63). The arbitrary standards by which bodies are evaluated, marked, and (potentially) othered are being established (through hypothesis rather than based on any actual analysis of performance) by the testing agency that has a vested interest in articulating standards which reify their privileged position as arbiter of knowledge.

By incorporating noncognitive behavioral assessments that, as Camara et al. explain, provide "a measure of a student's level of motivation, social engagement, and self-regulation" as early as grade school (8), this framework works to codify behavior from a young age. One of the "selling points" that ACT touts as predictive of patterns of success includes standardized assessments to indicate such qualities as acting honestly, getting along with others, keeping an open mind, maintaining composure, socializing with others, and sustaining effort. Then, in trying to establish behavioral values in the interest of predicting potentiality for success, social/emotional behavioral characteristics—carefulness, cooperation, creativity, discipline, goodwill, influence, optimism, order, savvy, sociability, stability, and striving—are evaluated in order to identify normativity and to quantify bodies with the goal of "amending" them in relation to their speculative, hypothesized, normative expectations and assumptions. These behavioral skills domains are subjective, often gendered, and racialized character evaluations, shaped by histories of colonization and domination.

Although seldom viewed as violence, classification categorizes with intent; through classification, power is consolidated as "the other" is named (Dolmage 2018, 2014, 2012; Tuhiwai Smith 2012; Gould 1996). Classifying, then, can be understood as one way of performing the slow violences of assessment's neoliberal colonial agenda. By prescribing valued behavioral characteristics—and by purportedly measuring the extent to which an individual embodies these valued identities, locating these bodies on a continuum of potentiality for success, and then disclosing this information to potential future employers—the neoliberal assessment practices carried out through ACT's Framework rely heavily upon systems of decontextualized evaluation and classification and are but one example of assessment as slow violence.

Within a neoliberal culture of standardization, success is uniform, and prescriptive normativity is valued. As Gallagher (2011) explains, "When education is viewed only 'in terms of' the market, accountability becomes a matter of providing data to feed that market. And assessment becomes the means by which those data are collected and reported" (456). In effect, the neoliberal economic obsession with measurable results and outcomes is performed in the name of gathering data for the purpose of standardization. It is important to identify this connection between measurable outcomes, standardized job preparedness screenings, and a neoliberal sense of success (i.e., monetary accumulation), and it is equally as important to complicate it. In the case of ACT's Framework, the neoliberal understanding of success (accumulated wealth) drives the creation, promotion, and use of career-readiness screenings (like the Framework's suite of assessments) in order to identify those who are normal (occupying a privileged positionality) and manage (colonize) those determined to be abnormal. These assessments reduce test-takers to quantifiable and measurable attributes that can be hierarchically categorized in relation to potential for success in the neoliberal economy.

The Framework shapes itself in response to this neoliberal exigency, performing slow violences in the process. That performance begins with format. A report included in the 2017 ACT Research Report Series explains the format: "The highest level contains broad domains of personality. The following and more detailed level contains components, or 'facets.' Next . . . are the subcomponents. The final and most specific level of the Behavioral Skills framework is composed of Performance Level Descriptors, which are specific observable behaviors that can lead to success in applied settings" (Colbow et al. 2017, 1–2). Table 3.1 (Domains, Components, and Subcomponents of the ACT Behavioral Framework) was included as a visual depiction in the report of the Framework. This hierarchical taxonomy of neoliberal values is based on a structure of "normative" predictive behavioral characteristics/components, each followed by definitions situating them within a neoliberal perception of what it means to be a desirable employee. These broad domains, components, and subcomponents provide opportunity for subjective evaluation while the responsibility is placed on the

Table 3.1. Domains, components, and subcomponents of the ACT behavioral framework

Domains	Components	Subcomponents
Acting Honestly (Honesty-Humility) Describes the extent to which a person values and adheres to ethical and moral standards of behavior, as well as personal level of humility	**Genuineness** Being sincere and truthful in interactions, appropriately giving others credit, and acknowledging his or her mistakes **Fairness** Acting in ways that are intended to be unbiased and fair to everyone **Modesty** Being humble about achievements, presenting a realistic view about himself or herself, and avoiding boasting or acting superior to others	Truthfulness Acceptance of Responsibility Fairness Modesty
Keeping an Open Mind (Openness to Experience) Describes a person's level of open-mindedness and curiosity about a variety of ideas, beliefs, people, and experiences	**Creativity** Generating original ideas, using existing ideas or things in new ways, and having an active imagination **Curiosity** Seeking out information to better understand a wide range of topic areas and/or obtaining a depth of understanding in one topic area that goes beyond what is required **Flexibility** Adapting to new environments and making adjustments to accommodate changes **Accepting Differences** Being open-minded and accepting of ideas, cultures, and ways of doing things that are different from his or her own	Originality Active Imagination Information Seeking Depth of Knowledge Environmental Adaptability Accommodation Open-mindedness Embracing Diversity
Maintaining Composure (Emotionality) Describes the extent to which a person is relatively calm, serene, and able to manage emotions effectively	**Stress Tolerance** The degree to which a person can control feelings of anxiety and other negative emotions in order to function effectively in a range of situations **Self-Confidence** A tendency to be self-assured and to make decisions without needing a lot of input from others	Worry Management Negative Feeling Management Decisiveness Independence

continued on next page

Table 3.1—*continued*

Domains	Components	Subcomponents
Socializing with Others (Extraversion) Describes a person's preferred level of social interaction, behavior in interpersonal situations, and optimism	**Assertiveness** Influencing others and preferring to be in charge in social interactions and group activities **Optimism** The degree to which a person expresses a positive mood and a positive outlook **Sociability** Seeking out and enjoying situations involving interpersonal interaction and building relationships with others	Taking Charge Influence Cheerful Mood Positive Outlook Interacting with Others Networking
Getting Along with Others (Agreeableness) Describes the degree to which a person interacts positively and cooperates with others, and is generally kind, friendly, and tactful	**Cooperation** Being respectful, polite, collaborative, and skilled at working through conflict with other people **Perspective Taking** Identifying, acknowledging, and understanding the emotions of others, showing concern for others, and considering the audience when providing information **Goodwill** Assuming others have good intentions, trusting others, being able to forgive and not holding grudges **Helpfulness** Helping others and being generous with his or her time and/or resources despite personal cost **Patience** Tolerating frustrations presented by others or by situations without expressing irritation or hostility	Respect for Others Collaboration Conflict Management Interpreting Emotional Reactions Showing Concern Considering the Audience Forgiveness Trust Assisting Others Selflessness Tolerating Frustrations with Others Tolerating Situational Frustrations

continued on next page

Table 3.1—continued

Domains	Components	Subcomponents
Sustaining Effort (Conscientiousness) Describes a person's level of diligence, effort, organization, self-control, and compliance	**Dependability** Reliably fulfilling responsibilities, meeting deadlines, and producing quality work	Timeliness Follow Through Quality
	Order Planning and organizing tasks and materials, creating schedules, monitoring progress, and paying close attention to details	Organization Planning Monitoring
	Persistence Working hard, making progress on relevant tasks, and maintaining focus despite setbacks or difficulties	Overcoming Challenges Maintaining Effort Focusing
	Rule Consciousness Following rules and procedures and complying with authority	Compliance Respect for Rules/Authority
	Goal Striving Setting challenging goals, doing tasks without being told. and working to improve or learn new skills	Self-Improvement Initiative Goal Setting
	Self-Control Managing impulses and weighing the consequences of one's behavior before acting	Restraint Thinking Before Acting

Source: ACT Research Report "Beyond Academics: A Holistic Framework for Enhancing Education and Workplace Success"

individual being assessed if they do not meet expectations. Though normativity is asserted and success is predicted by evaluating the social/emotional behavioral characteristics/identities ACT has identified, the "subcomponents" category does a great deal of this rhetorical work by offering a list of things that one *is not* if they should be assessed poorly on one of the behavioral characteristics (located in the components category) being evaluated. For example, in the "Getting Along with Others" domain, "Helpfulness"—defined as "helping others and being generous with his or her time and/or resources despite personal cost"—is listed as a normative behavioral characteristic required for success. Based on the inverse relationship set up by this chart, being poorly evaluated in this category means that the individual is both selfish and uncooperative. By setting up this inverse relationship, the Framework prescribes a sort of violent normativity in which the test-taker feels more and more to blame as they are evaluated as less and less successful. In addition, the focus on sacrifice "despite personal cost" is foundational to both enactments of colonization and structural violence—placing the responsibility on the individual rather than on the system—while framing helpfulness in relation to sharing resources monetizes those contributions, thus reflecting the neoliberal focus on economics.

If neoliberalism is all about governmentality through market-based logic, then there is an enormous stake involved in the determination of which individuals will be the most desired contributors to participate in and bolster the economy. ACT's Framework serves a neoliberal colonialist agenda of conformity and control in order to identify and achieve economic viability articulated in terms of its concept of success. For example, consider the domain of "Sustaining Effort." The subcomponents assessed in order to determine capacity for successful sustainability of effort include compliance, restraint, and monitoring. Establishing a parallel relationship between success and compliance, success and restraint, and success and monitoring works to locate bodies that will accept governmentality as a function of the norm. Like colonization, this established relationship is sneaky and covert but enacts violence on bodies assessed as deficient in compliance, restraint, and self-monitoring (in the neoliberal sense).

Establishing normative standards/characteristics for success is justified as a way to identify those in need of support (or amendment) to be more successful or as a tool that can boost corporate productivity by locating workers destined for success. At a base level, these assessments inflict harm and enact slow violences that are difficult to spot until the damage has been done. Even when violence has been identified, the responsibility for being unsuccessful is deflected onto the individual rather than the system. This is a neoliberal performance of power whereby "normalcy is used to control bodies" in relation to the results of these assessments while an assessment practice such as ACT's Framework "marks out and marginalizes those bodies and minds that do not conform" (Dolmage 2012, 110). And, in marking out and marginalizing, violences impact those being assessed as the burden to fit in is placed on "nonnormative" bodies. If, as ACT asserts, the data from the Framework's assessments is aggregated as a means by which to track and chart an individual's progress towards (or away from) standards of success, then poor performance on these tests could have lifelong consequences for the bodies marked for exclusion. When measurements are amassed, bodies can be tracked and classified indefinitely and, as a result of these assessments, individuals can lose access to a variety of opportunities.

Often, when access to opportunity and privilege is determined by socioeconomic class, violence is obscured by systemic pressures to overlook it. When this structural violence occurs—where value, potential, and success are evaluated through neoliberal assessment practices—the burden "lies on individuals to acclimate to the existing structures of the institution" (Stenberg 2015, 99). These violences are imposed through neoliberal discourses that would "have us believe that individuals, not values or structures, are in need of change—and often, that individuals are best served by acclimation to a more standard mode of being and doing" (102). When bodies are evaluated in relation to neoliberal values, as in ACT's suite of evaluative tools, then assessments become both the means by and the ends toward which systemic values are upheld and served. This narrative of normativity maintained throughout neoliberal discourse pushes bodies to adapt to violent systems in order to maintain systemic power and privilege. To think about this in terms of ACT's Framework: success (a monetized neoliberal value) is articulated as a goal to be adopted and maintained that can (and should) be evaluated (through the means of a standardized assessment) to reaffirm one's ability (or to locate the lack of ability) to contribute (economically) to the system in place (neoliberal capitalism). Thus, individuals are pressured to adapt to even violent (in terms of the potential negative impacts) assessment practices (like ACT's Framework) in order to (possibly) be assessed as normal which, in turn, publicly affirms one's potential to appropriately (normatively) participate in (maintain) the system.

Neoliberal assessment practices, as demonstrated in ACT's Framework, impact the students we work with, the programs we work in, and the corporate values that direct the institutions we work at. But, as Tony Scott and Lil Brannon argue, assessments are often sanctioned and adopted without considering some important questions, like "Who mandates assessments? Who is in a position to determine what is valued? What views of literacy do various values reflect and enact? How do scores (valuations) circulate beyond the program and what are the consequences?" (Scott and Brannon 2013, 292). As scholars and teachers in the field of composition studies, we need to be asking: Whose agenda is served by these evaluations of potential, and through what means do they gain velocity? What neoliberal values are reflected in these assessments and whose bodies are—and are not—privileged through the sanctioning of these values? What are the consequences—the violences—resulting from the circulation of the results of these assessments, especially as they are accumulated over a long period of time? In asking these questions and in considering embodied identities—shaped by a multitude of different realities and experiences and impacted by a variety of cultural and belief systems—Gabriela Rios (2016) calls us to consider "Rhetoric and Composition Studies [as] a site ripe with decolonial potential" (115).

REDRESSING SLOW VIOLENCE: ASSESSMENT AS DECOLONIAL WORK

This chapter is situated in the "Recognizing" section of this edited collection, and I understand recognizing as doing the work of witnessing and illuminating. In fact, the work being done throughout this collection—recognizing violences, intervening in the performance of violences, and ameliorating the effects and impacts of violences—involves illuminating: illuminating when recognizing, illuminating when intervening, illuminating when ameliorating. Specifically, the illuminating that I engage in throughout this chapter emerges from my commitments to decolonization, to altering the colonialist orientation within which neoliberal assessment practices damage so many. With this in mind, this final section describes decolonial approaches that center on (student) bodies and commits to actionable response to colonizing practices.

As discussed by Gomes (2018), assessment—a colonial project riven with neoliberal values—requires decolonization. Colonization prescribes, substantiates, and perpetuates a cycle of violent normativity. In response, advocating for nonstigmatized acknowledgment of nonnormative bodies and experiences means arguing against culturally determined bodies and the othering process that makes this determination possible; it means arguing for the multiplicity of embodied realities and experiences. Banks and his colleagues (2018), alongside Inoue and Poe (2012), posit rethinking assessment as social justice. If, in recognizing violent assessment practices and utilizing nonviolent methods, we can diminish the reach of violences and reduce their further impact and material consequences on our students, then as compositionists and pedagogues committed to social justice, we should bear witness to and disrupt these violences. This can be done in a variety of ways, including, as modeled in this chapter, performing rhetorical analyses of slow violences present in neoliberal assessment practices in an attempt to direct attention to some of the ways that constructions and evaluations of abnormality do violences to those being assessed. The social justice end espoused by Banks et al., as well as Inoue and Poe, intersects with Gomes's call for decolonization.

Decolonization is a process of social justice that addresses and redresses colonization, colonizing practices, and embedded histories of coloniality; confronts the violences enacted; and creates spaces for theory, practice, methodologies, and methods that recognize and value all humans and embodiments. It involves making apparent how humans *are already* being colonized; decolonial work actively contests colonial approaches to knowledge production and assessment of that production while offering alternative rhetorics and methods that witness, disrupt, and reimagine assessment. When bodies are assessed and otherness is marked by neoliberal assessment practices—such as the ones discussed in this chapter—attempts to justify exclusion are made, and categories of inclusion and exclusion are maintained rhetorically through assessments of proximity to and/or deviation from "the norm." In response, decolonial approaches aim to redress colonial impacts by recognizing and bearing witness to the violences of colonization (Haas 2015; Anzaldúa 2012); doing critical work to support all people, cultures, histories, and lived embodied experiences and realities (Haas 2012; Driskill 2010); supporting respectful and reciprocal dialogue (Haas 2015); and maintaining a commitment to constantly revisit, review, and analyze as relationships shift over time and space (Haas 2015, 2012; Agboka 2014). Decolonization impacts how one writes, which narratives they amplify, the methods they conceptualize, the curriculum they design, the pedagogy they practice, the assessment practices they utilize and problematize, and which sites become the focus for decolonial disruption.

Neoliberal assessment practices are phenomena in need of decolonization. As illuminated by this chapter, such practices work to code bodies—by marking them, ascribing their value, and assigning subjective meaning through methods of quantification and location on a continuum of normativity—and, in doing so, propose a monolithic experience promulgating essentialism and universalization. Though the problem of the Framework itself remains, as compositionists we have the skills and responsibility to develop nonviolent and noncolonizing/ decolonizing assessment practices. In relation to this understanding of coding as a violent performance of neoliberalism, decoding becomes a decolonizing assessment practice and involves conceptualizing, articulating, and utilizing assessment methods that contextualize, situate, and elucidate rather than prescriptively assign meaning. Though it is impossible to decode others, we can *self-(de)code*. While there is not space in this chapter to discuss self-(de)coding in much detail, I would like to provide a brief pedagogical example. As compositionists, we can design courses that prioritize student-led evaluation and understand experiential knowledges as acts of self-decoding that depend on students' reflection and contextualized articulation of their lived self-value as writers. In my courses I ask students to think deeply about, and journal often in reaction to, their own compositions and those that are introduced throughout the course (articles we read; videos that we watch; social media posts that we discuss; multimodal compositions of all sorts). Because reaction is a deeply personal experience shaped by lived experiences, embodied knowledges, and positionality, the space of the journal is private and becomes an unmediated space of self-reflection that can then be referenced, across time, to better understand what impacts one's sense of self-value and compels their work. After reflecting upon their journal reactions, students use their experiential knowledges to create individualized project plans that prioritize their understanding of self and articulate both values (what they see as important in their writing and why) and pitfalls (things to avoid and why). Then, to articulate their project grade, they assess their work in relation to their project plan and alongside collaboratively constructed assignment prompts. The important part of this self-decoding work, and what differentiates it from the contract grading that been around for decades, is the journaling/ reaction component. Identifying one's own strengths and pitfalls (while considering what impacts and influences these understandings) and determining one's own values (rather than them being determined by others) matters and works to counteract decontextualized assessment practices that code, mediate, and ascribe value to another person's work.

At the beginning of the chapter, I began the work of recognizing by positing neoliberal assessment practices as inflicting layered violences on those being assessed.[8] I end the work of recognizing with decolonization, which is not really an end at all. Rather, it is a reimagination of futures. In fact, imagination and reimagination are significant parts of decolonization (Driskill 2010), pushing the conversation beyond critique to generative and productive potential and asserting that inclusion and accommodation be reimagined as shared social responsibility to create an inclusive discipline. In order to mitigate the impact of slow violences and engage in decolonization, we must reimagine our fields, our academic institutions, and our pedagogical commitments through the use of decolonial methodologies, pedagogies, and practices. This being said, it is important to underscore that the work I do in this chapter bears witness to *just one* instance of colonization's slow violences: these violences operate on many levels and in many different versions. Slow violence is not just a part of neoliberalism but of all colonizing assessment practices. I have chosen to focus on ACT's Framework because it is one of the violences that impacts the students that we work with, particularly those that are multiply marginalized. Since assessment practices writ large are implicated in this critique of colonizing methods, I make the call to analyze—carefully, critically, and compassionately—the assessment methodologies, methods, and approaches that we use in our own classrooms as one way to engage in decolonial analysis while we conceptualize pedagogies that respect and uphold *all* students.

NOTES

1.   Also known as "ACT Behavioral Skills Framework" and "ACT Holistic Framework," for the purposes of this chapter, I will refer to it as the "Framework" or as "ACT's Framework."

2.   Embodied identity is contextualized identity, emergent from the cultures, histories, ethnicities, and interactions that impact and shape one's life and experiences.

3.   I want to make clear that when I use the word "bodies" in this chapter I am doing so purposefully. N. Katherine Hayles (1999) reminds us that "the body is always normative relative to some sort of criteria" (196). By invoking this term, I am critiquing the normative construction of humans and their identities that takes place through colonizing practices and institutions and through the processes of colonization.

4.   I define erasure as marking some bodies as excludable, tagging them for omission and negation.

5.   Introduced in 2014, ACT's Framework was designed "to provide a more holistic and integrated picture of education and work readiness from kindergarten to career" (Camara et al. 2015, 3). The Framework combines preexisting and newly created cognitive and noncognitive assessments to evaluate and "articulate what students need to know and be able to do at numerous points along the K–Career continuum" (3) in order to be successful. Marketed to K–12 educators, parents, and corporations, this suite of assessments attempts to draw connections between measurable results and social/emotional and psychosocial behavioral characteristics in order to mark one's propensity for college and career success.

6.   I choose to focus on ACT WorkKeys Suite and ACT Engage due to their early imple-
mentation (beginning in grade school) and their claims to establish and evaluate
social/emotional learning characteristics.

7.   Social/emotional learning assessment ACT Engage has recently (2017) been
rebranded ACT Tessera. I will refer to it as ACT Engage since the reports referenced use that name.

8.   *Recognizing* is an act of intervening and, in the case of ACT's Framework, is the first
step in disrupting its attendant slow violences.

REFERENCES

Agboka, Godwin. 2014. "Decolonial Methodologies: Social Justice Perspectives in Intercul-
tural Technical Communication Research." *Journal of Technical Writing and Communications* 44, no. 3: 297–327. doi: 10.2190/TW.44.3.e.

Anzaldúa, Gloria. 2012. *Borderlands/La Frontera: The New Mestiza.* 4th ed. San Francisco:
Aunt Lute Books.

Banks, William, Michael Sterling Burns, Nicole I. Caswell, Randall Cream, Timothy R.
Dougherty, Norbert Elliot, Mathew Gomes, J. W. Hammond, Keith L. Harms, Asao B.
Inoue, Josh Lederman, Sean Molloy, Casie Moreland, Karen S. Nulton, Irvin Peckham,
Mya Poe, Kelly J. Sassi, Christie Toth, and Nicole Warwick. 2018. "The Braid of Writing
Assessment, Social Justice, and the Advancement of Opportunity: Eighteen Assertions."
In *Writing Assessment, Social Justice, and the Advancement of Opportunity,* edited by Mya
Poe, Asao Inoue, and Norbert Elliot, n.p. Fort Collins: WAC Clearinghouse.

Broad, Bob. 2003. *What We Really Value: Beyond Rubrics in Teaching and Assessing Writing.*
Logan: Utah State University Press.

Camara, Wayne, Ryan O'Connor, Krista Mattern, and Mary Ann Hanson. 2015. "Beyond
Academics: A Holistic Framework for Enhancing Education and Workplace Success."
In *ACT Research Report* 2015 (4). http://www.act.org/content/dam/act/unsecured
/documents/ACT_RR2015-4.pdf.

Caswell, Nicole I., and William P. Banks. 2018. "Queering Writing Assessment: Fairness,
Affect, and the Impact on LGBTQ Writers." In *Writing Assessment, Social Justice, and the
Advancement of Opportunity,* edited by Mya Poe, Asao Inoue, and Norbert Elliot. Fort
Collins: WAC Clearinghouse.

Caswell, Nicole I., and Stephanie West-Puckett. 2019. "Assessment Killjoys: Queering the
Return for a Writing-Studies World-Making Methodology." In *Re/Orienting Writing
Studies: Queer Methods, Queer Projects,* edited by William P. Banks, Matthew B. Cox, and
Caroline Dadas, 169–85. Logan: Utah State University Press.

Chaput, Cathy. 2010. "Rhetorical Circulation in Late Capitalism: Neoliberalism and the
Overdetermination of Affective Energy." *Philosophy and Rhetoric* 43, no. 1: 1–25. doi:
10.5325/philrhet.43.1.0001.

Colbow, Alexander, Christian Latino, Jason Way, Alex Casillas, and Tamara McKinniss.
"The ACT Behavioral Skills Framework: How Does It Compare to Other Behavioral Models?" *ACT Research Report* 2017 (6). http://www.act.org/content/dam/act
/unsecured/documents/ACT_RR2015-4.pdf.

Cushman, Ellen. 2016. "Decolonizing Validity." *The Journal of Writing Assessment* 9, no. 1:
n.p. http://www.journalofwritingassessment.org/article.php?article=92.

Dingo, Rebecca. 2012. *Networking Arguments.* Pittsburgh: University of Pittsburgh Press.

Dolmage, Jay. 2018. *Disabled upon Arrival.* Columbus: Ohio State Press.

Dolmage, Jay. 2014. *Disability Rhetoric.* Syracuse: Syracuse University Press.

Dolmage, Jay. 2012. "Writing Against Normal: Navigating a Corporeal Turn." In *Composing
Media Composing Embodiment,* edited by Kristen Arola and Anne Wysocki, 110–26. Boulder: University Press of Colorado.

Driskill, Qwo-Li. 2010. "Doubleweaving Two-Spirit Critiques: Building Alliances between Native and Queer Studies." *GLQ: A Journal of Lesbian and Gay Studies* 16, no. 1–2: 69–92. doi: 10.1215/10642684-2009-013.

Elbow, Peter. 1973. *Writing without Teachers.* New York: Oxford University Press.

Elliot, Norbert. 2005. *On a Scale: A Social History of Writing Assessment in America.* New York: Peter Lang.

Gallagher, Chris. 2011. "Being There: (Re)Making the Assessment Scene." *College Composition and Communication* 62, no. 3: 450–76. JSTOR.

Galtung, Johan. 1990. "Cultural Violence." *Journal of Peace Research* 27, no. 3: 291–305. doi: 10.1177/0022343390027003005.

Galtung, Johan. 1969. "Violence, Peace, and Peace Research." *Journal of Peace Research* 6, no. 3: 167–91. doi: 10.1177/002234336900600301.

Gomes, Mathew. 2018. "Writing Assessment and Responsibility for Colonialism." In *Writing Assessment, Social Justice, and the Advancement of Opportunity,* edited by Mya Poe, Asao Inoue, and Norbert Elliot, 201–25. Fort Collins: WAC Clearinghouse.

Gould, Stephen Jay. 1996. *The Mismeasure of Man.* New York: W. W. Norton.

Haas, Angela. 2015. "Toward a Decolonial Digital and Visual American Indian Rhetorics Pedagogy." In *Survivance, Sovereignty, and Story: Teaching Indigenous Rhetorics,* edited by Rose Gubele, Joyce Rain Anderson, and Lisa King, 188–208. Logan: Utah State University Press.

Haas, Angela. 2012. "Race, Rhetoric, and Technology: A Case Study of Decolonial Technical Communication Theory, Methodology, and Pedagogy." *Journal of Business and Technical Communication* 26, no. 3: 277–310. doi: 10.1177/1050651912439539.

Hayles, N. Katherine. 1999. *How We Became Posthuman: Virtual Bodies in Cybernetics, Literature, and Informatics.* Chicago: University of Chicago Press.

Inoue, Asao. B. 2009. "The Technology of Writing Assessment and Racial Validity." In *Handbook of Research on Assessment Technologies, Methods, and Applications in Higher Education,* edited by C. Schreiner, 97–102. Hershey, PA: Information Science Reference.

Inoue, Asao B., and Mya Poe, eds. 2012. *Race and Writing Assessment.* New York: Peter Lang Publishing.

Lederman, Josh, and Nicole Warwick. 2018. "The Violence of Assessment: Writing Assessment, Social (In)Justice, and the Role of Validation." In *Writing Assessment, Social Justice, and the Advancement of Opportunity,* edited by Mya Poe, Asao Inoue, and Norbert Elliot, 229–55. Fort Collins: WAC Clearinghouse.

Medina, Cruz, and Kenny Walker. 2018. "Validating the Consequences of Social Justice Pedagogy: Explicit Values in Course-Based Grading Contracts." In *Key Theoretical Frameworks for Teaching Technical Communication in the Twenty-First Century,* edited by Angela M. Haas and Michelle F. Eble. Logan: Utah State University Press.

Nixon, Rob. 2011. *Slow Violence and the Environmentalism of the Poor.* Cambridge, MA: Harvard University Press.

O'Neil, Peggy, Cindy Moore, and Brian Huot. 2009. *A Guide to College Writing Assessment.* Logan: Utah State University Press.

Rios, Gabriela. 2016. "Mestizaje." In *Decolonizing Rhetoric and Composition Studies: New Latinx Keywords for Theory and Pedagogy,* edited by Iris Ruiz and Raul Sanchez, 109–24. New York: Palgrave Macmillan.

Scott, Tony, and Lil Brannon. 2013. "Democracy, Struggle, and the Praxis of Assessment." *College Composition and Communication* 65, no. 2: 273–98. JSTOR.

Stenberg, Sheri J. 2015. *Repurposing Composition: Feminist Interventions for a Neoliberal Age.* Logan: Utah State University Press.

Stuckey, J. Elspeth. 1991. *The Violence of Literacy.* Ann Arbor: University of Michigan Press.

Tuhiwai Smith, Linda. 2012. *Decolonizing Methodologies.* London: Zed Books.

Villanueva, Victor. 1999. "On the Rhetoric and Precedents of Racism." *College Composition and Communication* 50, no. 4: 645–61. doi: 0.2307/358485.

4

BY DESIGN
Violence and Digital Interfaces in the Composition Classroom

Katherine T. Bridgman

Reflecting on his experiences as a young college student, Kiese Laymon (2016) calls out the ideologies that shape our classrooms and the violence that stems from these ideologies. Laymon shares an experience he had in a course that emphasized students finding their own voices. He quickly found that, instead of discovery, the course encouraged students to mimic "the kind of voice that sat with its legs crossed, reading *The New York Times*" (121). In other words, while his teacher urged him to find his voice, he quickly realized she was merely looking for the "one education necessitated I lead with" (121). Laymon's description of the voice his teacher fostered—the body of cross-legged reader of the *New York Times*—is telling. This particular body, one that I will discuss more throughout this chapter, is a body granted what Nirmal Puwar (2004) describes as the "power of invisibility" (57). The power of this cross-legged reader "emanates from its ability to be seen as just normal, to be without corporeality" (57). This body of the voice expected in so many of our composition classrooms, however, is not without corporeality. Instead, this body that Puwar describes as the ostensible "universal human" (56) is a cisgendered, able-bodied, middle-class, white male, the voice and corporeality of which we teach students to approximate—despite claims to do otherwise (Dolmage 2014; Garland-Thomson 1997; Puwar 2004; Villenas et al. 2006).

Carmen Kynard (2018) describes what happens to bodies that resist these approximated embodiments of the crossed-legged reader of the *New York Times* when she shares how, a month after she joined her institution, she was teaching in a computer lab, and her course was observed by a white man who asked to hover over a student named Zeek while he was writing. Zeek, who described himself as having the "thickest accent in the class" (129), experienced what Heidi Safia Mirza (2009) describes as the "'weight' of living a non-white existence" (235), wherein bodies

https://doi.org/10.7330/9781646422807.c004

that are not white become at once hypervisible, yet silenced—unable "to speak for themselves" (Patricia Hill Collins, quoted in Mirza 2009, 239). This "weight" results from the increased surveillance experienced by students like Zeek. Kynard offers an example of this surveillance, of both Zeek and her as his instructor, describing how the observer "literally stood over Zeek's body as he was sitting at the computer, watched every letter that he typed on the keyboard, and then criticized the form of those words in the public document of a required, institutional form" that remains part of Kynard's permanent file as a faculty member (130). The violences experienced by both Zeek and Laymon (as well as Kynard) emerge from what Rosemarie Garland-Thomson (1997) describes as the "social processes and discourses that constitute physical and cultural otherness" (8). These violences are "the kind of violence that higher education has not only sustained but always justified as right and good for classrooms with brown and black college students, always using the trope of language correctness to do its dirty work" (Kynard 2018, 130). Not simply confined within the walls of our classrooms, this violence accretes through teaching practices that "actively promote White language supremacy, which is the handmaiden to White bias in the world, the kind that kills Black men on the streets by the hands of the police through profiling and good ol' fashion prejudice" (Inoue 2019, 11). This violence is normalized, reframed as benefitting students because teachers successfully approximating "the universal human form" are ostensibly of "pure mind, their bodies [. . .] of no consequence" (Puwar 2004, 57), so they can do no harm. Such bodies exist in opposition to the highly marked bodies of students who do not embody this normative corporeality. In other words, at the same time student "figures of otherness are highly marked in power relations, even as they are marginalized, their cultural visibility as deviant obscures and neutralizes the normative figure that they legitimate" (Garland-Thomson 1997, 8–9). This normative figure is enacted and approximated by so many, largely white, instructors and further replicated through the accepted pedagogies of our field.

As we seek to recognize and confront this violence in our classrooms, Adam Banks (2015) reminds us that we must look more deeply into our pedagogical practices and examine the technologies these pedagogies rely on:

> As composing becomes more and more enmeshed in digital environments, tools, practices, and networks, we need to see this as a crossroads moment for our scholarship too. That crossroads for me is one where we see that we have to embrace technology issues not as part of what we do,

but as central to what we do. Technology is what we do, or what we need to do, not just because literacy is always technologized, not just because of computers AND composition, but because of the big picture technological issues that are always brought to bear on all facets of our lives and work. (274)

While our field has a considerable history of scholarship on the interfaces present across our classrooms—from social media interfaces, to word processing interfaces, to course management system interfaces—much remains to be done in recognition of the physical violence enacted across so many of these interfaces through the normative embodiments they perpetuate and frequently demand from users.

In the remainder of this chapter, I apply this recognition of embodied violence to an examination of a commonly used interface in our classrooms, the Blackboard course management system, to examine how digital interfaces enact embodied violence in the writing classroom through the normative embodiments they perpetuate among students (and teachers). Although these interfaces have been examined extensively by scholars in our field, this chapter stands to extend that work by turning our attention to recognizing the ways in which digital interfaces enact violence within our classrooms by demanding approximations of the normate body from students (and instructors).[1]

I begin this discussion of strategies for recognizing violence enacted against students across digital interfaces with a brief discussion of several different forms that violence takes. Developing a more nuanced understanding of violence enables instructors to recognize the enforcement of students' approximations of the cross-legged reader of the *New York Times* as an act of violence. Next, I examine how instructors can recognize the cultural violence introduced by digital interfaces and work with students to help them also recognize this violence. Throughout this discussion of digital interfaces, I will draw from the course management system Blackboard as an example of a digital interface that frequently enters our classrooms under the assumption that it functions as a transparent extension of our pedagogies. With over one hundred million users across over ninety countries (Blackboard 2019), Blackboard has become such a mainstay of many classrooms that it frequently goes unseen by instructors. However, as Blackboard promises to support instructors in providing students with the "optimal educational experience" (Blackboard 2019), it elides the assumptions behind what this optimal experience is and the potential violence that is enacted through the educational experience enabled by Blackboard's interface.

VIOLENCE, DIGITAL INTERFACES, AND THE NORMATE BODY

In his examination of violence, Johan Galtung (1990) reiterates the interlocking forms of violence that maintain acts of direct violence, the latter of which are perhaps most readily and visibly apparent through acts of war, hate, and bigotry. These acts of direct violence exist alongside structural violence, which "hides from immediate perception, spreading its violence through laws, education, official policies, and social practices that privilege some people and embodiments over others" (Bridgman, Fleckenstein, and Gage 2019, 89). These forms of violence are enabled by what Galtung refers to as cultural violence, which maintains and normalizes both direct and structural violence: "Cultural violence makes direct and structural violence look, even feel, right—or at least not wrong" (Galtung 1990, 291). This violence "hinders [a student's] pursuit of self-affirmation as a responsible person" and "interferes with the individual's ontological and historical vocation to be more fully human" (Freire 2000, 55). While an extended discussion of the forms of violence that unfold across digital interfaces would address the structural and direct violence enacted in these spaces, this chapter will focus on recognizing the cultural violence that thrives across digital interfaces, "legitimiz[ing] and thus render[ing] acceptable in society" direct and structural violence (Galtung 1990, 292). This cultural violence is allowed to flourish and goes unrecognized within pedagogies that treat digital interfaces as simply "a repre sentation of computational processes, a convenient translation of what is 'really going on'" within our digital technologies (Drucker 2013, 213). To the contrary, interfaces are locations of dynamic interactions "between user and computer, user and software, computer and software, user and content, software and content, user and culture, and the user and other users" (Carnegie 2009, 165). These interactions are imbricated with the power dynamics sustained by ideologies shaping our classrooms, such that interfaces are also "sites within which the ideological and material legacies of racism, sexism, and colonialism are continuously written and re-written along with more positive cultural legacies" (Selfe and Selfe 1994, 484). Such cultural violence unfolds through ideologies that perpetuate what Iris Ruiz and Damián Baca describe as the "colonial unconscious" of the field of writing studies (Ruiz and Baca 2017, 226), an unconscious that is normalized through the design of writing interfaces such as Blackboard. Such interfaces support the pedagogies of a field that continues to "theorize and teach writing as an alphabetic technology that emerged in Western Europe and spread throughout the world from ancient Greece to imperial Rome to enlightenment Germany, to eighteenth-century Anglo-North America by way of Western global expansion" (226).

Central to the cultural violence enacted by digital interfaces is the normate body that is not only privileged but perpetuated through the embodiments that constitute effective interface use. Jay Dolmage (2014) describes this normate body as "able-bodied, rational-minded, autonomous, polite and proprietary, and so on. In North America, the normal position is also middle to upper class, white, male, western European, preferably American, overconfidently heterosexual, right-sized, and so on. These norms change, but the presence of a desired, central and privileged position persists" (21). The body of the cross-legged reader of the *New York Times* in the experience of Laymon is one manifestation of this normate body promoted through the cultural violence of a pedagogy claiming to support students in finding their voices, a pedagogy that masks the expectation that students approximate another body.

The direct and structural violences enacted by this coercion, however, are masked by the cultural violence of the digital interface. This violence manifests as "our culture also mark[s] out and marginaliz[es] those bodies and minds that do not conform," as we saw reflected in the experiences of Laymon and Zeek when we witnessed the eruption of direct and structural violence as their bodies were surveilled and punished (Dolmage 2014, 9). Additionally, the normalcy of the cross-legged reader of the *New York Times* is "a social construct" that "*acts* upon people with disabilities" (9, original emphasis) and others who cannot "easily ignore their bodies" (Dolmage 2012, 116). These facets of violence are perpetuated through design tropes enacting a form of cultural violence that "legitimiz[es] and thus render[s] acceptable" the direct and structural violence committed by this normate body (Galtung 1990, 292).[2]

When composition instructors approach the digital interfaces across which students write as neutral, merely "a thing, static, stable, and fixed" (Drucker 2013, 213), we perpetuate the cultural violence that legitimates, even renders invisible, the direct and structural violences that surveil and punish the embodiments students bring to our classrooms. In doing so, we ourselves embody the instrumental reason of the normate body, a reason emphasizing the efficiency of an interface while eliding the ways in which "the electronic interface influences the actions and writing practices of its users/inhabitants," ourselves included (Carpenter 2009, 143). As it does so, interfaces such as Blackboard become "a positioning of subjectivities" (Walls, Schopieray, DeVoss 2009, 284) that seeks to replicate the normate body Kynard's observer sought to enforce on Zeek. In the context of digital interfaces, those users' bodies that do not conform to these active norms are subject to direct and structural violence as they are coerced to approximate the normate body, eliding the embodiments they bring to these interfaces and projecting onto them the "impossibly idealized universal user through the repetition of common design tropes and metaphors, as well as physical functionality" (McCorkle 2012, 174).

As interfaces such as Blackboard perpetuate the prioritizing of this normate body, a key component of the cultural violence enacted by interfaces is the transparency of their design. As industrial designers Laurie Vertelney and Sue Booker point out, "good industrial design is transparent" and "enable[s] users to access the functionality of the product without tripping over the interface" (Vertelney and Book 1990, 60). Kristin Arola (2010) underscores a tension between the rhetoricity of these interfaces and their lauded transparency, commenting that when "design remains primarily beyond the user's control, the interface seemingly functions in an arhetorical way; an interface that allows an easy post is a success" (7), regardless of the violence inflicted on the user. Such transparency is perceived to be key for institutional interfaces such as Blackboard, for which users receive very little, if any, training. Promising an "optimal educational experience" (Blackboard 2019) means providing students and instructors with an interface that is seamless and easy to use and, therefore, unseen within the classroom. This transparency also elides the rhetoricity of these interfaces and what may be at stake for users. Anne Wysocki and Julia Jasken describe this rhetoricity, writing that "interfaces are thoroughly rhetorical: Interfaces are about the relations we construct with each other—how we perceive and try to shape each other—through the artifacts we make for each other" (Wysocki and Jasken 2004, 33). As such, they are also frequently locations of cultural violence that reiterate the accepted "centrality, naturality, and neutrality of this normate position" (Dolmage 2014, 22), thus legitimizing the violence performed through and by this normate body.

As instructors embrace this transparency of the interface, we perform what Wysocki and Jasken (2004) describe as "forgetful seeing," a visual habit that highlights the use-value of interfaces while hiding their rhetorical function and ignoring the body. Forgetful seeing frequently thrives within university classrooms, as "we have convinced ourselves that we and the students with whom we work are made of much finer stuff than the machine in our midst" (Selfe 1999a, 414), and, as a result, we do not pay attention to the technologies we engage alongside our students, sometimes every day. As we see forgetfully within our classrooms, we ignore the ways in which these interfaces implicate our classrooms "in unthinking ways in political agendas, legislative initiatives, or educational systems that support a very narrow version of official literacy"

(Selfe 1999b, 160). This happens as instructors automatically require students to use Blackboard to submit work, participate in discussion boards, and make course material available, all without consideration of how this use of the interface is impacting both teachers and students. Cynthia Selfe (1999b) reminds us that when this happens "we all lose, and we are all implicated in the guilt that accrues to a system of violence through literacy" (160).

SEEING THE INTERFACE: INSTRUCTORS' RECOGNITION OF VIOLENCE

A first step in recognizing the cultural violence operating across a digital interface is to acknowledge our own forgetful seeing of digital interfaces. For instructors able to successfully approximate the normate body, mostly notably white instructors, this means that we must recognize the ways in which our bodies are replicated and privileged across interfaces such as Blackboard at the expense of our students. This "whiteness exists as an unmarked normative position" (Puwar 2004, 58) and intersects with a range of other embodiments, most notably maleness and able-bodiedness. For example, Puwar (2004) writes, "the male body is invisible as a sexed entity. Its absence of gender entitles it to take up the unmarked normative locale" (58). In their discussion of a Black feminist disability framework, Moya Bailey and Izetta Autumn Mobley extend Puwar's work, writing that "the tropes utilized to distinguish between supposedly superior white bodies and purportedly inferior bodies of color have relied on corporeal assessments that take the able white male body as the center and 'norm.' Notions of disability inform how theories of race were formed, and theories of racial embodiment and inferiority (racism) formed the ways in which we conceptualize disability" (Bailey and Mobley 2019, 27). Thus, if instructors embodying intersections of whiteness, maleness, and able-bodiedness want to intervene in the perpetuation of violence within their classrooms, and across digital interfaces in particular, we must begin by recognizing our own performances of invisible bodies within the classroom, performances that are themselves a form of cultural violence.

This violence is recognized by learning to "look at, as well as through" the interfaces embodied by students in our classrooms (Haas 2009, xii). Doing so prompts us to recognize the rhetorical work of digital interfaces such as Blackboard that map student-users within broader ideological landscapes that are "oriented simultaneously along the axes of class, race, and cultural privilege [and] aligned with the values of rationality, hierarchy, and logocentrism characteristic of Western patriarchal cultures" (Selfe and Selfe 1994, 491), maps in which the normate body comfortably resides and across which it gets replicated. Course management systems perpetuate these maps, creating a need for instructors to have "a more critical edge when it comes to technology studies so that we don't become hoodwinked every time governments and corporations unite to try to sell us utopian visions about the next new technological hotness that will heal everything that ails us" (Banks 2015, 275). The "utopian vision" sold by course management systems is one of efficiently supporting assessment paradigms existing "solely to serve the interests of (white) academic management," a manifestation of cultural violence that ignores the range of direct and structural violence enacted by such "management" and "efficiency" (Kynard 2018, 132).

In order to disrupt the cultural violence circulated through and by digital interfaces, we must first recognize the ways in which a course management system such as Blackboard enacts a form of cultural violence that makes the normate body seem natural within our classrooms. Harkening back to the blackboards of the nineteenth century, Blackboard privileges the flow of communication from the instructor out to students. Instructors are the only members of a class permitted to post announcements and initiate blogs, wikis, and other forums for student writing. Additionally, the interface supports a uniform digital experience of the course by pushing out the instructor's organization of the course site and course information to students, without giving students the option to reorganize this content on their own screens. This uniformity is reiterated by Blackboard's support of standard-language ideologies through visually highlighting student writing that may not be conforming to what Trinh T. Minh-ha describes as "well-behaved, steeped-in-convention-language of 'clarity' " (1989, 16). Finally, the normate body of the course is restricted to its membership in the course and university community, isolated from the other communities that students are a part of. At the same time that Blackboard deemphasizes digital connections between a course and extracurricular digital contexts beyond the university, so too does its default settings remove markers of students' community memberships beyond the classroom and the university more generally. This membership is visually reiterated through the university branding of Blackboard via default color schemes and headers that frequently top each page with a university logo, along with the ways in which Blackboard prevents students from choosing the name they go by within a course.

In addition to the tacit assumptions that privilege Western epistemologies and hierarchical relationships between teacher and student,

Blackboard's interface also replicates the normate body through its privileging of print literacies. In moving her students' writing outside of a course management system, Kynard (2018) was able to create digital spaces with her students that mobilized "a black vernacularized pedagogical space" (137) that is not available within Blackboard's interface. Within this space, "the language of African America (AAL) [was used] not merely as a set of linguistic moves that operate against an imagined standardized norm. AAL is also a languaging/meaning-making system that represents its own epistemological and ontological systems. It is a sonic, visual, and spatial intervention in white ways of knowing and shapes the contours of how I attempt to mobilize a race-radical black feminist pedagogy" (137–38). In moving student work outside of the institutional interface of a course management system, Kynard was able to create more antiracist and nonviolent digital spaces, within which her students could evoke embodiments that resisted the normate body of her institution's course management system by inviting the creation of a wider range of texts and stepping outside of Blackboard's perpetuation of standard-language ideology. For instructors hampered by their inhabitation of the normate body, such strategies as those provided by Kynard require that first step of recognition. Only then can we provide a pedagogy that disrupts rather than reinforces the interface's cultural violence.

COMING TO BODY: STUDENTS' RECOGNITION OF VIOLENCE

While our recognition of the cultural violence abetted by digital interfaces such as Blackboard is critical, the recognition of cultural violence must not stop with instructors. Instead, this recognition can be pivotal for many of our students, both those who benefit from having their bodies centered by this cultural violence and those who are marginalized by the normate body within institutions of higher education. For the latter, such recognition is less likely to reveal something they did not already know but, instead, provides an opportunity for naming and making visible their experiences of violence. For all of our students, recognition of this violence is a key prelude to ameliorating this violence. Students equipped with frameworks for recognizing the cultural violence operating across a digital interface are set up "to become critical thinkers about technology and the social issues surrounding its use" who can understand and assess the "social, economic, and pedagogical implications of new communication technologies and technological initiatives [. . .] that affect their lives" (Selfe 1999a, 432).

Students' recognition of the embodied violence enacted across so many digital interfaces starts with "discovering the who, what, when, where, and how of things," so that we may then use "that knowledge in a manner that enables you to determine what matters most" as students decide how they will negotiate the covert and overt violence they experience across digital interfaces (hooks 9). This critical thinking prompts students to stop seeing themselves as passive users of digital interfaces; instead, in answering these questions, students develop a vocabulary to name the embodied violences enacted across digital interfaces, share their recognition with others, and come to see themselves as agentive embodied users of digital interfaces. As we embrace these strategies with interfaces such as Blackboard within our classrooms, we also make explicit the role of these interfaces in our pedagogies. When students are taught only to be proficient users of technologies, rather than critical users of technologies, they "learn only to *fill up* those templates and *fill in* those electric boxes—which, in their ability to invite intellectual work, are the moral equivalent of the dots on a multiple choice test," and, as they "complete someone else's software package[,] they will be the invention of that package" (Yancey 2004, 320, emphasis original).

Aside from merely talking about digital interfaces in our classrooms, instructors can employ these interfaces in ways that model and prompt a further recognition of cultural violence circulated across the interface. In the case of Blackboard, one way to do this would be to visually reinforce students' critical awareness by using the interface in ways other than how it was intended to be used. For example, choosing visual backgrounds or colors for the sidebars that disrupt the carefully branded nature of this space disrupts Blackboard's managerial focus on efficiency, and such modifications can be used as a visual cue for students that disrupts the interface's transparency and underscores their embodiment of these spaces. A writing course could choose the background design meant for a chemistry course. Such design decisions visually disrupt the transparency of the interface and fracture the cohesion of the normate body that would ostensibly be universally embodied in the same way within a chemistry course and a writing course. Additionally, under "Course Tools," instructors can change the name of their course, their course banner, or the layout of the Blackboard site for their course, as well as the color scheme. Customizing these settings allows instructors to disrupt the seamless branding of their course that further circumscribes the work of students within the context of the university and isolates our classrooms from both the rich embodied experiences students have outside of the classroom and the communities outside of the university they are part of. Instructors can also adjust the visual design of the sidebar menu to make clearer where buttons are, thus resisting assumptions about the literacy practices that students are bringing into our classrooms. While all of these actions are circumscribed by what Blackboard allows and are certainly nothing like hacking the interface, in a course that invites their critical thinking about the interface these decisions can prompt students' recognition of the cultural violence enacted across Blackboard and other digital interfaces.

Additional ways to extend students' recognition of the cultural violence circulated across a digital interface such as Blackboard is to challenge the normate body coded into Blackboard's interface through the (mis)use of Blackboard's functionality. For example, instead of reiterating students as passive consumers of course information by posting information such as the syllabus or reading schedule as a PDF in a folder titled Course Documents, faculty can post such documents in discussion boards. Doing so reiterates students' roles as active participants and knowledge creators within the course. Instructors can also involve students in this playful reimagining of the interface by asking students to design alternative interfaces. This strategy draws from classroom activities suggested by a number of other scholars teaching in the field of computers and composition that engage students directly with the design of the interface. For example, Arola (2010) concludes her discussion of Web 2.0 templates by suggesting that teachers ask students how these interfaces would be different with various changes to their design. "Such interrogations," she contends, "help students see how the design of every element impacts the overall effect. In particular, making seemingly ludicrous suggestions (for example, what if every element on Facebook appeared in concentric circles) helps interrogate the ways in which seemingly neutral or invisible interfaces shape our understanding and use of the space" (12).

Another facet of students' recognition of cultural violence across Blackboard includes the ways in which the interface legitimates the direct and structural violence of standard-language ideology. Instructors can support students' recognition of this cultural violence by highlighting the ways in which the interface surveils students' language use, for example by marking writing as in error when it does not conform to the standard-language ideology of the university. Such policing excludes not only students' linguistic practices from their work within the university but also excludes the ways of knowing that are embodied by students. Furthermore, Blackboard's monitoring of student language practices contributes to the hypervisibility of many nonwhite students, eliding the fact "that don't nobody all the time, nor do they in the same way, subscribe to or follow standard modes of expression. Everybody mix the dialect they learn at home with whateva other dialect or language they learn afterwards[. . . .] Yet, even folks with good jobs in the corporate world don't follow no standard English" (Young 2011, 64). Such policing of student writing demonstrates Kynard's (2018) observation that language and writing are the "place and space where we most often impose the most violence and social control in higher education" (127), and interfaces such as Blackboard are key locations of cultural violence that make the structural and direct violence described by Kynard seem natural within institutions of higher education.

CONCLUSION

As we work to recuperate and honor the embodiments of our students within the classroom, we also expand the meaning-making potential of composition classrooms. The normate body, after all, not only enacts violence on the bodies of students entering our classrooms. It also enacts violence on the communities these students represent and the ways of knowing they embody. This has perhaps never been more clear than during the onset of the COVID-19 pandemic, when millions of students across all levels were asked to move to e-learning models, within which institutional interfaces such as Blackboard took center stage as ostensibly neutral providers of access. This historical moment for considering the use of technology in and outside of our classrooms has underscored, among many other things, the precarity of student and instructor bodies within these interfaces and the embodied violences enacted through the design of these digital spaces. This moment highlights the ways in which so many bodies have always occupied a precarious position within the digital interfaces relied on in our classrooms.

As we work toward the recognition of the violence enacted across digital interfaces such as Blackboard, we are reminded to be agile in both how we work with students to recognize the cultural violence enacted across digital interfaces and how we work with students to ameliorate this violence. The high-stakes nature of this recognition and amelioration is particularly clear as students and faculty members struggle to survive and thrive in a world overshadowed by a global pandemic and the entrenched inequities it is exacerbating. The strategies discussed here reflect their origin in a prepandemic world, when I had the luxury of working with students in a classroom where we could come together for discussion by looking together at these interfaces. Working across digital interfaces of any type during a pandemic underscores the "positioning of subjectivities" that occurs as we work across digital interfaces with our students (Walls, Schopieray, DeVoss, 2009, 284). As so many classrooms moved online during the pandemic, many instructors were asked to use interfaces such as Blackboard under the auspices that our classrooms could be recreated online across the neutral interfaces of course management systems. Such an approach ignores the "constant formation [of the user] in relation to the interface" (Drucker 2013, 216). "Organiz[ing] our relationship to complex systems" (213), digital interfaces during the pandemic have (as much as ever) perpetuated the marginalization of those communities hit hardest by COVID-19. For many of these students, their success in a course became ever more closely tied to their ability to approximate the normate body as they completed all of their coursework across institutional interfaces such as Blackboard. This context underscores the degree to which faculty must model their recognition of the cultural violence enacted across the digital interface in ways that do not reenact the very violences they are working to also disrupt and ameliorate. For example, while the strategies above would be appropriate for a face-to-face classroom where student and teacher could look at and discuss the interface together, these strategies in the context of a pandemic, when an entire class might be held virtually, would risk enacting the very violence they sought to recognize.

Teaching across institutional digital interfaces during a pandemic highlights the ways in which institutional interfaces such as Blackboard create façades that ostensibly remove our classrooms from the fraught contexts that surround them. As these interfaces provide some of the only links we have to students, many are recognizing that these interfaces have *never* been removed from the contexts that surround them—even in the best of times. In other words, the violence discussed above is not violence that originates within the composition classroom. Rather, this violence extends from discourses originating beyond our classrooms, including "public discourse on the education of low-income students of color" that remains deficit-focused, emphasizing "the notion that youth of color lack the language, the culture, the family support, the academic skills, even the moral character to succeed and excel" (Bucholtz, Casillas, and Lee 2017, 43). Such discourse shares its roots with the perpetuated normate body of "a middle-class Euro-American" (Villenas et al. 2006, 3) that Dolmage (2012) describes as "white, male, straight, upper middle class; the normal body is his, profoundly and impossibly unmarked and 'able'" (115). These discourses and their materializations within composition classrooms inflict cultural, structural, and direct violence on our students by refusing to recognize student embodiments and by denying students "self-affirmation as a responsible person" (Freire 2000, 55). Although our classrooms can never be neutral spaces untouched by ideologies (Berlin 1988) and their resulting violences, we can work with students to recognize these contexts that they are always already inhabiting in both the digital and physical spaces of their lives. For many students, such recognition will not be telling them something they did not already know. Instead, such recognition may provide a language for naming their experience and disrupting the cultural violence that feeds the direct and structural violence many know all too well.

NOTES

1. While in this chapter I explore the violence enacted against students, this does not mean there is not also violence enacted across digital interfaces against the bodies of instructors who use these technologies. Thus, although this chapter focuses on the violence enacted against students, more work remains to be done toward recognizing the ways in which a similar violence is enacted against instructors as well.

2. Johan Galtung (1990) describes direct violence as the "event" and structural violence as the "process" (294). One example Galtung provides relates to the environment, wherein normate bodies enact a direct violence against nature—such as the slashing and burning of forests—that is coupled with the structural violence of industrial activity, "leaving non-degradable residues and depleting non-renewable resources" (294). Such direct and structural violence enacted by the normate body, although environmental in nature, reiterates the privileges of the bodies that benefit the most from the "world-encompassing commercialization" that leads to environmental destruction, leaving those bodies unable to approximate the normate body to live with little to no defense against the impacts of this direct and structural violence.

REFERENCES

Arola, Kristin. 2010. "The Design of Web 2.0: The Rise of the Template, the Fall of Design." *Computers and Composition* 27, no. 1: 4–14. doi: 10.1016/j.compcom.2009.11.004.

Bailey, Moya, and Izetta Mobley. 2019. "Work in the Intersections: A Black Feminist Disability Framework." *Gender and Society* 33, no. 1: 19–40. doi: 10.1177/0891243218801523.

Banks, Adam. 2015. "Ain't No Walls Behind the Sky, Baby! Funk, Flight, Freedom." *College Composition and Communication* 67, no. 2: 267–79. JSTOR.

Berlin, James. 1988. "Rhetoric and Ideology in the Writing Class." *College English* 50, no. 5: 477–94. JSTOR.

Blackboard. "Blackboard for Higher Education." Accessed October 14, 2019. https://www.blackboard.com/higher-education/index.html.

Bridgman, Katherine, Kristie S. Fleckenstein, and Scott Gage. 2019. "Reanimating the Answerable Body: Rhetorical Looking and the Digital Interface." *Computers and Composition* 53, no.: 86–95. doi: 10.1016/j.compcom.2019.05.007.

Bucholtz, Mary, Dolores Inés Casillas, and Jin Sook Lee. 2017. "Language and Culture as Sustenance." In *Culturally Sustaining Pedagogies*, edited by Django Paris and H. Samy Alim, 43–59. New York: Teachers College Press.

Carnegie, Teena. 2009. "Interface as Exordium: The Rhetoric of Interactivity." *Computers and Composition* 26, no. 3:164–73. doi: 10.1016/j.compcom.2009.05.005.

Carpenter, Rick. 2009. "Boundary Negotiations: Electronic Environments as Interface." *Computers and Composition* 26, no. 3:138–48. doi: 10.1016/j.compcom.2009.05.001.

Dolmage, Jay. 2014. *Disability Rhetoric*. Syracuse: Syracuse University Press.

Dolmage, Jay. 2012. "Writing Against Normal." In *Composing (Media) = Composing (Embodiment)*, edited by Kristin Arola and Anne Wysocki, 115–31. Boulder: University Press of Colorado.

Drucker, Johanna. 2013. "Reading Interface." *PMLA* 128, no 1: 213–20. doi: 10.1632/pmla.2013.128.1.213.

Freire, Paulo. 2000. *Pedagogy of the Oppressed*. Translated by Myra Bergman Ramos. New York: Bloomsbury.

Galtung, Johan. 1990. "Cultural Violence." *Journal of Peace Research* 27, no. 3: 291–305. doi: 10.1177/0022343390027003005.

Haas, C. 2009. *Writing Technology: Studies in the Materiality of Literacy*. New York: Routledge.

hooks, bell. 2009. *Teaching Critical Thinking: Practical Wisdom*. New York: Routledge.

Inoue, Asao. 2019. "How Do We Language so People Stop Killing Each Other, or What Do We Do about White Supremacy?" Paper presented at the Conference on College Communication and Composition, Pittsburgh, March 14, 2019. http://tinyurl.com/y374x2r6.

Garland-Thomson, Rosemarie. 1997. *Extraordinary Bodies: Figuring Physical Disability in American Culture and Literature*. New York: Columbia University Press.

Kynard, Carmen. 2018. "*This Bridge*: The Black Feminist Compositionists' Guide to the Colonial and Imperial Violence of Schooling Today." *Feminist Teacher* 26, no. 2–3: 126–41. doi: 10.5406/femteacher.26.2–3.0126.

Laymon, Kiese. 2016. "Da Art of Storytellin' (a Prequel)." In *The Fire This Time*, edited by Jesmyn Ward, 117–27. New York: Scribner.

McCorkle, B. (2012). "Whose Body?: Looking Critically at New Interface Designs." In K. Arola and A. Wysocki, *Composing (Media) = Composing (Embodiment)*, 174–87. Boulder: University Press of Colorado.

Minh-ha, Trinh T. 1989. *Woman, Native, Other*. Bloomington: Indiana University Press.

Mirza, Heidi Safia. 2009. "Postcolonial Subjects, Black Feminism, and the Intersectionality of Race and Gender in Higher Education." *Counterpoints* 369: 233–48. JSTOR.

Puwar, Nirmal. 2004. *Space Invaders*. New York: Berg.

Ruiz, Iris, and Damián Baca. 2017. "Decolonial Options and Writing Studies." *Composition Studies* 45, no. 2: 226–29. https://compstudiesjournal.com.

Selfe, Cynthia. 1999a. "Technology and Literacy: A Story About the Perils of Not Paying Attention." *College Composition and Communication* 50, no. 3: 411–36. JSTOR.

Selfe, Cynthia. 1999b. *Technology and Literacy in the Twenty-First Century*. Carbondale: Southern Illinois University Press.

Selfe, Cynthia, and Richard Selfe. 1994. "The Politics of the Interface: Power and its Exercise in Electronic Contact Zones." *College Composition and Communication* 45, no. 4: 480–504.

Vertelney, Laurie, and Booker, Sue. 1990. "Designing the Whole-Product User Interface." In *The Art of Human-Computer Interface Design*, edited by Brenda Laurel, 57–63. Boston: Addison-Wesley Longman.

Villenas, Sofia, Francisca E. Godinez, Dolores Delgado Bernal, and C. Alejandra Elenes. 2006. "Chicanas/Latinas Building Bridges." In *Chicana/Latina Education in Everyday Life*, edited by Dolores Delgado Bernal, C. Alejandra Elenes, Francisca E. Godinez, and Sofia Villenas, 1–10. Albany: State University of New York Press.

Walls, Douglas, Scott Schopieray, and Dànielle Nicole DeVoss. 2009. "Hacking Spaces: Place as Interface." *Computers and Composition* 26, no. 4: 269–87. doi: 10.1016/j.compcom.2009.09.003.

Wysocki, Anne, and Julia Jasken. 2004. "What Should Be an Unforgettable Face . . ." *Computers and Composition* 21, no. 1: 29–48. doi: 10.1016/j.compcom.2003.08.004.

Yancey, Kathleen. 2004. "Made Not Only in Words: Composition in a New Key" *College Composition and Communication* 56, no. 2: 297–328. JSTOR.

Young, Vershawn. 2011. "Should Writers Use They Own English?" In *Writing Centers and the New Racism,* edited by Laura Greenfield and Karen Rowan, 61–74. Logan: Utah State University Press.

5

THE PRODUCTIVE VIOLENCE OF PEDAGOGY
Argumentation and Change in the Writing Course

Trevor C. Meyer

Today, we inhabit a conflict between one side, who see themselves as defending True American Values against their violation by vicious enemies, and another side, who see themselves doing the exact same thing. In this revived Culture War, many terms are read in opposing, mutually exclusive ways: "Black Lives Matter" is read as containing an implicit "(Only) Black Lives Matter" or as "Black Lives Matter (Too)," and "feminism" means both gender equity and cultural castration. One person's attempts at reasonable critique can be seen by another as a personal attack, certain differences in opinion are acceptable while others are decidedly not, and which is which depends on who the person happens to be. Whatever common ground there once was, if there ever was, is now tentative and contingent, even if people consider their own common ground neutral and objective. Therefore, there is a serious need to educate people in argument—that is, how to disagree better.

As a field, composition is already invested in better disagreement, as shown by the commonplace commitment to argument. In a survey of argument in composition textbooks, A. Abby Knoblauch (2011) describes arguments as occasions "in which a rhetor attempts to convince or convert an opponent" (245). This article shows how textbook authors also work to explicitly "contrast argument marked by quarreling, fighting, winning, [and] defeating opposition," with the proper approach of "mature reasoning, civil conversation, mediation, and truth seeking" (250). Even so, both are ways of overcoming opposition, and, rather than turn away from such opposition, as many in the rhetorical tradition have, I suggest we turn toward it and look more closely. Indeed, the current state of public discourse suggests that we need to reexamine the tools, approaches, and premises of our understanding of argument, because, without it, friction will increase until discourse across ideological divides is not only difficult but impossible, leaving physical force—blade, bullet, and bomb—as the only means to deal with disagreement.

As James Crosswhite (2013) writes in *Deep Rhetoric*, argument, and rhetoric more broadly, is "defined as the other to violence . . . able to accomplish exactly what violence accomplishes," but in a non- or anti-violent way; however, to be "an alternative to violence, rhetoric must in some way resemble it" (134). This resemblance means that when "argument fails," as Jennifer Bay (2002) writes, "wars are fought, violence committed, vengeance inflicted" (694). If argument is either a form of violence or an alternative that resembles it, we might reasonably seek to reduce or eliminate such violence, or even move beyond argument altogether, as Catherine E. Lamb (1991) suggests. However, I see this drive to reduce or eliminate violence as impossible at best and, at worst, as a way of perpetuating and justifying violence that serves our own ends while demonizing that by others.

Instead, we must recognize the "violence in language and sociality that cannot be fully eradicated without eradicating language and sociality themselves," meaning that even the most explicitly nonviolent approach is violent too, although not in the most usual sense of the term (Crosswhite 2013, 135). To begin this recognition, I suggest we follow Crosswhite in considering "violence" more broadly, as "any force that is exerted without complete assent and participation—physically, emotionally, symbolically, in any way at all—on a person or group or on the things which are valuable to them, or on the cultural and linguistic and symbolic and physical habitats out of which they come to understand what is valuable to them and what is not" (162). While students assent to our teaching by taking our class, they cannot completely know to what they have assented. Outside of vigorous, ongoing, affirmative assent or specific structures like labor-based grading contracts, knowing whether students' assent is full, knowledgeable, and complete becomes a challenge, especially as assent connects to questions of consent and assault, which are too complex to deal with fully and ethically here.

While Crosswhite's (2013) expanded definition does not equate the violence of argument to the violence of assault—which is not only "a kind of madness but also a kind of evil"—it does illustrate violence as more than the simple, cliché image of a punch to the face (135). Under this broader definition, the destruction of symbols (whether the Star of David or the Stars and Bars), the establishment of policy (whether "nondiscrimination" or "freedom of religion"), or the negative description of any particular values ("family values," "reproductive rights," or

"America") are all examples of violence, but that does not mean that all violence is the same or to be similarly valued.

While we might easily characterize cruel words, raised voices, or physical aggression as violence, we must recognize that violence is also the coercive norms and prohibitions that delimit appropriate and ethical action; both the disruption of the status quo and the enforcement of it are forms of violence. But whether we call it "violence" depends on whether we're fighting "tyranny" to produce "freedom" or fighting "terrorism" to produce "peace," or whether any particular violence is seen as "just," either enacting "justice" or merely "justified." By ignoring the violence at work in normative practices, we do not erase the violence committed but rather obscure it to emphasize its desirable products.

Rather than a distinct category, my term "productive violence" refers to an orientation toward violence as generative, useful, or even desirable. This seeming paradox illustrates the pervasiveness of the narrow definition of violence as mere destruction, despite destruction being only one of the many products of violence. Other products include health and hygiene (we eat dead plants and animals and eradicate microorganisms), rigor (we reject insufficient scholarship), and even common ground itself, which is produced by the violent exclusion of ignorant, biased, or bigoted ideas in favor of compromise.

In this chapter, I want to help us recognize the violence always already lurking within our pedagogies, and which is always already productive, despite its negative connotations. To do so, I will review the major forms of argumentation in the composition field, illustrating the productive violence of each: the problem of the eristic within Aristotelian argument, the coercion required by the Rogerian method, and the potential of invitational rhetoric, which recognizes the ethical viability of violence. Finally, I will address how this recognition affects how we teach student writers. If we recognize the violence we can, do, and must commit for our own pedagogical goals, we can see that, rather than an objective entity in itself, "violence" is a rhetorical construct by which we evaluate, and justify or demonize, any action. Through this recognition, we might see our own violences as they seem to those with different or opposing ideologies, who value different products of violence, which is vital if we are to teach argument in the new Culture War.

MODES OF TRADITIONAL ARGUMENT: ERISTIC AND AGONISTICS

To illustrate the violence always already present in argumentation, I turn to Aristotle's *On Rhetoric*—translated by George Kennedy (1991)—an influential part of ancient foundation of not only the larger rhetorical tradition but also for argument in college composition. However, Aristotle's cultural context—Greek "agonism," in which argument is a kind of contest or fight—suffers from the misunderstanding wrought by centuries of distance and the dominance of hostile ideologies. By looking through the lens of productive violence, we can see that when faced with an eristic wrangling aiming to rouse emotion, Aristotle constructs his own coercive set of irenic rules in response, which are no less violent, but only differently so.

Before his more famous definition of rhetoric as the "ability to see in a given case the available means of persuasion," earlier Aristotle (1991) writes that people use rhetoric "to defend themselves and to attack others," making rhetoric an art of fighting with words (1.1, 2). Furthermore, Aristotle finds it "absurd to hold that a man ought to be ashamed of being unable to defend himself with his limbs, but not of being unable to defend himself with rational speech," when rational speech is the more distinctly human means of self-defense (1.1, 5). However, even if an argument is a fight, what "fight" means for Aristotle and his contemporaries is not necessarily the same for us today. The agonistic approach is not the bloodthirsty brutality it often seems but instead something explicitly opposed to such brutality.

In *Bodily Arts*, Debra Hawhee (2004) argues that the ancient *agōn* emphasized "the contestive encounter rather than strictly the division between opposing sides" (16). Whether competing in running, wrestling, or oratory, the goal of the contest was not simply victory but *arête*—more properly translated as "virtuosity" or "excellence" rather than the more common and static "virtue"—which is only earned through agonistic enactment (17, 25). That is, there is no *arête* without *agōn*, no excellence without contest. On the battlefield, where it's kill or be killed, the risk of death far outweighs the potential for *arête*. But within the contest, with its rules and judges, *arête* becomes far easier to perform and recognize, which is why Pindar (1990) calls it the "finest" of "the gifts of war" (10.56). Therefore, *agōn* is produced by the rules delineating the contest, including safety and consent as well as respect and honor when engaging an opponent, who is a loved rival we struggle with rather than an obstacle to overcome or an enemy to destroy.

Considering this agonistic context, Aristotle's (1991) attempt to "give some account of the systematic principles of rhetoric" aims to make argument an *agōn* so that rhetors might succeed through merit and skill, rather than through privilege, brute force, dishonesty, or simple luck, because while "things that are true and things that are better are, by their nature, practically always easier to prove and more persuasive," this is not always or necessarily the case (1.1, 1). With these rules, Aristotle distinguishes logical, proper argument and "wrangling" (*erizō*)—from Eris, goddess of discord and associate of Ares, god of slaughter—an "arousing of prejudice, pity, [and] anger" within the judge, audience, or opponent, which is often more successful than rational argument (1.1, 5). Here we have a binary that persists throughout the tradition and into the twentieth century: productive, nonviolent argument and destructive, violent eristic.

We can see this binary in Edward P. J. Corbett's (1969) essay, "The Rhetoric of the Open Hand and the Rhetoric of the Closed Fist." Discussing contemporaneous civil rights protests, Corbett metaphorically describes the two different—and mutually exclusive—models of argument, which provides further insight into the violence at work even in supposedly nonviolent approaches to disagreement. Corbett's "open hand" approach is "an older mode of discourse which was verbal, sequential, logical, monologist, and ingratiating," the style of academic argument inherited from Aristotle (295). In contrast, Corbett describes the tactics of civil rights protestors as the "closed fist," eristic disruption that is "often non-verbal, fragmentary, coercive, interlocutory, and alienating," a common response to such protests, even today (295). While Corbett concedes that sometimes the closed fist is useful, it is clear that he prefers the one with calm "logical" discussion, not eristic marching and "coercive" chanting. While we might not prefer eristic as a method of argument, Corbett's identification of civil rights protest as eristic shows that sometimes it is the only option when fighting oppression.

Discussing how John Quincy Adams was accused of "wrangling" for his opposition to slavery, Patricia Roberts-Miller (2006) writes, "in situations of oppression, when univocality is enforced through aggressive, if not openly coercive, discourse, then dissent will necessarily be perceived as equally aggressive," especially if the tone in which these rules are articulated is gentle, calm, or *reasonable* (148). When the norms of proper argument have been constructed as neutral, natural, and objective, then it is easy to dismiss dissenters as wranglers, and "a situation in which violence has triumphed, and continues to triumph by silencing dissent, may look very nonconflictual" (142). When the rules are established to legitimize and justify oppressive political institutions or social structures—excluding particular views and people from the onset—the only option is eristic. While we might easily justify eristic in cases like racial justice, it is still violence that breaks the norms of peaceful civility: the coercive means of maintaining an exclusionary social status quo.

Likewise, the rules of logic that circumscribe so-called rational argument also maintain an exclusionary conceptual status quo. That is, coercion is not imposed on innocent, rational argument from without, but rather coercion is how rational, peaceable argument is violently produced.

Both the irenic coercion of argumentative norms and the eristic disruption of such norms are instances of productive violence. In the violence of law, irenic coercion produces peace, order, and regularity, a set of rules that allows differing positions to be judged on equal ground, even if inequality is the result. In the violence of revolution, eristic disruption breaks rules to change an audience, challenge assumptions, or overcome opposition, even if such disruption is destructive. However, both violences can be useful to most any ideology, making neither more nor less just, evil, nor violent than the other, but merely different. This double risk of irenic coercive restriction and eristic wrangling disruption endemic to contestatory argument has led teachers and scholars to try to minimize this risk of violence as much as possible, employing noncontestatory or even anticontestatory alternatives.

ALTERNATIVE MODES OF ARGUMENT: ROGERIAN RHETORIC

One prominent alternative to traditional argument was developed by Carl Rogers (1952). Rather than focusing on who is "right" or "wrong," Rogers approaches disagreement as a lack of mutual understanding, a therapeutic approach that was appropriated by Richard E. Young, Alton L. Becker, and Kenneth L. Pike (Young, Becker, and Pike 1970) and promoted by Maxine Hairston (1976) and others. In the Rogerian method, participants overcome emotionally charged disagreement through compassionate expression, which avoids both eristic wrangling and "rational, disinterested argumentation" (Hairston 1976, 373). As Rogers (1952) asserts, "the major barrier to mutual interpersonal communication is our very natural tendency to judge, to evaluate, to approve or disapprove, the statement of the other person," a form of productive violence fundamental to the human condition (130). Once we eliminate this sense of threat, miscommunications become much easier to resolve. However, we should recognize that such "elimination," even of something like "threat," is an instance of productive violence fundamental to the Rogerian project.

As Hairston (1976) outlines it, Rogerian argument has five phases. First, there is a "brief, objective statement" of the facts of the case presented as neutrally as possible (375). Second, one party summarizes the other's position "in impartial language," avoiding hostility and demonstrating care for the other party's "interests and concerns," which is followed by, third, an equally objective statement of one's "own side of the issue," avoiding "loaded language or any hint of moral superiority" (375–76). Fourth, the party must outline both common ground and irreconcilable differences, and fifth, they "must suggest a reasonable solution that he believes both parties can live with" and "pointing out what both sides may gain" from this solution (376). In theory and often in practice, this approach works well, as Paul Bator (1980) explains: "through discovery of each other's points of view, we are all encouraged to revise our image of the world" (431). While such a call for understanding is certainly reasonable, as a whole-cloth replacement for argumentation, it has met with some resistance that addresses the violence at work in this supposedly nonviolent alternative.

Lisa Ede (1984) argues that Young, Becker, and Pike (1970) both misunderstood and appropriated Rogers' method by assuming that a therapeutic engagement between two people over a specific issue is easily adapted to larger, more complex disagreements. This method produces a problematic, yet common, "arhetorical view . . . in which language functions ideally as a transparent means of self-expression," rendering contextual consideration, genre convention, and audience adaptation as forms of eristic wrangling (40). Additionally, aside from acknowledging their possibility, I argue that Rogers' approach delegitimizes irreconcilable differences, because this method implies that if we simply state truth objectively and neutrally, whatever that is, any disagreement would result from ignorance, arrogance, or willful stupidity. Furthermore, offering Rogers (1952) as an alternative to Aristotle (1991) is based on a "stereotyped view of classical rhetoric," ignoring the complex, nuanced, and agonistic ancient Greek rhetoric in favor of a caricatured "classical tradition" (40).

Andrea Lunsford (1979) explains that there is no specific "Rogerian" corollary in Aristotle, because his argument does not begin with "the point of breakdown in communication or of ignorance of the facts, but at the point of possible communication and with a full knowledge of the facts. Hence, the techniques used in Rogerian argument are not neglected by Aristotle—rather they form the foundation which is necessary before successful argument begins" (148). That is, Rogers and Aristotle simply emphasize two parts of the same complex system of violent coercion imposed on argument to produce peaceful conformity and predictable regularity. Rogers emphasizes the coercive foundations of the system that make disagreement possible, and Aristotle emphasizes the coercive restrictions of what legitimate disagreement must be. In sum, both Aristotle and Rogers produce irenic coercion to combat eristic disruption, focusing on conduct and preconditions, respectively. However, even if the Rogerian method has its problems, its popularity exemplifies writing teachers' "long-standing discomfort with persuasion" (Ede 1984, 41), which we can now see as the fear of wrangling and of coercion in all argument.

Beyond the risks of an agonistic approach to disagreement, the "classical tradition" also carries the violence of patriarchal norms: the exclusion of women from power, privilege, and public speech. The privilege of men to not only acquire learning but also to dictate what learning, argument, and reason *are* has led some recent feminist scholars of argumentation to provide an alternative to the tradition itself, another productive violence: the eristic disruption of feminism revolting against the irenic coercion of patriarchy.

ALTERNATIVE MODES OF ARGUMENT: INVITATION

While both Rogers and Aristotle use irenic coercion to reject eristic disruption, they only do so within a system of patriarchy that promotes a toxic masculinist agonism as the only legitimate means of engagement. In "Beyond Persuasion: A Proposal for an Invitational Rhetoric," Sonja K. Foss and Cindy L. Griffin (Foss and Griffin 1995) argue that while persuasion has its place, persuasion itself is motivated by a "desire for control and domination" because "the act of changing another establishes the power of the change agent over that other" (3), which often produces "feelings of inadequacy, insecurity, pain, humiliation, guilt, embarrassment, or angry submission on the part of the audience" (6). As an alternative that avoids these negative feelings, Foss and Griffin (1995) explain that in the invitational approach "resistance is not anticipated, and rhetors do not adapt their communication to expected resistance in the audience. Instead, they identify possible impediments to the creation of understanding and seek to minimize or neutralize them so they do not remain impediments" (6). In doing so, "rhetors recognize the valuable contributions audience members can make . . . [and] do not engage in strategies that may damage or sever the connection between them and their audiences" (6). This openness to the audience creates conditions of *safety* from reprisal in offering perspectives, *value* in the worth of those perspectives and those offering them, and *freedom* of any participant to engage any topic without explicit prohibition or assumed superiority.

However, as with Rogers (1952), this more robust alternative has been challenged, and, recently, Jennifer Emerling Bone and others, including

Griffin (Bone, Griffin, and Scholz 2008), responded to the major critiques of invitational rhetoric, some of which are more complicated than others. In addressing these critiques, Bone, Griffin, and Scholz deftly counter reductive readings of invitational rhetoric and complicate the ways we can understand and practice it. But, in so doing, they make the violence of invitation more easily recognizable, troubling the ease with which invitation can be a "nonviolent" alternative to traditional persuasion. Therefore, I will examine some of the critiques Bone, Griffin, and Scholz address, rather than all that they engage in the original essay. I cannot present their full arguments here, so I must rip words from the body of their text, manipulate them to suit my present purposes, and stitch everything together following the coercive norms of academic writing and academic integrity. I have been committing this typical, scholarly form of productive violence throughout this chapter, one that Bone, Griffin, and Scholz explicitly promote in their article.

Responding to "the critique that only women can and do use invitational rhetoric, that it is a 'feminine' rhetoric, or that feminist and patriarchal argumentation styles are mutually exclusive," Bone, Griffin, and Scholz (2008) argue that such a critique is "quite simply, not supported by the original article" (441). Indeed, to place persuasion and invitation into a mutually exclusive, restrictive, essentialist gender/sex binary is itself a patriarchal move. Nevertheless, scholars must risk such essentialism, because "definitions remain a necessary part of academic scholarship," and the violent elimination of complexity and nuance produces "clarity" for "scholars and their audiences" (445). That is, even as Bone, Griffin, and Scholz note the violence of a restrictive definition, they concede that such a violence is needed to produce effective scholarship and clear writing. Not only do they argue for the productive violence of essentialism in order to be understood and taken seriously, but Bone, Griffin, and Scholz also offer further productive violence in its most obvious and recognizable form by asking "what would it mean to say that persuasion, at times, can be violent, that there may be a continuum of 'violence,' or that rhetorical violence may, at times, be desirable?" (439).

In response to the critique that invitation is offered as a panacea for disagreement, Bone, Griffin, and Scholz (2008) argue that sometimes "no amount of persuading or inviting is going to be useful" and that assuming so "places undue responsibility and accountability on the rhetor and the type of communication used" (441). Even though the invitational approach "assumes that we listen to and communicate with those whom we would rather not listen to or communicate at all," in some situations nonviolent listening does more harm than good (448).

In such situations, using "an extreme and unnatural verbal interruption or reproach may halt a dangerous or desperate situation and open up a space for further negotiation before decisions are made and actions taken. To employ symbols to bring about a forceful alteration or a harsh and painful change may, in fact, be a necessary step to prevent harm or bring about a greater good. To interfere may not always be appropriate, but in certain contexts, verbal interference may cause individuals or groups to think differently about complex situations" (439). Even though Bone, Griffin, and Scholz question the drive of persuasive domination, sometimes domination is needed "to prevent a racist, classist, sexist, homophobic act, or even to prevent someone from hurting themselves or another person or entity" (457). In the approach to disagreement that explicitly advocates for conditions of safety, freedom, and value for all participants, some positions should not be safe, free, or valued, because their very inclusion excludes other, usually marginalized, perspectives. In such instances, the safety, freedom, and value of such perspectives must be violated to protect the safety, freedom, and value of all others.

While "the theory of invitational rhetoric suggests that at times knowing what is best for another is less than clear," in these instances, when we *do* know "what is best" for others, we are performing an instance of violence because "obvious" cases of knowing what is best for another are not as obvious as they might seem to us (Bone, Griffin, and Scholz 2008, 457). To the person we *do* know better than, our help is paternalistic violence against their agency; deplorable acts must be fought, even if doing so violates the autonomy of those committing them. Like the irenic coercion required by civility and logic in traditional argumentation, the productive violence of invitation can also work to produce oppressive power structures, even if its products are desirable. We might then justify our own violence, explain how it is not *really* violent, or whatever easy defense we might offer when confronted by the other with differing values and different ideologies. In the end, neither persuasion nor invitation is *the* answer.

Indeed, the complex problematic of how to disagree is not a single problem with a single solution. The most productive models of disagreement might then require multiple approaches and question the conditions of the problem itself in order to develop a more flexible "ontological orientation" to engage with others across multiple dimensions (Bone, Griffin, and Scholz 2008, 446). There are some examples of such flexible approaches that combine or multiply the binaries of invitation and persuasion, eristic disruption and irenic coercion. While they do not go far enough, they provide useful insight for a pedagogy of productive violence.

INTEGRATIVE MODES OF ARGUMENT: PARADOX AND PLURALITY

While many approaches might inhabit traditional or alternative argument in different ways, others complicate argument to address many of the complexities I have discussed. Such integrative approaches provide several advantages over remaining strictly within one side of the binary, even though they do not sufficiently overcome the limitations or risks that motivate them.

One approach by Dennis Lynch, Diana George, and Marilyn M. Cooper (Lynch, George, and Cooper 1997), "agonistic inquiry" or "confrontational cooperation," explicitly foregrounds the mutual co-constitution of the oppositional productive violences by having "people struggle over interpretations together, deliberate on the nature of the issues that face them, and articulate and rearticulate their positions in history, culture, and circumstance" (63). By foregrounding differences in perspective, attempting argument without aggression, and situating perspectives within their contexts, this integrative approach is certainly more productive than dwelling in reductive binaries. In questioning the traditional paradigm, they begin to see the productive violence of pedagogy: not "productive" inquiry *or* "violent" agonism, cooperation *or* confrontation, but rather both together.

As examples, the coauthors describe two different classes that used this approach. One questioned the foundations of a political controversy—the racism of Native American mascots—through reading articles from "both sides," and the other addressed water resource use and conservation through the common assignment sequence of topic exploration, position development, consideration of limitations and opposition, and reflection on the overall process. Their pedagogical attempts helped students consider issues with more nuance, engage with the complexities of real world issues, practice argument as more than mere eristic, and so on. However, in attempting to overcome the strict division between traditional argument and eristic disruption, persuasion, and invitation, without addressing the conceptual structures that produces this division, the authors end up reaffirming the mutually exclusive binary: in order for confrontation to happen, there must be cooperatively generated and enforced norms, norms that are challenged and maintained through confrontational tactics, returning us to eristic disruption and irenic coercion.

In Patricia Roberts-Miller's (2004) *Deliberate Conflict*, we can see another approach that identifies the disagreement about what constitutes proper and productive argument in the differing notions of "public" assumed by various composition pedagogies. To illustrate these differences, Roberts-Miller posits the intersection of two axes, what I term the method of language use and the orientation to disagreement. The methodic axis ranges from expressive to deliberative, whether persons primarily use language to present their perspective or to ask questions and respond to answers. In an expressive method, a person "expresses (or declares) certain ideas . . . [without] any attempt to interweave a fair discussion of the views of his opposition," which we can see in both invitational rhetoric and eristic wrangling (48). In contrast, deliberation requires engaging with opposition, asking questions and answering them, and coming to conclusions after careful consideration, which we can see in both Rogers (1952) and Aristotle (1991). The other axis concerns the orientation to disagreement, and it ranges from irenic to agonistic: "In an irenic public sphere, a productive argument results in the persons reaching agreement about the issue about which they originally disagreed (or one about which there was never any disagreement in the first place) . . . [whereas] in an agonistic sphere, a productive argument leads to appropriate policies, raises interesting questions, brings up injustices, or draws attention to points of view that had been obscured" (12). The two axes create four different notions of productive disagreement: *irenic expressive* (invitational rhetoric), *irenic deliberative* (Rogerian argument), *agonistic expressive* (eristic wrangling), and *agonistic deliberative* (traditional argument).

Through Roberts-Miller's (2004) four-fold model, we can see the binaries of argument more broadly and the productive violence required by all of them. In order to create the conditions for deliberation, the common ground needed to disagree, persons need to express their views; in order to get to deliberation, we need expression, and we need deliberation to establish the conditions for that expression. Conversely, in order to achieve agonism, we need irenic agreement on proper conduct, and, to achieve irenicism, we need agonistic participation by all involved. While the distinction between orientations to disagreement and methods of using language is important and useful, to privilege one over the other as inherently superior, ethical, or effective (aside from the fittingness of the approach to a given situation, which we can never know in advance) renders participants vulnerable to other, differing approaches. This drive to "designate some specific rhetoric as a discourse beyond reproach or criticism, [is] to be in principle blind to whatever coercion or violence it might harbor" (Crosswhite 2013, 135). All four approaches require both eristic disruption and irenic coercion, even though the ability to see this is limited not only by conflating all argument with eristic disruption, and demonizing it as anything other than destructive, improper, and violent, but also ignoring the coercive foundation of deliberative norms. In sum, none of these four is more or less violent than any other, but rather each differs in their particular products of violence and their emphasis on the productivity of particular violences.

Both Lynch et.al. (1997) and Roberts-Miller (2004) move us forward, but a tendency persists to privilege whatever "we" value and what pro-ductive, violence, and argument mean to *us*. That is, violence is a term we, whoever we are, use for things we don't like or agree with, things *they* do, while our own actions, no matter how hard a choice they may be, are justified, usually by their product, and thus not *really* "violent." Furthermore, for those opposed to our ideology, either in fact or only in seeming, such justification of violence as nonviolence is hypocritical and often leads them to reject our arguments (and us, and even academics writ large) altogether.

Perhaps instead of resting in our comfortable assumptions about violence, we might recognize that it is all violence all the way down, and it is all productive. That does not therefore mean that all violence is the same or similarly valued, nor that all its products might be useful, beneficial, or desirable in a specific instance. We might instead attend closely to the conditions of particular disagreements and recognize which specific kinds, degrees, and intensities of violence would be most appropriate in a particular case and most productive of desired ends. While we are constrained by our coercive governmental, institutional, and departmental norms, each of us must decide in our own classes how best to balance eristic disruption and irenic coercion, what violence we practice explicitly and what implicitly, and what products we intend our pedagogical violence to produce.

PEDAGOGICAL CONDITIONS FOR PRODUCTIVE VIOLENCE

When we teach argument in the classroom, we must do much more than simply offer traditional, clichéd understandings and attempt to apply them normatively in expected ways; nor can we lord over our students, coercing them to accept our views, norms, and values simply because we have the violence of assessment at our disposal. Rather, we might foreground our violence as violence so students might fully engage with it themselves; I have three recommendations.

First, we can look more closely at the coercive conditions and eristic possibilities surrounding the basics of our discipline: what words to use and how to put them together. To illustrate, while so-called correct grammar will help our students to be taken seriously by the future academic and professional audiences for whom they will write when they leave our class, we can also share how restrictive, exclusionary, and linguistically fictional such an "objective norm" is. We might share how this approach comes directly from the Eurocentric, urban, elite population that historically dominated higher education (and largely still does today). We can point to the exclusionary Greco-Roman inheritance of language education that understands error as ethnic otherness (barbarism) or rural deficiency (solecism). However, if an employer or another professor cannot understand a piece of writing, then they have power to treat it as nonsense, even if they do so because of reductive and antiquated linguistic attitudes. In sum, even if we need to teach our students to be able to write with the voice of power, we need to do so explicitly or perpetuate and obscure our participation in a history of unjust "white language supremacy" (Inoue 2019).

Second, we might teach our students the rules of logic to both defend their own claims and question those of others, but we need to illustrate the circular fallacy at the root of logic: a claim is wrong because it is illogical. We might show that the claim "your experience of racism is not necessarily representative of a larger trend because you're just one person" is logical, yet violent and dismissive, while the fallacious *ad hominem* "Daniel Tramp is wrong about immigration policy because he hates immigrants" might be worth considering. We can teach students to gather evidence to support their claims and evaluate their credibility. But we might also teach them to question the authority of that evidence, the material conditions and power dynamics by which a source is granted "authority" in a particular argument, field, or situation. We also can teach them that authoritative evidence does not necessarily guarantee that an argument is persuasive, or even correct (*ad verecundiam*). We need to talk about the fact that ethical arguments are not always, or maybe even usually, effective, and that effective arguments are not necessarily ethical. Telling the truth can put you in chains as often as it can set you free.

Third, we need to foreground the contemporary coercive norms of our own academic contexts: our assessment metrics as well as departmental and university policies. We need to explain why the view that "black people are more criminal than white people" is unacceptable and not something about which we can simply agree to disagree. We must also explain that seeing such views as unacceptable is not "indoctrination," but part of what once might have been the core of civil society, and to espouse such views might be a violation of the ethical guidelines to which students assent when they enter university. Moreover, we need to understand the coercive nature of these norms, not just advocate their justness, productivity, or commonality. We need to discuss the material conditions immanent to the classes we teach, the students in those classes, the reasons why we have this assignment in this class, the justification for requiring composition for everyone but no additional writing courses, not even requiring majors in technical fields to take technical writing, or whatever the particular situation might be at your particular institution. We need to explain that forcing students to meet word counts and use outside sources is not an attempt to "stifle a unique voice" but part of helping them "write better" or becoming "better writers" or whatever we claim to do, attempt to do, or actually accomplish in a particular writing class.

We need to explain that explanation is not always enough, that, no matter what we say, we might not be heard. We might write thousands of words, follow all the coercive norms, revise for years, and yet, because of the eristic disruption we offer, we might be rejected as insufficient, confused, or not offering productive contributions to the field. *As I might be so rejected here with this writing.*

A pedagogy of productive violence, in which we explicitly account for the violence we can, do, and must commit, in as many dimensions as we can, is extremely difficult with no guarantee or even a great possibility of success; violence is *both* a necessary condition for *and* a risk to productive human interaction. Nevertheless, this is what argumentation has been since the beginning; we look for alternatives to physical force as the foundation for life. When Aristotle (1991) saw fear directing policy, he sought to make it a fair contest. When we saw the violent implications of traditional argument, we looked to therapy for different ways to practice and teach it. When Foss and Griffin (1995) saw the patriarchal heritage of persuasion, they offered invitation. When others saw them as overreaching, Bone, Griffin, and Scholz (2008) responded that sometimes violence is the answer. We look for comfortable and justifiable ways to do the things we must, ways that require the exclusion of what we deem irrelevant, ignorant, or unimportant.

In short, we have always had a pedagogy of productive violence, and all I argue is that we recognize it, affirm it, and move forward, especially if we are supposed to give students the skills to disagree better in the contemporary Culture War: win, lose, draw, forfeit, or disqualification. In any case, we must keep fighting for a better way to disagree.

REFERENCES

Aristotle. 1991. *On Rhetoric.* Translated by George Kennedy. Oxford: Oxford University Press.

Bator, Paul. 1980. "Aristotelian and Rogerian Rhetoric." *College Composition and Communication* 31, no. 4: 427–32. JSTOR.

Bay, Jennifer. 2002. "The Limits of Argument: A Response to Sean Williams." *Journal of Advanced Composition* 22, no. 1: 684–97. http://wwwjaconlinejournal.com.archives/vol 22.3/bay-limits.pdf.

Bone, Jennifer Emerling, Cindy L. Griffin, and T. M. Linda Scholz. 2008. "Beyond Traditional Conceptualizations of Rhetoric: Invitational Rhetoric and a Move Toward Civility." *Western Journal of Communication* 72, no. 4: 434–62. doi: 10.1080/10570310802446089.

Corbett, Edward P. J. 1969. "The Rhetoric of the Open Hand and the Rhetoric of the Closed Fist." *College Composition and Communication* 20, no. 5: 288–96. JSTOR.

Crosswhite, James. 2013. "Rhetoric and Violence." In *Deep Rhetoric,* 134–73. Chicago: University of Chicago Press.

Ede, Lisa. 1984. "Is Rogerian Rhetoric Really Rogerian?" *Rhetoric Review* 3, no. 1: 40–48. JSTOR.

Foss, Sonja K., and Cindy Griffin. 1995. "Beyond Persuasion: A Proposal for an Invitational Rhetoric." *Communication Monographs* 62, no. 1: 2–18. doi: 10.1080/03637759509376345.

Hairston, Maxine. 1976. "Carl Roger's Alternative to Traditional Rhetoric." *College Composition and Communication* 27, no. 4: 373–77. JSTOR.

Hawhee, Debra. 2004. *Bodily Arts: Rhetoric and Athletics in Ancient Greece.* Austin: University of Texas Press.

Inoue, Asao B. 2019. "CCCC Chair's Address: How Do We Language So People Stop Killing Each Other, Or What Do We Do about White Language Supremacy." *College Composition and Communication* 71, no. 2: 352–69. JSTOR.

Knoblauch, A. Abby. 2011. "A Textbook Argument: Definitions of Argument in Leading Composition Textbooks." *College Composition and Communication* 63, no. 2: 244–68. JSTOR.

Lamb, Catherine E. 1991. "Beyond Argument in Feminist Composition." *College Composition and Communication* 42, no. 1: 11–24. JSTOR.

Lunsford, Andrea. 1979. "Aristotelian vs. Rogerian Argument: A Reassessment." *College Composition and Communication.* 30, no. 2: 146–51. JSTOR.

Lynch, Dennis A., Diana George, and Marilyn M. Cooper. 1997. "Moments of Argument: Agonistic Inquiry and Confrontational Cooperation." *College Composition and Communication* 48, no. 1: 61–85. JSTOR.

Pindar. 1990. *Olympian Odes.* Translated by Diane Arnson Svarlien. Perseus Project. http://www.perseus.tufts.edu/hopper/text?doc=Perseus:text:1999.01.0162.

Roberts-Miller, Patricia. 2006. "Agonism, Wrangling, and John Quincy Adams." *Rhetoric Review* 25, no. 2: 141–61. JSTOR.

Roberts-Miller, Patricia. 2004. *Deliberate Conflict: Argument, Political Theory, and Composition Classes.* Carbondale: Southern Illinois University Press.

Rogers, Carl. 1952. "Communication: Its Blocking and Its Facilitation." *ETC: A Review of General Semantics* 9, no. 2: 83–88. EBSCO.

Young, Richard E., Alton L. Becker, and Kenneth L. Pike. 1970. *Rhetoric: Discovery and Change.* New York: Harcourt, Brace, and World.

6

"I'VE GOTTEN A LOT OF SYMPATHY AND THAT'S NOT WHAT I'M LOOKING FOR"
Epistemic and Ontological Violence in Writing-as-Healing Pedagogies

Cathryn Molloy and James Zimmerman

Writing as healing assignments have a more than thirty-year history in composition studies, and scholars have written compellingly in favor of and against such pedagogies. This chapter suggests that there is subtle, yet problematic, violence inherent in these approaches, especially those that force students' disclosures of painful experiences. Using data from a mixed-methods study to define these terms, we argue that compulsory disclosures enact violence we call *epistemic* and *ontological*. We define *epistemic violence* as knowledge creations warped into predetermined narrative arcs and tropes suggested in writing prompts, confining writers to archetypes that they might feel compelled to take on as new identity markers. Likewise, *ontological violence* is the term we use for the pruning of students' available forms of being, or the tendency of prompts to offer them limited inventional purviews within which to make sense of themselves and their experiences.

After presenting a review of literature, we use our data to provide insight into violence in well-intentioned writing-as-healing prompts. These terms emerged from a troubling contradiction in our data: students mostly agree that writing about their personal lives for graded assignments is advantageous but often do not see these assignments as spaces where they can create new meaning or explore various states of being. While publications on writing as healing in our discipline have declined, cross-disciplinary publications continue to appear, notably in the health sciences (Kersting et al. 2011; Fogarty 2010; Duncan et al. 2007; Ogle 2005). This work has evolved without the aid or knowledge of composition scholarship,[1] an issue that Jessica Singer and George Singer (Singer and Singer 2007) identify. Moreover, writing-as-healing

https://doi.org/10.7330/9781040422007.c006

scholarship outside of composition studies provides evidence of the efficacy of written emotional disclosures for alleviating the suffering associated with a number of physical and mental health struggles. Importantly, though, these studies are proposing writing as healing in largely clinical contexts and not for use in classrooms. The literature arguing in favor of writing-as-healing approaches in composition studies often relies on anecdotal evidence and/or studies conducted with and on the researcher's own students. We contend that student writers will not necessarily be forthcoming with the instructors for whom they produce such work due to the uneven power dynamics. Keeping these two issues in mind—reliance on the anecdotal and focus on instructors' own students—we endeavor to add new insight to debates on whether written emotional disclosures are advantageous or even appropriate in classroom settings.

THE HOPE FOR WRITING AS HEALING

Though writing as healing likely has origins that reach as far back as antiquity (Baumlin and Baumlin 1989, 247), it was in the 1980s that this pedagogical strategy became a popular approach to college writing assignments as evidence emerged that writing expressively seemed to accelerate physical and emotional healing (Pennebaker and Smyth 2016).[2] The writing as healing trend is attributed to social psychologist James W. Pennebaker (1997), whose many early studies conclude that there are numerous and indisputable benefits to emotional disclosures and that there are psychological and physiological repercussions from withholding painful pasts.

Pennebaker's approach asks writers to externalize inner trauma without the fear of audiences' judgments, with the idea that such compositions have ameliorative effects. Judith Herman (1997) similarly offers a system of recovery that involves calling up traumatic experiences in order to move on with life, the dominant belief being that writing about painful pasts leads to better writing and thinking and to healthier human beings. Likewise, Charles Anderson and Marian MacCurdy (Anderson and MacCurdy 2000) explain that "personal essays begin with the individual but end with the universal, a process which itself creates connections that can heal" (197), indicating that there is a social dimension to writing as healing work. Indeed, for many, "writing a story about a personal tragedy connects one with others who have gone through a similar trauma and thereby universalizes it" (Moran 2004, 94). Others point out the irony in scholar-practitioners who critique students' narrative disclosures while using these approaches themselves from their places of privilege (Robillard 2003).

In the 1990s, the bulk of writing-as-healing scholarship emerged in the wake of debates over whether expressivist approaches were antithetical to social epistemic frameworks. In order to capitalize on that kairotic moment, some proponents argued that writing as healing is an expressivist approach that makes students more socially responsible since they write about painful experiences that grow out of larger social issues. Wendy Bishop (1993), for example, argued that personal writing is at the fraught dividing line between composition theory's social turn and expressivism (508). Wendy Ryden (2010) likewise astutely explored the "fault line" of writing-as-healing pedagogies, "the narrative divide between public and private" (243). For Ryden, creative nonfiction and personal narrative assignments open an "aperture for healing to take place" (243). In the same way, the "make the personal political" mantra made popular in various feminist works paved the way for writing as healing.[3] Writing as healing also gained traction as an indictment of the conservative notion that the personal has no place in academic discourse. In reference to students writing their rape narratives, for instance, Michelle Payne (2000) maintained that "essays about such oppression are crucial to the projects of critiquing power and ideology" (153). Louise DeSalvo (2000), too, believed that written personal disclosures "force us into an awareness about ourselves and our relationship to others and our place in the world that we wouldn't otherwise have had" (5).

Varied and valid sources of enthusiasm have animated writing instructors' and scholars' excitement for writing-as-healing approaches. In cases like Pennebaker (1997), there is even strong empirical data to back his assertions on the capacity of writing to heal traumas. That said, it is important to note that Pennebaker's research is not about the use of writing as healing in graded settings or even in writing classes. Moreover, studies in the field of composition either draw from anecdotal evidence alone or use data that enthusiastic writing-as-healing instructors gather from their own students. We, thus, designed a study to determine students' dispositions toward writing-as-healing approaches from across the curriculum. We were especially interested in learning what students would say if they were invited to speak with researchers they'd never met or worked with before.

A STUDY OF WRITING AS HEALING

We conducted a mixed-methods study composed of anonymous survey research that included an invitation for non-anonymous follow-up interviews.[4] Our survey, which went out to the entire student body at our state university, including approximately 19,000 undergraduate and 1800 graduate students, and elicited 206 completed responses, with 15 survey participants indicating interest in the interview, 13 of whom followed through. As the interviewers, we used six questions, with minimal follow-up questions for clarification, all designed to be intentionally open-ended to capture participants' dispositions toward this subject without influence.[5]

We asked for no information on the courses, instructors, assignments, or disclosures, so that the focus would be on students' experiences. This decision allowed participants to answer freely without fear that they were "outing" a particular course or instructor. The thirteen interviewees included two graduate students and eleven undergraduate students. After data collection, we culled the quantitative data for major takeaways and used that information to inform what we are calling a "holistic approach to coding." Similar to precoding, we independently annotated printed transcripts in order to note "rich or significant participant quotes" and relevant passages (Saldaña 2010, 16). Then, we examined major trends in the survey data alongside our annotations, developed a coding scheme, and coded the data. We call this approach "holistic" because we included informal discussions of our survey data alongside our original annotations of the interview transcripts. Our version of holistic coding highlights the fact that "coding is a heuristic . . . an exploratory problem-solving technique without specific formulas to follow" and is often "cyclical" (8). After redoing the coding several times to parse this data in a meaningful way, we determined that the concepts of epistemic violence and ontological violence best captured the contradictory nature of our data.[6] Our discussion below will use two representative students as examples of the perils of writing-as-healing assignments.

HARM INSTEAD OF HEALING

Our study indicates that epistemic and ontological violence can ensue from writing prompts that invite a personal response while demarcating specific expectations on the level of form. They presuppose certain kinds of content (and experiences), forcing student writers into narrow and limited compositional spaces. As a result, students are unable to articulate versions of self that fall outside of these limited tropes. Two of our respondents, Lisa and Jason, demonstrate the operation and effects of both kinds of violence. The cases of Lisa and Jason, alongside other data, indicate that epistemic and ontological violence can be the unintended consequences of course-based, for-credit writing-as-healing assignments. Epistemic and ontological violence can not only confuse students regarding their experiences, but they can also cause students to call into question their public and private identities. While students self-report positive outcomes of writing-as-healing assignments, they also suggest that these compositional conditions alter them and their experiences in ways that exceed the expected learning outcomes of a typical college course. We term these alterations "violent" since they happen by force in the context of uneven power dynamics. Asking students to revisit moments of trauma outside of a safe therapeutic setting is hazardous. Since these writing assignments are shared with instructors and often with classmates, students' public personas and senses of self can be violated. Another way that they constitute violence is in their tacit nature; students seem not always to be aware of the potentially negative outcomes of these pedagogies. Indeed, writing-as-healing prompts presuppose certain kinds of content (and experiences), which is problematic since the benefits of writing expressively rely on completely uninhibited and open possibilities rather than generic, constraining forms. Epistemic and ontological issues often overlap, as questions of knowledge influence feelings and behaviors.

Rather than providing Lisa,[7] a white graduating senior from a poor rural family, an opportunity to contend meaningfully with a troubling socioeconomic reality, the writing prompt she was assigned forced her, first, to fit her narrative into a form involving the amelioration of a private trauma that would be familiar to audiences—a form of epistemic violence—and, second, to moderate or edit her experiences to better align with her audience's backgrounds—a form of ontological violence, since her available forms of being were reduced rather than multiplied. As Lisa explained in response to the third question of our interview, a particularly fraught and deeply private circumstance led Lisa's family to split up into multiple households. When she found herself assigned to write about her personal life in a creative nonfiction course, she understood the initial prompt from her instructor to be asking her for narrative symmetry and for a "happy ending" in the form of a resolution to the conflict the narrative introduced. She responded by writing in a narrative arc that was only about herself and her sister. She eliminated her brother to avoid revealing very personal details of her family's situation, realities that would eclipse the opportunity to offer the expected "all is well now" ending to the narrative of suffering. Lisa's story did not necessarily get told as the experience occurred, nor did the writing necessarily allow her space to reflect meaningfully on events as they'd taken place. Instead, she felt pressured to succumb to what she believed were audience (and instructor) expectations in terms of what her story could contain and how it should end.

This alteration of her narrative to fit the prompt had an impact on the rest of her experiences in the course. As she put it, "I will never be able to bring him [her brother] up again, so I had to write him out of another story because it didn't make sense. Now I was almost crafting something that I was against doing." Here, to further complicate her situation as a student in a for-credit course, she felt that sharing her original piece in class prevented her from writing about her brother in subsequent assignments. In fact, Lisa saw the other writing assignments as spaces where she had to "craft" explicit stories that would make sense to her audience given her previous version of her family history, thereby doing violence to her own memories and doing damage to her feelings. Thus, both her ability to learn from the class and her psychological well-being were jeopardized by the prompt.

In addition to having her self-knowledge called into question, she also felt pressure to behave—to be—differently. "I didn't feel comfortable in the classroom atmosphere that I could totally write about that. I feel like I get that a lot because I don't feel like other people's experiences are like mine," Lisa reflected. Clearly, there is an assumed linearity to experience suggested in Lisa's responses—a hallmark of epistemic violence—and there is a paradoxical sense that the prompts are asking her to write about anything at all at the same time that they are restricting her compositional purview—a mark of ontological violence: "I think it seems so easy to write about what you know, *it's what they tell you to do.* But then you have to put a lot of that bargaining of what you feel comfortable to reveal" (emphasis added). She adds, "I think I grappled with whether or not I was presenting it properly." As Lisa makes clear, she sees the space of her writing class as a place where she is doing what she is told and where she is meant to present a specific and singular version of self. The fact that Lisa had to grapple in that way with her own legitimate experiences indicates the struggle that can occur when a student tries to respond not only to a prompt but to the tacit genre expectations of their instructor and peer audiences implicated by the prompt. We argue that these pressures and expectations enacted harm, coercing Lisa into being different than she was.

Finally, Lisa reveals that she writes about her family for these graded pieces even though, as she also says, "I don't like to talk about my family very often, because I don't prefer to." Lisa also makes it clear that she is very conflicted on her decision to disclose in response to prompts for graded work: "I don't feel like I disclose more in my writing than I do in my personal life. But I don't know. Now I'm questioning it. I don't feel like I do. In theory, I don't . . . I feel like the student that's writing about trauma as a means to get an *A*." Her self-knowledge is forcibly called into question, with no professional therapeutic support. Lisa found what Peter Goggin and Maureen Goggin (Goggin and Goggin 2005) argue so compellingly: that classrooms are not safe spaces (45). They contend that writing about a traumatic past "poses powerful problems for the rhetor, for it is by its very nature both beyond language a rhetor possesses and yet can only be constituted by the language s/he produces" (32). Melissa Goldthwaite (2003) develops an analogous line of argument when it comes to confession and power: "I puzzle over the impulse to confess—not just the desire and need to tell—but also the power play of certain confessional situations" (57). Lisa's confusion surrounding writing about her family and its specific traumas aligns well with these critiques of writing as healing, all of which indicates the unintentional infliction of what we identify as epistemic and ontological violence with their attendant damage.

The case of Lisa represents the dynamics of course-based writing-as-healing approaches that can impair rather than benefit the student. Lisa's interview makes it clear that she has had some traumatizing experiences related to poverty, and she does write about them for graded work. That said, she is "crafting something" she is "against doing" in order to fit the prompts and attempting simultaneously to control the level of disclosure; she discloses even though she "doesn't prefer" to talk about her family. Just as the scholarship in the field makes it clear that there is a violent potential in classroom settings when writing-as-healing approaches are taken, Lisa's way of talking about her experiences raises red flags in terms of epistemology and ontology. She does not feel free to "craft" the kind of narrative that she would compose if the writing were anonymous—the kind of writing on trauma that Pennebaker (1997) would say is beneficial—and, instead, takes genre considerations and audience expectations as first orders of concern. These assignments seem to offer agency to writers, but they ironically foreclose on the generative proliferation of possible ontologies since students like Lisa and the family members she represents become "characters" in their own narratives, with all of the fictional insinuations that go along with that term. The result is accidental, but perhaps not incidental, violence, perpetuated on a young person's identity and way of being.

Similar to Lisa, Jason,[8] an African American graduating senior in a helping field, did not find opportunities to explore dynamic forms of being or invitations to move away from archetypal narrative arcs in writing-as-healing prompts in his courses. In fact, he found that the prompts asked him to edit his experiences to better fit with audience expectations—a form of epistemic violence Lisa also experienced. In addition, he found that his available forms of being were limited to stereotypes, a form of ontological violence. He described, for example, how his instructors expected him "to omit certain things" and to "fit" his writing into "a set mold." Such prompts, Jason's responses suggest, present writers with a hermeneutic imperative that is innately psycho-analytic in that it asks writers to press their experiences into a narrative arc and to interpret their pasts in ways that might inform the present. We call these circumstances *epistemic violence* since the narrative tropes suggested in the prompts lead to students rightfully feeling subjected to instructor and peer invasions of privacy.

More importantly, writing-as-healing prompts can even alter the students' sense of their own experiences and their significance. When writing prompts interrupt and limit students' senses of themselves, ontological violence is at play since available forms of being are stifled rather than multiplied. This kind of constraint does subtle violence to ways of both knowing and being in the context of the classroom. Jason reports that "oftentimes, it feels like, they were more worried about what our darkest moments were, rather than the moments we've had success in, or some of our privileges." He reflects, "I kind of felt like I was selling myself to be more interesting than what I really am, day-to-day, because you're taking these stories, and you put them on the page, and you think, 'Oh wow! He's been through so much in such a short time!' and it's like 'You know that happened one day, but the rest of the week went by well.'" Jason is, thus, clear that his writing assignments led his classmates to interpret him in limited ways. Jason's story reveals that writing-as-healing approaches can be risky, and paradoxically, the care taken by instructors to mitigate such dynamics can complicate the hazards. These risks are due to audience expectations that operate as the backdrop of genre expectations. The result is an invisible violence, more harmful because of its imperceptibility.

Leaving a mark of ontological violence, these prompts meant that Jason felt compelled to "sell" himself, which goes against the stated intentions of writing-as-healing pedagogies, which would presumably offer him safe space to break free of the past rather than force him to become stuck in the past. Jason continues, "Looking back at some of the things that I've written, it's like, 'Man! I really did go through that.' It starts almost shifting my own view of my life. I think, 'Man! I really did have it tough.' It makes me forget." Jason's experiences would seem to align with what writing-as-healing's critics have feared: that these approaches could inadvertently cause traumatization (Carello and Butler 2014; Wood 2011; Herrick 2002; Micciche 2001). Rather than lifting him up, recalling his painful past leads him to lose track of his own sense of progress, efficacy, and growth. This shift in self-perception would seem to be the purview of a trained therapist and not something that should be taken on—or evoked—in a classroom setting. Equally important, Jason feels forced to write about painful, traumatic memories at the expense of sharing some of his moments of personal empowerment. This is an instance of epistemic and ontological violence rather than an opportunity for students to carefully craft an ethos for a given circumstance. It is, in a word, toxic.

Clearly, both epistemic and ontological violence are related to ideological force; even when the push for students to tell certain kinds of stories in specific ways is tacit—as it seems to have been in Jason's case—the pedagogies are potentially problematic as they change the student's understanding of how things went and influence the way their peers see them. As Theodore Jacobs (2011) explains, psychoanalysis is largely an exercise in "reading a human text" (985). Writers are not simply asked to write about their experiences, but they are directed to interpret their musings. In part, this interpretive disposition plays out on the level of recognizable confessional tropes (e.g., the breakup narrative or parents' divorce story). Asking student writers to identify their experiences via these narrative tropes assumes that they fit with a predetermined arc or, more importantly, that they cannot remain tentative about their experiences if they wish to focus instead on cultivating the kinds of experiences they'd like to have moving forward. Such constraints harm rather than heal.

Moreover, as an African American student in a mostly white classroom, Jason's experiences were perhaps even more vulnerable to archetypal influences. His instructor and classmates indicated that they wanted to hear more about those of his experiences that fit their idea of the struggles of a young Black man, rather than about Jason's particular successes. Jason's story shows that writing-as-healing discourses ultimately perpetuate epistemic and ontological violence, since they promote a tropes-driven form of narrative that too often fixes the writer/speaker in the role of victim and other people, by default, in the role of benefactor or, conversely, aggressor. Jason observes on writing about his past, "It kind of made me forget the good that has happened as well. Like, 'This bad situation happened, then this bad situation happened,' then 'Man, I almost went to prison,' that kind of thing. I've lived a rough life, but that's not the total story." In a poignant and complicated admission, Jason also notes, "I've gotten a lot of sympathy and that's not what I'm looking for. Like the things that I tell, and the things that I write about did happen, but I did not allow it to shape my whole life or my whole destiny or my whole life outlook. Just because bad things happened doesn't mean I am a pity case, and oftentimes . . . like 'oh I feel so bad for you.' And it's like, 'No I'm fine. Look!' " This kind of subtle violence forces Jason to be on the defensive as he listens to classroom critiques: "They often think, 'this happened, so he looks good on the outside, but what's really going on in the inside.' And I'm like, 'Nope. Nothing.' "

Jason's analysis of the rhetorical situation is telling: "If a prompt is given that is supposed to be our personal life, it's more than just what happened, but how do we interpret what happened, and how do we feel about what happened, and how have we used what happened to grow as individuals . . . So take your stories and make it fit. I don't know exactly what it is they want." The idea of expectations clearly suggests the ways in which students can feel powerful forces distorting their own experiences, feelings, and even senses of self. These forces can do untold violence to unsuspecting students, even when their well-intentioned instructors believe the assignments promote self-knowledge and increased well-being. What the experiences of Lisa and Jason illustrate is a danger inherent in overzealous attempts to help students resolve personal problems or process emotional trauma in the context of for-credit writing assignments. While the instructors' intentions are laudable, the effects can be damaging. The classroom can become threatening to students' identities and to their agency.

THE DANGERS OF WRITING AS HEALING

As Lisa and Jason's experiences show, enthusiasm for writing-as-healing approaches can overshadow the potential for epistemic and ontological violence, especially given the conditions of classroom discussion, feedback, and grading. When past suffering is packaged under these conditions for college credit, there is an inherent potential for unintended violence. Assignments can become spaces of harm where students' knowledge creations and forms of being are interrupted or repressed. Their experiences further demonstrate how claims to writing as healing's virtues ironically form the basis of its propensity to slip into epistemic and ontological violence. The act of writing out a trauma story, for example, could encourage self-indulgent, elitist tendencies. Such narratives might ultimately be of dubious social and personal value—even as they promise writers engagement with relevant publics as they heal themselves. The complexity of Jason's case is even clearer when considered in light of Lynn Worsham's (2006) provocative analysis of narrative disclosures. Using the Freudian distinction between pleasurable "narrative fetishism," or "the construction of a narrative that is consciously or unconsciously designed to purge the traces of the trauma," and "the work of mourning," or "an effort to integrate a traumatic event that so overwhelmed the individual or social psyche that it could not be integrated as it occurred" (177–78), Worsham asks, "How can teachers of writing know that a personal narrative about traumatic experience fosters the work of mourning rather than substituting for this important word-work the pleasure of storytelling?" (180). Worsham concludes that most classroom settings are spaces in which narrative fetishism occurs at the expense of clinically appropriate ways to process traumas, and Jason's case would seem to substantiate Worsham's claim.

Writing-as-healing pedagogies, thus, enact epistemic and ontological violence when they include narrowly defined, psychoanalytic-leaning hegemonic dispositions toward trauma and recovery or promote constricted inventional purviews within which to imagine and recast experience, potentially leading to limiting and damaging representations of self. Some students may think of composition instructors as voyeurs (Herrick 2002, 274), and some instructors may see extraordinary personal disclosures even when they don't ask for them, forcing instructors into uncomfortable ethical conundrums (Morgan 1998).

Existing scholarship shows the potential for epistemic and ontological violence, yet it falls short of sounding the alarm bells loud enough to dampen enthusiasm for such pedagogical moves. Focusing on the politics of disclosure, on voyeurism, and on trauma's ultimately unspeakable nature are critiques that do not go far enough. The real danger in epistemic and ontological forms of violence is that instructors and students are often equally unaware of what is being done. Using epistemic and ontological violence as a framework, the data we share above adds gravitas to critical scholarship on writing as healing for composition studies in ways that we hope will inform other instructional spaces.

The literature in trauma studies consistently indicates that true mourning and healing are best approached anonymously and without the inhibitions inherent in audience expectations and feedback, both hallmarks of classroom settings. As Didier Fassin and Richard Rechtman (Fassin and Rechtman 2009) explain in *The Empire of Trauma*, "In contrast to the many works that psychiatrists and historians, philosophers and anthropologists have devoted to the subject, we believe that the truth of trauma lies not in the psyche, the mind, or the brain, but in the moral economy of contemporary societies" (275). Importantly, classrooms are sites of moral economic exchange where students must contend with how they believe we would like to see them through and in their writing. Fassin and Rechtman argue that claims to traumatic events give speakers an automatic uptick in credibility: to have suffered a lot in life is to be an unquestionably good person. "We know nothing, or almost nothing, of their subjectivities—or interiority—as victims," the authors remind us (279). Trauma "speaks of the painful link that connects the present to the past" (284), but, in Jason's account, the past, in all of its literary-worthy pain, does not impact the present as much as the writing-up of his experiences based on prompts make it appear. Trauma writing is a complex enterprise that is best undertaken in carefully constructed clinical settings where the threat of epistemic and ontological violence may be diminished.

Of course, there can be other consequences of writing-as-healing assignments that, even while risking the violence we are concerned with, may have neutral or even positive outcomes as well. For example, Lisa expresses confidence that she was "still gaining positive ground writing about the stuff [she] was struggling with." She believes that she benefited from writing as healing, although doing so caused her to "craft something [she] was against doing." Interestingly, Lisa thinks of writing as healing as a freeing genre: "I don't really feel like anything can be off-limits. It can be stuff that you're merely grappling or currently working through, or even stuff that you've gotten over." She also noted: "You have to know crafted ways of talking about larger issues in life that are more acceptable." Another possible positive outcome could be that, by becoming more aware of the ways in which everybody suffers to one degree or another, at one time or another, students may gain greater empathy. It's even possible that students will help each other, or that a student will be encouraged by the therapeutic intentions of the experience to seek professional help. Our argument is that these outcomes are all uncertain and that the hazards of mandating explorations of past traumas or troubles outweigh the potential benefits.

HEALING THROUGH FUTURE-ORIENTED WRITING

As our study indicates, epistemic and ontological violence generate dangers associated with writing about trauma for credit. Students asked to process the traumas that mark contemporary life in general as well as their own unique experiences are exposed to complicated course-based experiences that may do more personal harm than compositional good.

In the context of the hyperpublicity of contemporary media, we see that opportunities for safe and productive metacognition are crucial if writing instructors really want to help students grow and develop as young adults. Creating a curricular space for reflective writing would seem to be consistent with the missions of colleges and universities; however, our research suggests that writing-as-healing prompts often fall short of providing opportunities for safe processing of the large and small traumas students bring into college and the ones they subsequently experience as college students. Worse still, we see evidence that students' ways of knowing and ways of being can be further damaged by misguided feedback from peers and instructors.

We believe that written emotional disclosures can best be used to prepare students for future social performances rather than offering space to process their pasts. Indeed, some of our interview participants indicate that they use writing-as-healing prompts as "metacognitive space," or cognitive affordances that enable individuals to "reflect purposefully and systematically on their performance and, in turn, to use this information to modify or redirect their future performance and thinking" (Schraw and Moshman 1995, 360). Five responses by interviewees make it clear that personal reflective writing, rather than reifying the traumatic mark the past leaves on the present, might help them to determine an advantageous communicative course of action for the future. For example, one of our participants explains, "If I'm asked that question in real life, now I would be better equipped or better prepared to answer it, if that is something I feel comfortable with." This is, to be sure, outlier data; however, we think it is intriguing since it does not appear to be as fraught with the potential for inadvertent violence as are some other forms of writing as healing.

In metacognitively oriented assignments, we might ask students to tell us less about their past and articulate more about who they want to become and how they might work toward becoming that person. We know from our own cautious experimentation with "writing the future" that research-based writing about a healthy future life can be rich with detail and emotion. In every instance of highly personal writing in the classroom, however, the priorities and the challenges are consistent: it is a matter of encouraging meaningful writing and variations on "publication" without straying into inappropriate counseling and rehabilitation. We have to work to protect the health of our student writers by helping them gain greater self-regulation and opportunity through writing competence.

One assignment we've found that is able to harness all that is advantageous in written emotional disclosures without falling into the territory of epistemic or ontological violence is the "my possible futures" assignment, where we ask students to list their aspirations and do research on various timeframes from a few months way to beyond graduation or even as far into the future as ten years. This assignment encourages students to address the challenges of adult life they might have already experienced or observed up to this point, yet it resists asking students to tell the stories of their personal or family traumas. Another example of an assignment that might tap into the strengths of written emotional disclosures without risking ontological or epistemic violence is the "everyday suffering" assignment, where we ask students to do research into types of trauma that are common to ordinary people as they grow and develop from childhood through full maturity. This assignment allows students to consider specific kinds of trauma without requesting them to reveal their own experience with such things.

We acknowledge that required writing courses—especially freshman courses—are more prone to inflict epistemic and ontological damage than elective courses with older students, but even in elective courses there is the possibility of doing more harm than good when it comes to graded, for-credit writing about trauma. Moreover, forms of epistemic and ontological violence are inevitably woven into the fabric of everyday life in the various subtle and overt demands that a person "tell their story" to heal and to help other people in the process. We, thus, suggest that any writing assignment (or, indeed, any social, political, or private statement) that invites or requires expressive writing or "writing about what you know" should be undertaken with more care than it is often given. By avoiding any assignments that can become spaces of violence where students' knowledge creations and forms of being are interrupted or stifled, writing instructors can still offer challenges that are meaningful and that can take advantage of students' knowledge of themselves. There are many other examples we know writing instructors could develop if they relied on the basic sentiment behind the two terms we articulate in this chapter: that written emotional disclosures should only be required of student writers in ways that allow them to maintain control of their multifarious and proliferative meaning-making potential and to experiment with possibilities that are beyond one-dimensional forms of being.

NOTES

1. One notable exception is Janice Carello and Lisa Butler (2014).
2. Writing expressively emphasizes affective benefits and connections that are achieved through externalizing the writer's internal landscape. This popular approach to the teaching of writing emerged in the 1980s alongside two other

dominant approaches: cognitive process and social epistemic. Scholar-practitioners debated which of the three approaches was most advantageous for students.

3.   See, for example, Carol Hanisch (1970).

4.   Recruitment mechanisms and data-collection procedures were designed in consultation with our Institutional Review Board (IRB). The project went through review in February 2014 and was approved after revisions in March 2014 prior to data collection. Data collection was completed in September 2014.

5.   See Appendix A: Interview Questions.

6.   We also coded data that indicated students' contradictory beliefs about writing as healing—they find the genre to be helpful, but share misgivings—and we charted a few interesting instances of students using written emotional disclosures to explore potential, future social performances.

7.   This participant name is a pseudonym, as are all others used in this essay.

8.   Cathryn Molloy (2016) uses quotes from Jason in a *Composition Studies* course design essay.

REFERENCES

Anderson, Charles M., and Marian M. MacCurdy, eds. 2000. *Writing and Healing: Toward an Informed Practice. Refiguring English Studies.* Urbana: National Council of Teachers of English. https://eric.ed.gov/?id=ED436788.

Baumlin, James S., and Tita French Baumlin. 1989. "Psyche/Logos: Mapping the Terrains of Mind and Rhetoric." *College English* 51, no. 3: 245–61. JSTOR.

Bishop, Wendy. 1993. "Writing Is/and Therapy?: Raising Questions about Writing Classrooms and Writing Program Administration." *Journal of Advanced Composition* 13, no. 2: 503–16. JSTOR.

Carello, Janice, and Lisa D. Butler. 2014. "Potentially Perilous Pedagogies: Teaching Trauma is Not the Same as Trauma-Informed Teaching." *Journal of Trauma & Dissociation: The Official Journal of the International Society for the Study of Dissociation (ISSD)* 15, no. 2: 153–68. doi: 10.1080/15299732.2014.867571.

DeSalvo, Louise. 2000. *Writing as a Way of Healing: How Telling Our Stories Transforms Our Lives.* Boston: Beacon Press.

Duncan, Elaine, Yori Gidron, Eyal Rabin, Liza Gouchberg, Asher M. Moser, and Josef Kapelushnik. 2007. "The Effects of Guided Written Disclosure on Psychological Symptoms among Parents of Children with Cancer." *Journal of Family Nursing* 13, no. 3: 370–84. doi: 10.1177/1074840707303843.

Fassin, Didier, and Richard Rechtman. 2009. *The Empire of Trauma.* Princeton, NJ: Princeton University Press.

Fogarty, Colleen T. 2010. "Fifty-Five Word Stories: 'Small Jewels' for Personal Reflection and Teaching." *Family Medicine* 42 (6): 400–402.

Goggin, Peter, and Maureen Goggin. 2005. "Presence in Absence: Discourses and Teaching (in, on, and about) Trauma." In *Trauma and the Teaching of Writing,* edited by Shane Borrowman, 29–51. Albany: State University of New York Press.

Goldthwaite, Melissa. 2003. "Confessionals." *College English* 66, no. 1: 55–73.

Hanisch, Carol. 1970. "The Personal Is Political." *Notes from the Second Year: Women's Liberation.* http://carolhanisch.org/CHwritings/PIP.html.

Herman, Judith. 1997. *Trauma and Recovery: The Aftermath of Violence—from Domestic Abuse to Political Terror.* New York: Basic Books.

Herrick, Jeanne Weiland. 2002. "Telling Stories: Rethinking the Personal Narrative in the Contact Zone of a Multicultural Classroom." In *Professing in the Contact Zone: Bringing Theory and Practice Together,* edited by Janice M. Wolf, 274–90. Urbana: NCTE.

Jacobs, Theodore J. 2011. "Insights, Epiphanies, and Working Through: On Healing, Self-Healing, and Creativity in the Writer and the Analyst." *The Psychoanalytic Quarterly* 80, no. 4: 961–86.

Kersting, Anette, Kristin Kroker, Sarah Schlicht, and Birgit Wagner. 2011. "Internet-Based Treatment after Pregnancy Loss: Concept and Case Study." *Journal of Psychosomatic Obstetrics and Gynecology* 32, no. 2: 72–78. doi: 10.3109/0167482X.2011.553974.

Micciche, Laura R. 2001. "Writing through Trauma: The Emotional Dimensions of Teaching Writing." *Composition Studies* 29, no. 1: 131–41.

Molloy, Cathryn. 2016. "Multimodal Composing as Healing: Toward a New Model for Writing as Healing Courses." *Composition Studies* 44, no. 2: 134. https://www.questia.com/library/journal/1P3-4318388701/multimodal-composing-as-healing-toward-a-new-model.

Moran, Molly Hurley. 2004. "Toward a Writing and Healing Approach in the Basic Writing Classroom: One Professor's Personal Odyssey." *Journal of Basic Writing* 23, no. 1: 93–115.

Morgan, Dan. 1998. "Ethical Issues Raised by Students' Personal Writing." *College English* 60, no. 3: 318–25. doi: 10.2307/378560.

Ogle, Kathleen. 2005. "Where Medicine, Literature, and Healing Meet." *Minnesota Medicine* 88, no. 7: 40–43.

Payne, Michelle. 2000. "A Strange Unaccountable Something: Historicizing Sexual Abuse Essays." In *Writing and Healing: Toward an Informed Practice*, edited by Charles Anderson and Marian McCurdy, 115–57. Urbana: National Council of Teachers of English.

Pennebaker, James W. 1997. *Opening Up: The Healing Power of Expressing Emotions.* New York: Guilford Press.

Pennebaker, James W., and Joshua M. Smyth. 2016. *Opening Up by Writing It Down: How Expressive Writing Improves Health and Eases Emotional Pain.* 3rd ed. New York: Guilford Press.

Robillard, Amy E. 2003. "It's Time for Class: Toward a More Complex Pedagogy of Narrative." *College English* 66, no. 1: 74–92. doi: 10.2307/3594235.

Ryden, Wendy. 2010. "From Purgation to Recognition: Catharsis and the Dialectic of Public and Private in Healing Writing." *JAC* 30, no. 1/2: 239–67.

Saldaña, Johnny. 2010. *The Coding Manual for Qualitative Researchers.* 1st ed. Thousand Oaks, CA: Sage Publications.

Schraw, Gregory, and David Moshman. 1995. "Metacognitive Theories." *Educational Psychology Review* 7, no. 4: 351–71. doi: 10.1007/BF02212307.

Singer, Jessica, and George H. S. Singer. 2007. "Writing as Physical and Emotional Healing: Findings from Clinical Research." In *Handbook of Research on Writing*, edited by Charles Bazerman, 485–98. New York: Routledge. doi: 10.4324/9781410616470.ch30.

Wood, Tara. 2011. "Overcoming Rhetoric: Forced Disclosure and the Colonizing Ethic of Evaluating Personal Essays." *Open Words* 5, no. 1: 28–34.

Worsham, Lynn. 2006. "Composing (Identity) in a Post Traumatic Age." In *Identity Papers*, edited by Bronwyn T. Williams, 170–81. Boulder: University Press of Colorado.

PART 2

Intervening

7

KN K'ƏK'NIYAʔ / I'M LISTENING
Rhetorical Sovereignty and the Composition Classroom

Allison Hargreaves

On April 9, 2018, I gathered with colleagues, elders, students, and friends to hear our institution's apology for its participation in the residential school system. The occasion was the formal opening of the Indian Residential School History and Dialogue Centre on the Vancouver campus. Together we listened as our president, Santa Ono, spoke not only of the University of British Columbia's (UBC) historic role in training professionals who worked in the schools but also of its continued role in marginalizing Indigenous peoples and knowledges. We listened remotely from our Okanagan campus ballroom. Through the windows to the north, through a door left ajar—the courtyard, a cool breeze—and to the west—kłpapqłpiwaʔs, the little alkaline lake for which the campus grounds are named in the language spoken by the land, Nsyilxc.

In "Land Speaking," Syilx knowledge-keeper and poet Jeannette Armstrong (2017) says there is a "special knowledge in each different place" and that the land is a "constant teacher" in this. To thrive in a place, we must "listen intently to its teachings—to its language," she says (142). I have been wondering what it means to *listen*—both as an uninvited guest in Syilx lands and as a teacher at kłpapqłpiwaʔs. This is what I have heard from my Nsyilxc language teacher, Elder Richard Armstrong: the meaning of *teacher* is one whose job it is to tell a story over and again so that others may understand: suxʷmamayaʔəm. The word for *student* is very similar: atsmamayaʔəm—one whose job it is to listen and learn that which is being told to her. My job as a guest is to be a student; my job as a teacher, then, is two-fold and relational: to listen intently and then to tell others what I know. Armstrong also reminds us that to "speak is to create more than words, more than sounds retelling the world; it is to realize the potential for transformation of the world" (183). So a teacher listens and then tells the stories that will help the

https://doi.org/10.7330/9781646422807.c007

students survive and thrive, knowing the power in this to transform the world. This is what I have heard.

The transformative power of the word is well known to storytellers for whom speaking and listening are the means by which immaterial thought and spirit are made manifest in the world. In his guide to writing, *Writing with the Old Ones: From the Oral Tradition to the Printed Page*, Richard Wagamese (2012) explains: "In the Ojibway world, storytelling is recognized as energy. A story rides on our breath and makes the air move which in turn causes our ear drums to vibrate. Those vibrations become electrical signals that the brain translates into meaning" (33). "It all happens," he says, "because of energy" (33)—and the "astounding circle of creation" comprised by the acts of telling and listening (35).

Any meaningful work with words comes with considerable responsibility, as words can both heal and harm. Indigenous intellectual traditions attest to this power, as does the arrival on Turtle Island of European languages whose "forms of transmission (often forced or coerced)," were themselves a tool of colonial violence and assimilation (Justice 2004, 4). On the occasion of UBC's apology to survivors of residential schools, I was reminded of the physical, psychological, and spiritual violence committed daily by this system—but also of the discursive violence inherent to the stories of Indigenous deficit that were used to justify the schools' operation for over a century. Nor are these stories a thing of the past. Even as I learn to listen, so that I might teach in ways that heal instead of harm, I inherit this violent history as a white settler scholar and as a beneficiary of my institution's presence at kɬpapqɬpiwaʔs.

I came to kɬpapqɬpiwaʔs as an English-trained scholar of Indigenous literatures. An important part of my regular teaching assignment is the first-year composition course in the Aboriginal Access Program. This is an entrance program designed to transition Aboriginal learners into degree programs. The course itself is an initiation into University-level writing and research, and it's mandatory for all students entering the academy through the Access Program. The course is the credit equivalent to any other first-year composition course, and it's housed in the English program. What makes it different, however, is its engagement with what the academic calendar calls "Aboriginal perspectives." When I interviewed for this position, I was asked how I would teach this course. I said that I would use a traditional English writing handbook and that I would supplement this with Indigenous-authored essays for discussion and analysis. When I learned that I had landed the job and would be teaching this course in actuality, I remember a moment of panic: how would I design it? Being new to both teaching and kɬpapqɬpiwaʔs, I unfortunately designed it exactly as I'd said: traditional writing handbook and supplementary Indigenous-authored material.

Don't get me wrong; this approach "works," according to many of the metrics we might use. Most students pass the course and go on to their chosen degree programs with the communication skill set they need for academic success. They learn how to structure a sentence, a paragraph, an essay. They learn the hallmarks of persuasive academic writing. In teaching evaluations, students comment that they have gained greater confidence in their writing skills. But a tension was ever-present for me—one that other composition instructors seem often to share: a discomfort with the normalization of alphabetic writing, the conventions of the Greek rhetorical tradition, and—in a phrase—the course's overriding assumption that Indigenous students need what Malea Powell has called "the fix of Western literacy instruction" (401, quoted in Driskill 2015, 58). To put the problem in yet starker terms, Cherokee writer and rhetoric scholar Qwo-Li Driskill (2015) says of the writing classroom, "through a focus on rhetorical theories and compositional practices rooted in an Enlightenment concept of the Greco-Roman tradition, the discipline participates not only in a physical occupation of indigenous lands but also in intellectual colonialism" (57–58). So what are writing teachers to do?

In his landmark essay, "Rhetorical Sovereignty: What Do American Indians Want from Writing," Leech Lake Ojibway scholar Scott Richard Lyons (2000) offers a number of useful answers. For example he advises everyone, and teachers especially, "to think carefully about their positions, locations, and alignments: the differences and connections between sovereignty and solidarity" (466). This is actually the first thing I think writing teachers can do, and it involves listening deeply to the particular histories of the land and peoples where we teach. Concow Maidu poet Janice Gould (1988) reminds us "there is not a university in this country that is not built on what was once native land" (81). This is true for everyone, regardless of subject position or institutional affiliation. We acknowledge this truth whenever we acknowledge the traditional territories. Another thing writing teachers can do, then, is what writing teachers supposedly do best: pay attention to language. What could we know differently if we acknowledged territory in the language of the land? In my case, kn mypnwiłn Nsyilxcn ałi iʔ syilx əcmystis axaʔ iʔ təmxʷulaʔxʷ lut pənkin t'a səlmisəlx; I'm learning Nsyilxcn because the Syilx people know that this land has never been ceded. To learn this acknowledgment in the language is, I hope, one of the ways to become better acquainted with my location and responsibility at kłpapqłpiwaʔs.

Significantly, in the way that this acknowledgment has been taught to me, I am to understand and emphasize the Syilx knowledge of the land: what the *Syilx know* as unceded territory, rather than what *I know* and say is unceded territory—iʔ syilx əcmystis. And in this subtle difference of phrasing, we hear that difference and connection between sovereignty and solidarity that Lyons mentions. The knowledge we refer to is Syilx knowledge first. And Syilx knowledge is sovereign knowledge. While Lyons traces many shifting and contested definitions, he ultimately claims sovereignty as "the ability to assert oneself . . . It is a people's right [and] demand to exist and present its gifts to the world." It is also a "refusal to dissociate culture, identity, and power from the land" (457). To acknowledge territory in the language of the land is thus an act of solidarity for the non-Syilx guest and teacher who, in speaking, listens to the difference between Syilx knowledge and her own—between Syilx assertions and her own. But Lyons would have us go further yet.

He asks of writing teachers that we practice "more than a renewed commitment to listening and learning" but "a radical rethinking of how and what we teach as the written word" (450). This returns us to the curricular problem I noted before, of the English writing handbook and the "fix" of Western literacy—which is not merely a curricular conundrum, after all, but is, rather, a question of sovereignty. Forced instruction in the English language has been key to assimilation and colonization, and this is not an abstract history or present that teachers can choose to ignore. The university has inherited this history and continues to practice it today, both through its occupation of Indigenous lands and through its continued marginalization of Indigenous knowledges. In this context, the most important question may not be what can writing teachers *do* but rather the other question Lyons asks: "What do Indians want from writing?" This shifts the focus from what writing teachers might know and say about the written word to what Indigenous students and host communities know and say about their own communicative needs. Lyons calls *this* rhetorical sovereignty: "the inherent right and ability of peoples to determine their own communicative needs and desires in the pursuit of self-determination" (462). To engage the struggle for rhetorical sovereignty at the "scene of writing" (449), and at the site of postsecondary writing instruction at kɬpapqɬpiwaʔs specifically, the job of the writing teacher is thus *relational*—to ask, what do the people want from writing?

This is the learning in which I am now engaged, and the results of this will, I hope, transform our first-year writing course and what I teach as the written word. All writing teachers can take this next step, too—whether Indigenous or non-Indigenous, whether guests in the territory, or not: establish relationships and have conversations with local elders and knowledge-keepers. The first thing I did was talk with the Access Program's Syilx Elders-in-residence, Eric Mitchell and Chris Marchand. Eric and Chris have a formal role in Aboriginal Programs and Services. They support students through regular cultural programming and workshops at the centre and in the community. They are also engaged by the university, by the school districts, and by local faith-based organizations for an intensive twenty-four-hour training they offer in cultural safety. I worked closely with them over the past year as they delivered to my own academic unit the first-ever cultural safety training for faculty members at kłpapqłpiwaʔs. And when I asked them, "What do you want from writing, and what do you want for our students?," they said: first, empowerment, the empowerment for students in knowing and telling their own stories and the empowerment of having their stories told to them—stories that show what Eric termed as "*outside* to the white man's written word and law." And a key example they gave as an accessible teaching text is the 1910 Memorial to Sir Wilfrid Laurier.

An exemplar of local Indigenous public writing, the document is probably best known to literary scholars across Turtle Island as the textual inspiration behind renowned Cree playwright Tomson Highway's 2005 play *Ernestine Shuswap Gets Her Trout*, commissioned by the Secwepemc Cultural Education Society. In and around Syilx territory, however, the document is known first as a testament to Indigenous sovereignty. It hangs on the wall at the Okanagan Nation Alliance offices. It is cited at public gatherings. It figures prominently in the nation's public discourse about its historical and ongoing assertion of title and rights. And, because it is coauthored by the Chiefs of the Secwepemc, Syilx, and Nlaka'pamux nations, it also reflects nation-to-nation relationships and territorial borders that predate the arrival of the newcomers who came first for furs, then for gold, and then for the land itself. To teach this text is to bring local knowledges and Syilx rhetorical practice right into the classroom, and—as Eric pointed out—to build a web outward to include the related histories of neighboring nations. This emphasizes the "'here-ness' of both historical and contemporary indigenous peoples and practices"—which is to say that it is both grounded in place and deeply relational (Riley-Mukavetz and Powell 2015, 145).

When Eric and Chris recommended this teaching text, they did so first with the students in mind. I can see why; if sovereignty is "a people's right [and] demand to exist and present its gifts to the world" (Lyons 2000, 457), then the Memorial is as clear a statement on sovereignty as composition students are likely to find at kɬpapqɬpiwaʔs. Indigenous students routinely report that their experiences and knowledges are not reflected in university curricula and pedagogy; assigning local examples of Indigenous public writing is one way writing teachers can begin to address this problem. Through such texts, students might see their own ontologies, histories, and communication practices reflected. More than illustrative, however, the Memorial is also instructive—and this is the second reason why the Elders drew it to my attention. For the non-Indigenous teacher and guest, the Memorial can instruct the rethinking of one's teaching practice from and with Indigenous perspectives, because not only does it catalogue and perform a history of rhetorical resistance in the local territories, but it also provides firm instructions on the responsibilities of uninvited guests. These, particularly, are instructions I was meant to hear—because however meaningful the Memorial might be for the students, its use is arguably limited unless its teachers *take teachings* from it first. Listening to the Elders that day, my attention shifted from thoughts of how I might teach the Memorial in my writing classroom to what the Memorial might have to teach *me*, which I could then share with other instructors. Knowing that a teacher's task is to listen carefully before telling others what she knows, I wondered: what can the Memorial tell me about what the people want from writing? And what are the related responsibilities of the settler-identified writing teacher and guest? These questions occasioned my writing this piece, and for answers I look to the Memorial itself.

HISTORICIZING LOCAL RHETORICAL SOVEREIGNTY: THE MEMORIAL TO SIR WILFRID LAURIER

In 1910, Prime Minister Wilfrid Laurier embarked on a cross-Canada election campaign. On August 25 he made a brief stop in Kamloops, British Columbia, where he was greeted by a delegation of Chiefs from the Secwepemc, Syilx, and Nlaka'pamux nations. As hosts in the interior plateau, the Chiefs welcomed Laurier to their territories. And, as representatives of their sovereign nations, they delivered to Laurier a message: "the queen's law which we believe guaranteed us our rights, the BC government has trampled underfoot" (Memorial 1910, 3). Citing the provincial government's refusal to acknowledge the Aboriginal land title and rights guaranteed under international law, the Chiefs petitioned Laurier to bring the matter before the federal courts. "[W]e are becoming regarded as trespassers . . . [in] this our country," they said, and "[w]e demand that our land question be settled" (4).

The Chiefs recorded these grievances in a written declaration, and the Prime Minister departed for Ottawa with a copy in hand. While Laurier's subsequent efforts to address the land question were soon defeated, the Laurier Memorial lives on as an historic document with immediate political relevance for the Secwepemc, Syilx, and Nlaka'pamux nations, and for settlers in these territories today (*We Get Our Living* 1994, 61).

This is the story as I heard it when I was new to Syilx territory and first learning the patterns of invasion and settlement that preceded my own arrival. But to truly grasp the Memorial's (1910) contemporary political relevance, one needs to know more. One thing the expeditious version leaves out is the fact of continued Syilx presence and stewardship "since the beginning of people on this land" (*We Get Our Living* 1994, 1). Moreover, in the local history of colonial dispossession and resistance, the Memorial is but one public document among many in which the peoples' grievances are recorded and positions on the "land question" are eloquently expressed. In this sense, the Memorial is no haphazard response to the Prime Minister's visit in 1910; it is the product of many strategic preparations and a longer history of documentation as well as being a deeper expression of Indigenous diplomacy where conflict with newcomers is concerned. In *Unsettling Canada*, Arthur Manuel (2015) explains that the Memorial "was prepared . . . in mass meetings by our chiefs and people, who wanted to ensure that Canadians knew that we clearly remembered the betrayals of the previous century and that we demand redress in the current one. We called it a *memorial* because it represented, in a very precise way, our collective memories of our history with the settlers" (5).

The Memorial (1910) serves much the same purpose today, and its justice-seeking rationale is also reflected in its form. The *Oxford English Dictionary* (2019) defines "memorial" as a means of "preserving the memory of a person or thing" or as "something intended to assist the memory." Notably, there is a sense of both preservation and of mnemonic function to this kind of "record" or "chronicle." Manuel's (2015) comments reflect this conventional purpose but with the additional quality of remembering *for* someone else. After all, the Chiefs and people recalled very clearly the history of betrayals; it is the settlers and their government who (still) need reminding. In this way, the document also serves a diplomatic purpose: though composed from a distinctly Indigenous perspective, it petitions the "whites" and their government. Sir Wilfrid Laurier embodies this authority on the federal level, and the Chiefs' appeal to him is strategic. That is, in petitioning Laurier's authority, the Chiefs also draw attention to their own. They engage Laurier on a nation-to-nation basis, with the specific goal that "we may have a definite understanding with the government on all questions of the moment between us and them" (Memorial 1910, 4). And one of the main questions of the moment, both then and now, is this: axaʔ iʔ təmxʷulaʔxʷ lut pənkin t'a səlmisəlx. This land has never been ceded. Rhetorically, then, the Memorial works in several ways at once: it is a diplomatic dispatch, a storied record of events, an expression of collective memory, and a petition in protest of settler ignorance and amnesia. As a contemporary settler reader, I inherit this missive and become its present-day recipient. Though the Memorial is addressed to Sir Wilfrid Laurier ("Dear Sir and Father," it begins), I receive its message across the distances of time. And I am called to account.

The Memorial's historical account begins, strategically, with the arrival of fur traders and the establishment of Fort Kamloops in 1812: "One hundred years next year they came among us here at Kamloops and erected a trading post" the document begins. "They were the first to find us in this country. We never asked them to come here, but nevertheless we treated them kindly and hospitably and helped them all we could. They had made themselves (as it were) our guests" (1). At first, the Memorial tells us, relations with these uninvited guests were relatively good: "They did not interfere with us nor attempt to break up our tribal organizations, laws, customs. They did not try to force their conception of things on us to our harm" (1). But in 1858 a second wave of newcomers passed over the lands "in quest of gold," and things began to change (2). Following the discovery of gold in the Fraser Canyon and the foundation of the new colony of British Columbia in 1859, the interior was flooded with prospectors and other uninvited guests. Over the next few years, settlement progressed unchecked, and formerly diplomatic relations rapidly deteriorated. The spread of smallpox in the 1860s made matters worse; as the peoples' numbers were weakened by disease, so was their capacity to "fight back" (We Get Our Living 1994, 49). Meanwhile, to accommodate the growing population of settlers, reserve lands were rapidly surveyed and established—often without the peoples' participation or consent. Formerly allotted lands were illegally opened for white settlement with no communication or compensation. The people suffered the hardship of policies that restricted their movement and land use within their own unsurrendered territories (55). Thus, the "trust with which the Okanagans allowed the colonists to enter the Okanagan in peace, became a focus for outrage" (49). As the Memorial puts it:

What have we received for our good faith and patience? Gradually as the whites of this country became more and more powerful, and we less and less powerful, they little by little changed their policy towards us, and commenced to put restrictions on us. Their government or chiefs have taken every advantage of our friendliness, weakness and ignorance to impose on us in every way. They treat us as subjects without any agreement to that effect, and force their laws on us without our consent and irrespective of whether they are good for us or not. They say they have authority over us. (3)

Part of the Memorial's rhetorical power turns, then, on a descriptive contrast it establishes between how the people lived before—"supreme in their own territory" (1)—and how they are made to live now—"regarded as trespassers over a large portion of [their own] country" (4). The result is a nuanced history of the peoples' relations with newcomers, one that takes into account the long-standing history of Indigenous life on the land and forcefully "condemn[s] the whole policy of the B.C. government towards the Indian tribes of this country as utterly unjust, shameful and blundering in every way" (4).

Many aspects of this story are well documented in the colonial record, but rarely are the details told from Indigenous perspectives or with the presumed legitimacy of local Indigenous governance and resistance tactics. Seldom do we hear about how the Syilx resolved "to go to war to drive the liars out of their territory" (*We Get Our Living* 1994, 49) or how the Chiefs then formed a confederacy with their Secwepemc allies in 1874. Rather, these actions appear in the colonial record only as a source of anxiety to be managed. Government communications from this time reveal a growing unease regarding organized Indigenous resistance across the province and fears of an "Indian uprising" in the interior particularly (51). The Indian Reserve Commission of 1876 was the government's response. Significantly, this commission was given the power to renegotiate the sizes of reserves but not to deal with underlying issues of title and rights. Thus, it only *appeared* to address the land question but was, in fact, designed to "divide the confederacy" by making promises and offers "to the smallest bands of the confederacy" (52). This commission officially concluded its work in 1910, the year the Laurier Memorial was written. By this time, it had cut off or illegally opened up for settlement tens of thousands of acres in just the Okanagan valley alone.

Also, at this time, the BC government passed the University Act and first established my own institution and employer, the University of British Columbia (1908). Then, in 1910 the provincial government passed the University Site Act, which established 175 acres of Musqueam territory for the University Endowment Lands at ʔəlqsən, the present-day Point Grey campus location in Vancouver (Hives 1990). Later legislation would allow the lieutenant-governor to sell crown land on Point Grey for development, the funds from which would be put into an endowment for the university. In this way, the university is literally funded by the theft and subsequent sale of Musqueam land for residential development—a history which my own Okanagan campus inherits in addition to its occupation of Syilx land at the kɬpapqɬpiwaʔs site some four hundred kilometers inland.

When we think about the intersections between the "land question" and the history of education in the territories where we work and live, we must also consider the history of residential schooling. When the Memorial (1910) was written, nearly all of BC's residential schools were already in operation—including the major institutions in the interior: St. Joseph's at Williams Lake (1891), St. Eugene's at Cranbrook (1890), the Kamloops Indian Residential School (1890), and St. George's at Lytton (1902) (*Herstory* 2014, 347–55). This history is overlooked by most mainstream settler accounts of education and of place-making in the interior—precisely *because* this model of forced education was one of the key ways that Indigenous peoples were systemically removed from the land. Like boarding schools in the United States, residential schools operated for over a century in Canada, and their mission was explicitly assimilative. Children were removed from their families and communities and were forcibly delivered English-language Christian instruction with the expressed goal of solving the "Indian problem." As Syilx researcher Cathy Gottfriedsen (2014) observes in her contribution to *Herstory*, a collection of interior women's residential school stories, the impacts were complex and far-reaching: "Loss of land, resources, restrictions to small parcels of land, attacks upon the language and culture of the Indigenous peoples, introduction of diseases (which devastated our populations), loss of identity and the determining of who we are" (vi), hence what Lyons (2000) notes as the "duplicitous interrelationships between writing, violence, and colonization developed during the nineteenth[ ]century"—not only in residential schools, where the written word was violently imposed, but also in the halls of government, in courts of law, and on the land (449). Nor is this a "long ago history" (Gottfriedsen 2014, v). The last residential school to close its doors in the interior was St. Joseph's at Williams Lake in 1981 (*Herstory* 348). This means that many local Indigenous students are among the first generations not to have attended. The interrelationships between writing, violence, and colonization are felt deeply by students when they come to kɬpapqɬpiwaʔs, and necessarily inform the context in which composition instruction and its decolonization take place.

RELATIONALITY, DIPLOMACY, AND TEACHING AS GUESTHOOD

When Elders Chris and Eric spoke with me about the Memorial (1910) as a teaching text, they were thinking of the benefits to our students at kɬpapqɬpiwaʔs of learning a living, local example of Indigenous rhetorical sovereignty. But they were also referring me, as a writing teacher, to the Memorial. Why? Because the Memorial engages a deeply *relational* account of history. By this, I mean that it implicates its readers not only in the history of colonialism but also in the contextual process of meaning-making about it. As Shawn Wilson (2008) remarks on knowledge and relationality, "all ideas are developed through relationships," and none are "static in time or place. You must develop your own context" (134). This is certainly true of what the Memorial has asked of me. Although I have encountered this document many times since first arriving in Syilx territory, it's no accident that the Elders should remind me of it again at a time when I have questions about the violence inherent to the university and to the compositionist's teaching practice. The first thing the Memorial tells me in this context, then, is that to know your history is never enough. Of course, to know the history of Indigenous peoples' dealings with settlers in the interior is important to any teacher at kɬpapqɬpiwaʔs. But to stop there would be a refusal of relationality and a failure to hear the Memorial's deeper teachings. Rather, the Memorial calls on me to stretch my conventional understandings of responsibility and accountability, to take heed of my role in history and at this time and place. It does so by explaining invasion and settlement in the interior—but with distinctly Indigenous ontologies of diplomacy, hospitality, and guesthood in mind.

Apart from a much-needed history lesson, the Memorial (1910) embeds teachings toward just coexistence based on Indigenous diplomatic principles of mutual respect and reciprocity. These principles animate my interpretation of rhetorical sovereignty for the composition classroom, because they outline a local vision for how guest peoples and institutions (of which the university is certainly one example) should conduct themselves. This vision has direct implications for teaching practices, especially in the Memorial's expectation that guests should "do us no harm, but rather improve us by giving us knowledge" (2). Furthermore, the Memorial states, foreign institutions should never "force their conceptions of things on us" (1)—for it is Indigenous peoples themselves who must determine and assert, as Lyons (2000) puts it, their own desires and needs. While the Chiefs protest the authoritative and patronizing stance their guests have taken—"They say there are no lines except what they make" (3)—they also assert the peoples' "conceptions of things" by outlining the laws by which peoples should live together as partners in the same lands. These laws are *Indigenous laws*, as described in this often quoted passage: "With us when a person enters our house he becomes our guest, and we must treat him hospitably as long as he shows no hostile intentions. At the same time we expect him to return to us equal treatment for what he receives. Some of our Chiefs said, 'These people wish to be partners with us in our country. We must, therefore, be the same as brothers to them, and live as one family . . . We will help each other to be great and good.' " (2)

The uninvited guest may read this as a one-way statement of welcome. This is particularly tempting for the contemporary settler who imagines that the passing of time has released her from the expectation of returning "equal treatment" for what she has received. Too often, we imagine historical distance not only from the reality of dispossession and betrayal but also from the expectation of reciprocal relations by which Indigenous peoples often attempted negotiation with newcomers on matters of commercial, territorial, and political accord. However, the Memorial reminds us that these relationships and agreements aren't merely "historical"; as Leanne Simpson (2013) says of Indigenous diplomatic traditions, these are living "alliances with a commitment to continual renewal" (6). Nor should the peoples' "co-operative values" and hospitality be taken as unwitting vulnerability to invading systems "which promote domination and aggression" (Armstrong 2005, 244). Rather, expressions of welcome and aspirations for filial partnership are best understood as the living rhetorical demonstration of sovereignty. The Memorial (1910) reflects this approach at the very outset when it reframes the Prime Minister's campaign visit as an occasion warranting the Chiefs' formal diplomatic reception. This was noteworthy at a time when "status" Indians, considered legal wards of the state, were still fifty years out from even attaining the federal vote. Against this paternalistic relationship—enshrined in Canadian law through the 1876 Indian Act—the Chiefs instead address Laurier as a visiting statesman to their own sovereign territories: "We welcome you here," they say, "and we are glad we have met you in our country" (1). The magnanimous gesture of welcome conveys at once a governing ethic of hospitality and an assertion of sovereignty itself; they welcome Laurier because he is a visitor to *their* lands, where the hospitable reception of guests is a "social ethic" of both "good sense and obligation" (Armstrong 2009, 109).

To illustrate the importance of this practice for Syilx protocol specifically, Armstrong (2009) refers to a well-known teaching story involving Snk'lip, or Coyote, who, while on his travels, comes to visit the home of a giant. As Armstrong explains, the story turns on the expectation "that Coyote will be politely given food and acknowledged as a relative, no matter that he is a stranger or simply a visitor entering" (110). While some details are open to embellishment by individual storytellers, what remains foundational to this story is the protocol of "entering without invitation and expecting a formal greeting and the sharing of food" (111). With their words of welcome, the Chiefs establish these very principles of hospitality as key to the Memorial's (1910) rhetorical situation. That is, while the Memorial itself is occasioned by injustices for which the Chiefs seek resolution—"wrongs [that] may at last be righted" (1)— the legal foundation for their claim is first rooted in this teaching about the proper reception of guests. This lesson is embedded in many Syilx teaching stories, or captik^{w}ł, which form the narrative record of Syilx history and natural law (*We Get Our Living* 1994, 1). This teaching is also observed in Secwepemc law and custom as reiterated in the nation's contemporary retelling of the Memorial's significance: "the outsiders [are] guests who were invited and should be treated with kindness but were expected to show respect and reciprocity." In disregard of these "ancient laws of trespass and jurisdiction," however, the newcomers "defied the honour of being guests that we had bestowed upon them" (Shuswap Nation Tribal Council 2010).

As a guest in Syilx territory, and as a writing teacher at kłpapqłpiwaʔs, I want my teaching practice to honor rather than defy the responsibility of guesthood. The Memorial can guide this work, as well as the efforts of writing teachers elsewhere who seek to "reroot scholarly and pedagogical practices in the traditions of the Americas in order to interrupt ongoing colonization" (Driskill 2015, 74). As writing teachers, I think our first order of business is not teaching but learning. In my case, kn ckicx kl kłpapqłpiwaʔs kn sux^{w}mamayaʔəm. aʔpnaʔ sx̌əlx̌alt kn səcmamayaʔəm: I came to UBC as a teacher. Today, I am a student. I am listening to the language and the law of the land on which I work and live. By these actions, I hope to enact the responsibilities of guesthood, and of teaching, within the perimeters set out by my host nation, rather than by those set out by my employer, the university. This is a fundamental part of returning "equal treatment" for what I have received—to learn what Syilx teachers know and are willing to tell me, and doing so not for my institution's benefit but for the benefit of the students who often have yet to see their own rhetorical histories reflected in the academy.

For myself, part of this responsibility means that I acknowledge the authority of Indigenous community stakeholders in determining students' educative needs (Smith 2012; Kovach 2009; Archibald 2007).

With these principles in mind, I am now part of a collaborative effort to redesign compositions studies for Aboriginal Access Students on our campus. The project involves the co-creation of curricular goals and content in partnership with composition instructors, Elders-in-residence, lead administrators in our campus's Aboriginal Programs and Services, and the Okanagan Nation Alliance. The project brings Indigenous rhetoric to the fore, with emphasis on Syilx writing and research practices. While still delivering instruction on university-level discourse, the course will now integrate as core assigned readings the work of Syilx researchers, writers, and knowledge-keepers who animate the application of writing skills in real-world contexts in the local territory. But students will not merely read Indigenous-authored texts on which they can write traditional English essays; rather, they will work week by week to understand questions of research, argumentation, source documentation, and persuasive communication from Indigenous perspectives as well as Euro-Western norms—and by means of texts both written and oral. This is supported by weekly classroom visits from Elders who engage the students with oral storytelling and instruction on historical and contemporary Syilx rhetorical practice and in biweekly classroom visits from Syilx researchers and writers whose work exemplifies the application of composition and research skills to different career and life paths. Through these and related practices, including class field trips to local sites showcasing Syilx heritage and research practices, we hope to transform the experience of students in the mandatory first-year composition classroom.

On the larger scale, we know that the institution is founded on—and funded by—Indigenous lands. But there is also a way in which the university's present ameliorative strategies can themselves carry the same risks of appropriation and violence. In his apology for the university's involvement in the residential school system, UBC President Santa Ono (2018) acknowledged the fact that "UBC created educational opportunities for many Canadians [from which] Aboriginal people were largely excluded." This is the liberal framework by which the university still commonly operates—by the logic of inclusions and exclusions over which it maintains sole authority. To transcend this dynamic in our teaching, if such a thing is possible, we cannot merely create more inclusive classrooms in which Indigenous peoples and knowledges are made welcome. Particularly where our programming is ostensibly tailored to Indigenous-identified students, this supplementary approach will not do (I'm thinking here of my own novice approach to composition for Aboriginal Access students: a standard writing handbook, supplemented by Indigenous-authored essays). This approach positions Indigenous students as guests of the university rather than understanding the university as being a guest institution itself. If we take seriously the Memorial's (1910) teachings, then non-Indigenous teachers must learn to see ourselves as the *beneficiaries* of hospitality, rather than the benefactors. And as beneficiaries whose vocation is teaching, we have a particular responsibility in our engagement with and sharing of knowledge. Through its teachings on respect and reciprocity, the Memorial invites us to seek our teaching texts from local examples, to ground those examples in resident knowledges, and to build meaningful relationships to the benefit of our students, wherever our institutions might be.

Acknowledgments. For their teaching, I gratefully acknowledge Elders Richard Armstrong, Chris Marchand, and Eric Mitchell. For her insightful engagements with an earlier version of this paper, I thank Ruthann Lee. For their collaboration on a new composition studies course for Aboriginal Access Studies, I acknowledge Jordan Stouck, Pauline Terbasket, and Adrienne Vedan.

REFERENCES

Archibald, Jo-Ann. 2007. *Indigenous Storywork: Educating the Heart, Mind, Body, and Spirit.* Vancouver: University of British Columbia Press.

Armstrong, Jeannette. 2017. "Land Speaking." In *Read, Listen, Tell: Indigenous Stories from Turtle Island,* edited by Sophie McCall, Deanna Reder, David Gaertner, and Gabrielle L'Hirondelle Hill, 141–55. Waterloo: Wilfrid Laurier University Press.

Armstrong, Jeannette. 2009. "Constructing Indigeneity: Syilx Okanagan Oraliture and tmixʷcentrism." PhD diss., University of Greifswald.

Armstrong, Jeannette. 2005. "The Disempowerment of First North American Native Peoples and Empowerment through Their Writing." In *An Anthology of Canadian Native Literature in English,* 3rd ed., edited by Daniel David Moses and Terry Goldie, 242–45. Oxford: Oxford University Press.

Driskill, Qwo-Li. 2015. "Decolonial Skillshares: Indigenous Rhetorics as Radical Practice." In *Survivance, Sovereignty, and Story: Teaching American Indian Rhetorics,* edited by Lisa King, Rose Gubele, and Joyce Rain Anderson, 57–78. Logan: Utah State University Press.

Gottfriedsen, Cathy. 2014. "Introduction." In *Herstory: Indian Residential School Stories of Women from the Interior of British Columbia,* edited by Diane Pien, Margo Greenwood, Jessie Nyberg, Gwen Phillips, Kathleen Reynolds, Marie Abraham, and Cathy Gottfriedsen, v–vii. Vernon: Herstory Project. Funded by the Aboriginal Healing Foundation and the First Nations Health Authority.

Gould, Janice. 1988. "The Problem of Being 'Indian': One Mixed-Blood's Dilemma." In *De/Colonizing the Subject: The Politics of Gender in Women's Autobiography,* edited by Sidonie Smith and Julia Watson, 81–87. Minneapolis: University of Minnesota Press.

Herstory: Indian Residential School Stories of Women from the Interior of British Columbia. Edited by Diane Pien, Margo Greenwood, Jessie Nyberg, Gwen Phillips, Kathleen Reynolds, Marie Abraham, and Cathy Gottfriedsen, Vernon: Herstory Project.

Highway, Tomson. 2005. *Ernestine Shuswap Gets Her Trout.* Vancouver, BC: Talonbooks.

Hives, Christopher. 1990. "From Humble Beginnings." *The UBC Alumni Chronicle* 44, no. 3. https://archives.library.ubc.ca/general-history/from-humble-beginnings/.

Justice, Daniel Heath. 2004. "Conjuring Marks: Furthering Indigenous Empowerment through Literature." *American Indian Quarterly* 28, no. 1/2: 3–11. JSTOR.

Kovach, Margaret. 2009. *Indigenous Methodologies: Characteristics, Conversations, and Contexts.* Toronto, ON: University of Toronto Press.

Lyons, Scott Richard. 2000. "Rhetorical Sovereignty: What Do American Indians Want from Writing?" *College Composition and Communications* 53, no. 3: 447–68. JSTOR.

Manuel, Arthur. 2015. *Unsettling Canada: A National Wake-Up Call.* Toronto: Between the Lines Press.

Memorial to Sir Wilfrid Laurier, Premier of the Dominion of Canada. Chiefs of the Shuswap, Okanagan, and Couteau Tribes of British Columbia. 1910. Presented at Kamloops, BC, August 25, 1910. https://www.ceaa-acee.gc.ca/050/documents/42815/42815E.pdf.

Ono, Santa. 2018. "Statement of Apology." Speech delivered at the Opening Ceremony for the Indian Residential School History and Dialogue Centre, University of British Columbia, April 9, 2018, Vancouver. Printable copy available from the Office of the President of the University of British Columbia. https://president.ubc.ca/letter-to-the-community/2018/04/09/statement-of-apology/.

Riley-Mukavetz, Andrea, and Malea D. Powell. 2015. "Making Native Space for Graduate Students: A Story of Indigenous Rhetorical Practice." In *Survivance, Sovereignty, and Story: Teaching American Indian Rhetorics,* edited by Lisa King, Rose Gubele, and Joyce Rain Anderson, 138–59. Logan: Utah State University Press.

Shuswap Nation Tribal Council. 2010. "The Memorial to Sir Wilfrid Laurier: Commemorating the 100th Anniversary." Kanaka Bar Band. https://www.kanakabarband.ca/files/memorial-to-sir-wilfred-laurier-pdf.pdf.

Simpson, Leanne. 2013. "Politics Based on Justice, Diplomacy Based on Love." *Briarpatch* 42, no. 3: 4–7. http://ezproxy.library.ubc.ca/login?url=https://search-proquest-com.ezproxy.library.ubc.ca/docview/1349974166?accountid=14656.

Smith, Linda Tuhiwai. 2012. *Decolonizing Methodologies: Research and Indigenous Peoples.* London: Zed Books.

We Get Our Living Like Milk from the Land. 1994. Edited by Lee Maracle, Jeannette Armstrong, Delphine Derickson, and Greg Young-Ing. Penticton: Okanagan Rights Committee and the Okanagan Indian Education Resource Society.

Wagamese, Richard. 2012. *Writing with the Old Ones: From the Oral Tradition to the Printed Page.* Kamloops: Richard Wagamese.

Wilson, Shawn. 2008. *Research Is Ceremony: Indigenous Research Methods.* Winnipeg: Fernwood Publishing.

8

IN THE WEEDS

Joshua L. Daniel and Lynn C. Lewis

Since the 2016 presidential election, the rise of hateful discourse in national conversations, as well as overt and covert acts of violence, have manifested across our campuses and into our classrooms. As writing program administrators (WPA) at a large public university, we have witnessed an alarming change in the kinds of problems we are asked to solve, the concerns our instructors bring to us, and the day-to-day experience of administration. The 24/7 continual feeds ensure in us and in our instructors an always-present reiteration of fear narratives and a concomitant sense of anger at those in power who make and make up the news. Acceleration nips at our heels. We are "in the weeds."

The overt and covert violences we identify correlate directly with a political moment in which a candidate for the presidency of the United States boasted of his ability to assault women, to mock people with disabilities, and to encourage violence against his female opponent and *was still elected*. We saw the videos, viewed the photographs, heard the voices, and read the tweets. We witnessed angry mobs chanting "lock her up." These moments matter; they fill our media and social media feeds. We are experiencing, sharing, tweeting, and hearing instances of violence daily at an increasing drumbeat, and this cannot help but affect what goes on in our classrooms and in our work as writing program administrators. Of course, moments of violence are not new to any campus, and direct causality between this political moment and our experiences cannot be verified. Nevertheless, we have felt an increase in such moments–and we are not alone in marking it–and more and more of our time as administrators is devoted to discussing and intervening in fraught situations.

In this chapter, we describe four scenes in which we attempted intervention in moments of covert and overt violence in our first-year composition (FYC) program, and we reflect on the consequences of those interventions. We intend to illustrate how, while intervention strategies must be local, dialogic, process-oriented, and timely, consistent

https://doi.org/10.7330/9781646422807.c008

recognition of the presence and circulation of affect necessarily under-girds each scene of violence and each intervention attempt. Through the scenes we describe below, we explain how we came to understand how affect is bound up in each scene of violence, how best we adminis-trators can remedy some of its effects, and how making time to process, reflect, and discuss violence-tinged scenes, despite the speedy, weed-strewn pace of our days, is an absolute necessity.

We describe moments we have encountered as administrators that demonstrate how threats, intimidation, bullying, and the constant potential for further aggression lace our experiences as WPAs. We chose these scenes not only because they represent moments of violence we have encountered but also because they occurred within rhetorical situations common to writing program administration work: interven-ing when students interpret an instructor as hostile, assisting when an instructor is demeaned by students, and coordinating with partners on campus to help a student in crisis. We hope sharing these narratives might be helpful to other administrators when they inevitably encounter overt or covert moments of violence in their day-to-day work. From our own perspective and affective orientation, we have learned to lean on each other, the crucial first step while building an attentive, well-planned process that includes recognition of the violence enacted, collaborative and individual reflection across stakeholders—when possible—and generative response to the situation. Our purpose in this chapter is not to suggest that we handled each scene correctly—indeed, these scenes are infused throughout with our uncertainty about each situation and its resolution—but to describe their complexities as fully as possible to set the stage and reflect upon methods administrators might take up to help them productively intervene in moments of violence shaped by their local circumstances. We have come to understand that effective intervention will only occur through deep and recursive reflective prac-tices, theoretical inquiry, and collaboration. Each narrative is followed by reflection, where we explain what we came to understand about effective intervention and our attendant affective responses. Indeed, our dependence on collaboration between ourselves, as well as broader institutional structures and personnel, permits us to locate moments for dialogue and reflection even when in the weeds.

SCENE 1 (LYNN)

I begin directing the first-year composition program at my university a few weeks before my tenure decision is official. I am to be the immediate supervisor of 125 instructors consisting of 87 graduate student teaching assistants, 25 visiting assistant professors, and a sprinkling of lecturers and contingent faculty. I know some of the graduate students, but none of the others. They are a vast blur at first.

At the first mandatory all-instructor orientation meeting, I notice Dick.[1] He sits in the front row, arms folded across his chest, listening. He raises his hand to ask about whether he can use his own texts in the composition classroom. I hesitate. "Some," I say. "But the majority of the readings should come from the textbook." Dick nods. He offers me a thumbs up, and I smile back. Later, I realize this was a test: what would the limits of my authority be?

The semester rushes by, and in December, I read student evaluations and write a short note thanking each instructor, praising the abundant evidence of good teaching. However, Dick's evaluations stop me. Students across four sections remark on "meanness." He is insulting, some claim, and hostile, say others. The pattern is there, but inconsistent. Students in each section also comment on his intelligence and how their writing has developed. I know that sometimes students read wit as sarcasm, so I consider that perhaps this could just be a case of misinterpretation. When I've finished my half of the student evaluations, I meet with Josh so we can discuss any concerns. I tell him about Dick. He asks me what I want to do.

"Observe him, I guess? See how that goes?" Josh agrees.

Dick declines to answer my email requesting a time to observe. But I am busy, so I let it go.

The following semester, Dick misses the mandatory orientation. He emails Josh and says he was unsure about the meeting's location. Because we were in the same room as always, neither Josh nor I find this very convincing, but we decide it's not worth a battle. We've just moved from a print textbook to an e-book, and glitches abound for the first three weeks of the semester. I am fielding thirty-five to forty emails a day about the e-book, as is Josh. As the issues begin to resolve, I head upstairs to the instructors' floor to check for any remaining questions and thank folks for their patience. Dick is at his desk. I walk toward him and stand a few feet away. "Just checking in to see if things are going okay with the e-book," I say.

Dick folds his arms. "I'm sure I can figure it out," he tells me.

"Great," I say. "Let me know if I can help."

"I don't need help from you," he says.

I ignore the hostility. Not a big deal, I tell myself.

Three weeks later, I get an email from a university advisor with serious concerns about an instructor. The instructor has overtly threatened students. He has insulted them in class. He has name-called. What am I going to do about his behavior? I call the advisor immediately and ask for the instructor's name. It's Dick. Two days later, I am visited by two nervous first-year students from one of Dick's sections. One of them starts crying while the other describes Dick's rudeness and sarcasm. I hand her tissues and listen. I tell them they are doing the right thing speaking out. I email Dick repeatedly and tell him we need to meet. He doesn't answer.

Josh and I decide that it's time to start an official process: probationary status may help Dick get back on track. We discuss how best to do this and agree that concrete and achievable expectations are key. We create a specific list of objectives connected to the concerns that have been raised. I go to the department head and tell him I need to put Dick on probation. I show the head our list, and he agrees the expectations are entirely reasonable. Since Dick ignores my emails requesting a meeting, the head and I agree that he will meet with Dick to address that issue. A few days later, he sends me an email asking me to attend as well. When I arrive at the meeting, Dick is already sitting in the head's office. We discuss lines of communication and the importance of responding to emails. Dick seems agreeable in this moment and promises to do better. While not happy about the probation meeting he will have to attend with Josh and me, he listens attentively to my assurance that we want to support him. He leaves. I start to get up, and the head stops me: "Just a minute, Lynn," he says. He tells me that Dick has issued a complaint against me. "He says you bully him," the head tells me. "He says you tried to physically intimidate and bully him."

I am not proud of my response: I laughed.

There's more to this story, but beyond saying that Dick's behavior grew worse and, ultimately, his contract was not renewed, I stop the scene at the moment where the violences this instructor had enacted against his students under cover of his teacher mantle began to seep through and where he revealed what he believed to be—or perhaps what he hoped the head would believe to be—my violences towards him.

Reflection 1 (Lynn)

As I think back on this scene, I am cognizant of the covert violences evident from Dick—and from me. I note that perceptions of power structure in the interactions I have described and, as Josh and I discussed later, they are drastically uneven. I laughed at the idea that I, a five-foot-four woman, could possibly engage in physical bullying toward a younger and larger man. Dick's perception of me seemed oddly skewed. Later, I realize that Dick made this claim because he felt attacked from someone institutionally powerful. My physical stature had little to do with his emotional response.

At the same time, I realize that Dick had been challenging my authority from the first time we met. On the one hand, when I announced the adoption of our e-book, I was leading my first orientation as director and instituting major changes in the program while also signaling future changes. Dick, on the other hand, tested the waters by asking if he would have to stick to the rules about using a common textbook. As Josh put it, Dick's perspective may have been: "These changes I don't care for are happening just because she says so."

When Dick told me he didn't need my help with anything, he may have been seeking to end the conversation on his terms and maintain autonomy over his classroom. I failed to understand how my position as WPA limited my effectiveness at dialogue. Taken aback by Dick's accusation of bullying, I also failed to consider seriously Dick's emotions when he was told about his probation. Put differently, one consideration in a more effective intervention might have been to recognize and acknowledge the violence Dick was perceiving from the beginning. I did not understand that, by entering Dick's office space and affirming my power to do so, I was intimidating him because of my power as WPA.

SCENE 2 (JOSH)

I begin my work as associate director of first-year composition at Oklahoma State University in the fall semester of 2014, the same semester Dick begins working as an instructor in our program. Lynn will not become director until 2015, and my first year I work under the previous director.

In my first year, I am teaching graduate students, directing a mentorship program for graduate students, and overseeing the administrative work of four graduate students. My PhD was not added to my transcripts until August, so I had been a graduate student myself only a few weeks prior to my administrative assignment. FYC orientation overlaps with the university's orientation for new faculty, so I am stretched across multiple places my first week. I am learning new curriculum, departmental policies and procedures, and administrative practices. I am revising my dissertation for journal articles, attending faculty meetings, leading workshops, and trying to remember as many names as possible. I teach my first graduate seminar. I place an article. I win a teaching award. I forget about and miss an important meeting. Weeds abound.

Flash forward to when Dick presses Lynn about the program text-book. During the same meeting, he asks me questions about teaching his own assignments in place of the university-mandated common cur-riculum. I explain that we expect and encourage our instructors to teach each assignment based around their expertise and teaching styles, but they must stay within the curriculum and meet our outcomes. In other words, there are many ways to teach a literacy narrative, but he must still teach a literacy narrative.

Other small incidents occur over the following months. For instance, Lynn emails Dick multiple times about a teaching issue but receives no response. We note that he always emails me back promptly. Lynn suspects he is deliberately ignoring her, but I try to give him the benefit of the doubt because he has always volunteered to help with teacher training, and I cannot recall major issues with him during my first year. I reason that since he has worked with me before, maybe he feels we have a rapport. I imagine he figures anything he says to me is communicated to Lynn. I want him to be better about communicating with Lynn, but I am hopeful this will improve.

Lynn is concerned that Dick may have issues with a female author-ity figure. While I don't disbelieve Lynn's concerns, I don't fully grasp them until the three of us have a meeting to discuss his probationary status. He has been placed on probation because three different sources claim he is hostile to students: multiple student advisors have contacted Lynn; students have written about it in evaluations; and students have come to our offices to complain. One student tells me that Dick said, "If I ever even suspect you of plagiarism in my class, I will do everything in my power to see you expelled from this university and to make sure your academic career is ruined." Another student recalls an instance when Dick bragged that he would "crack some skulls" if he suspects plagiarism. Regardless of why Dick is evading Lynn and why he claimed she was bullying him, concern for his students is the priority. Lynn and I agree on a clear strategy: emphasize his previously good teaching record, make clear that we want to hear his side of the story, and provide clear expectations moving forward.

The meeting does not go well. Lynn explains the complaints, and Dick gets angry. He contends that complaints from students do not constitute valid evidence about his teaching. When I press him on the comments about "cracking skulls" and threatening to get a student expelled, he concedes that he made them, but claims they were neces-sary for impressing on students the seriousness of plagiarism. When we talk about setting up teaching observations, he argues that he is the only person qualified to evaluate his classroom. Still, he reluctantly agrees to what we outline. Both Lynn and I will observe his class during the semester to give him feedback. He will also send us assignment sheets and unit outlines so we can verify he is teaching the curriculum.

Throughout this conversation, I increasingly grow alarmed by Dick's body language. When Lynn speaks, Dick leans forward and raises his voice. Several times, he interrupts or misconstrues—deliberately, I feel—what she says. When I speak, he leans back and listens. He behaves one way toward Lynn and entirely differently toward me. Lynn and I both notice the disparity. Still, we communicate what we need to during the meeting, and we recognize that, in presenting him with this path, we have to give him a chance in good faith to take it.

Unfortunately, Dick does not meet the probation objectives. The only real successes are that he replies when I email to set up an observation and the observation is mostly successful. But he fails to send us any of the documents we had requested and does not respond to multiple emails from Lynn for an observation. When she goes to observe him, after emailing with her intention to do so, he confronts her loudly in the hallway: "This is not acceptable," he insists. She tells me later that his fury was palpable. She is shaken.

Shortly after, I receive an email from Dick beginning with a three-sentence description of his next unit plan, but with no assignment sheet or any other documentation. Beyond that, there is a long message about Lynn. He says he believes that she cannot be trusted and is determined to run him off, but he will not let her. He states that all future correspondence about his job will go through me.

This email makes me furious. I can't imagine why he would assume I share his opinion of Lynn or why he would think I would be willing to undermine my colleague. But he clearly does. I reply that this email is unacceptable and that it will be forwarded to both Lynn and the department head as part of the review of his probationary status. The department head eventually informs Dick that his contract will not be renewed.

Reflection 2 (Josh)

Questions about this scene still bother me. Did I give him the benefit of the doubt for too long? Why did I fail to recognize his hostility toward Lynn until I witnessed it? Moreover, when an instructor behaves this way, what is the appropriate response for a writing program administrator? As Lynn says in the previous reflection, perhaps Dick thought she was bullying him or undermining his classroom authority when she entered his office. Should I have seen this? Could I have intervened in the early days of the conflict? If so, how?

I admit to feeling angry when this happened. I felt offended that Dick felt comfortable insulting Lynn to me and that he believed he could get me to go behind her back. I wondered if I had handled the entire situation incorrectly and, moreover, I worried that I had let Lynn down. Was I direct enough in our conference? Had I made it clear that I agreed with his probationary status? Had I somehow signaled to him a *wink-wink*?: "Sure, I was in the meeting, but like you, I know how Lynn is. Just deal with me instead." I simulated scenarios like this in my mind a thousand times.

What strikes me now is how badly Dick must have misread the power differential. His claim that Lynn wanted to run him off suggests that Dick either believed that Lynn could fire him or perhaps that she would make his work so miserable that he would just quit. In that sense, reaching out to me, however clumsily, might be interpreted as digging in his heels and saying, "I'm not quitting. I'm not going anywhere." So, on the one hand, Dick misinterpreted how much power Lynn had, and he misconstrued how it might be wielded. On the other hand, Dick *did* go to the department head, which suggests he might not have been all that misinformed about the power dynamics. Though we do make recommendations, the head makes decisions about contract renewals. Really, it just makes me angrier to think about it in these terms, because Dick tried simultaneously to go behind Lynn's back to me while also going over her head to the department head. I have tried to imagine how badly I would have to be treated to do this to a colleague, and I have also tried to imagine how this instructor could have that impression of Lynn. I struggle with it. Lynn and I have spent a lot of time talking about what happened, and she has confessed that my anger made her feel better. "Maybe validated is a better word?" she corrected herself.

Makes sense to me.

Emotional labor is talked about a lot in writing program administration. If I'm being honest, it's a subject that I often rolled my eyes at when I was a graduate student. That's not to say that I was unaware emotional labor was a thing, but I saw it as a catchall for "yeah, this work can be exhausting, and you end up dealing with people who are angry or upset a lot." What I didn't account for was a moment where my own response might be anger and how that emotion could cause me to question if I were doing a good job. That's tricky, if unsurprising, when it comes to violence: how we can internalize it and wonder what we should have or could have done to prevent it. As junior faculty, I was grateful to work under a tenured colleague so that we had a chance to discuss what happened and plan how to respond, rather than feeling the full burden of response on my shoulders.

SCENE 3 (LYNN)

I arrive to observe Lucy's class ten minutes before the official start time and take a seat towards the back.[2] Lucy, a first-time teacher, raises a hand hello and continues logging on to the classroom computer while chatting with some students sitting just in front of her. There are nine students present, most of whom are men.

A group of five white male students is sitting in front of me talking loudly about the president-elect, Donald Trump. One says loudly, with a side glance at Lucy, "He's going to do really great things." Lucy ignores the statement. The students keep talking. One goes to the blackboard and writes, "It's my birthday. Leonardo DiCaprio." Lucy ignores the student as he laughs and sits down. When we reach the official class start time, Lucy looks around the room and says, "Let's wait and see if more students get here."

Lucy completed her undergraduate degree just months ago. Her hair is pulled back with an elastic band, and she is wearing comfortable sweats and a T-shirt. She offers a big smile as two more students arrive. She begins class by explaining that they will be discussing how to craft an argument.

She is nervous, I can see. That's normal when you are being observed and, when she gets into a tangle as she tries to define facts, inferences, and observations, she stops herself and asks, "Do you guys understand?"

One of the male students replies, "That was the best explanation ever. You're doing a great job." His tone is sharp and sarcastic.

Lucy smiles. She introduces a small group exercise to the class, in which she asks them to form arguments about an assertion. It's a complicated exercise involving a complicated topic: artificial intelligence. It asks students to craft an argument quickly, present it, and then be evaluated by other students, who are the designated judges. While she's explaining the exercise, the male student makes a comment under his breath to his friend, and they both snigger. I'm not sure what was said, but I am certain the comment was about Lucy from the glances they give her.

As the class works through the exercise, these troublesome dynamics persist. The cluster of male students continues to be sarcastic, especially one particular student. Lucy falls back on two phrases, "Did I make sense?" and "Was I clear?" Two students in the back look out the window, and one has earphones in, from which the class can hear tinny music. Lucy doesn't let everything go. She asks the student with earphones to remove them, though she is apologetic. She tells a student who gets up to leave at the end of the group exercise to sit back down as the class is not complete. She is working towards authority. At the end of class, she and I agree on a meeting time the next day.

I walk out into the hallway, thinking hard about what to say to Lucy when we meet. She is still Lucy the student and not yet Lucy the instructor, and I'm not sure how to approach the problem. I wonder if she sees the problem as I do. And that is where I start the conversation.

When we meet, we run through the standard questions about meeting the day's learning outcomes. Then I ask Lucy what she thinks about the class in general. She is noncommittal. I mention the assertive group of male students. She says, "They can be loud."

I pause, and then I say, "I thought they were disrespectful of you."

"Really?"

"Yes."

She says slowly, "Well, I have been thinking about some things I want to change for next semester. Like I'm going to update my wardrobe. I need to dress more like a teacher and less like a student."

This is an opening to a conversation about Lucy the instructor versus Lucy the student, so I nod and smile. She goes on to tell me that she's also going to wear makeup and ditch the flip flops.

I say, "There are little things you could do that might help you with your goal of 'more like a teacher.'" We talk through some ideas: making use of the classroom space, mixing students up more, asking for questions instead of validation from the students. But there's an elephant in the room as well—the gendered space of the classroom that a young woman is navigating, which I, who have the gravitas of age and authority—navigate very differently.

Reflection 3 (Lynn)

I remain troubled by both the young men's behavior and my own response. Why does Lucy have to invoke her authority through dress or cosmetics? On the one hand, I know she is right: if she dresses more like a teacher, she is more likely to be read that way. But, on the other hand, what violences were enacted in this moment, and how did I as WPA permit and normalize them?

My observation of Lucy's classroom does not differ from what I am seeing in other classrooms like hers—that is, taught by a new, young, and female instructor. When we discuss this scene, Josh and I agree that, despite efforts dating from the 1960s to constrain sexist and racist language, Trump has renormalized hateful discourse and licensed those who would normally behave with decorum in the classroom to use aggressive, demeaning, or hostile language toward immigrants, people of color, and women. For us, the feeling of an uptick in such behavior has been palpable in an adamantly pro-Trump region. More than once, I have listened to female instructors describe loud male students in MAGA hats silencing a classroom. I think about these conversations as I ponder Lucy's situation.

Lucy's remedy—alter her clothes and her makeup—is based on cultural beliefs about gender: a man would be less likely to see such changes as necessary. These male students are behaving aggressively due to a combination of Lucy's age, gender, and comportment. In other words, the scene feels nested in myriad complications. I recognize its complexities as I write. Intervention began by recognizing the nature of violence in Lucy's classroom. But what should come next?

In the end, support through dialogue was my essential intervention strategy. I still worry about what violences I may have enacted by failing to interrogate the classed and gendered notion that Lucy must dress "like a professor." However, I decide against pressing Lucy on assumptions about how she should present herself as an instructor. After all, this is Lucy's first semester of teaching, and the last thing she needs is for me to push her deeper into the weeds.

SCENE 4 (JOSH)

Here, I recount a situation we faced, in which physical violence in response to our program's attendance policy was a real concern. Because we are housed within General Education, our FYC courses are seen as important for improving retention rates. Like many programs, this means we have a standard attendance policy. Students are allowed a set number of unexcused absences. Beyond a certain number, their grade is reduced, and they can fail the course. All instructors are required to enforce this policy, and only Lynn can excuse absences. Most semesters include requests from either students or their instructors to excuse absences, but, generally, few problems emerge.

In this scene, we are concerned about a somatic act of violence, such as an assault or shooting. Mass shootings such as the ones at Marjory Stoneman Douglas High School in Parkland, Florida,[3] and at universities across the United States over the last few decades have made such concerns far too familiar. In this scene, Lynn and I and one of our instructors are anxious that a student in a classroom might harm an instructor or other students. This situation emerges near the end of the semester.

As anyone who has ever worked in writing program administration already knows, the final weeks of a semester can be stressful for students and instructors. Students are suddenly paying attention to their absences, since these might affect their grades. Graduate instructors are facing their own writing deadlines in their coursework and mounds of papers to grade. Everyone is exhausted and stressed. Undergraduates, graduates, and administrators get caught by the end-of-semester's many tangles.

One morning, while driving to the office, I receive a text message from Lynn informing me that we have a worrisome email from a student about a graduate instructor and that we should discuss it as soon as I arrive. The message does not ring alarm bells, since we frequently use text messaging to keep in touch.

When I arrive at the office, the email Lynn referenced is beyond anything I imagined. It begins by stating that the student's instructor has informed them of a grade reduction for excessive absences. The message then descends into what feels like rage. The student rants, claiming the instructor's grade reduction is an abuse of power that cannot go "unpunished." The email is long and confusing. The student writes, "blood shall spill." I am deeply alarmed.

As we talk through the situation, we realize that this is probably a student under a lot of stress, possibly in crisis. Maybe the student is making the threat unintentionally—the slightly archaic language sounds like something from *Game of Thrones*. At the same time, how can we possibly know? What are our responsibilities to this student? To the instructor? To the other students on campus? What if this student actually does "spill blood?"

No actual violence happens. Lynn contacts the Behavioral Consultation Team, and they seem relatively unconcerned. The ends of semesters are stressful for students, and apparently this is not outside the bounds of the situations they encounter regularly. But, for me, apprehension about this situation escalating into violence never fades. A sense of dread hangs in the back of my mind for the remainder of the semester. I think about it during my entire drive to campus every day and worry that I will receive an alert on my phone that something terrible has happened. The Consultation Team contacts the student and suggests a meeting to help, which the student accepts. The student drops the class. The remaining days and weeks of the semester tick forward. The semester ends.

Reflection 4 (Josh)

Scene 4 still troubles us greatly, because neither of us had encountered anything like it previously. Whether the student intended "blood shall spill" as an overt threat, this pseudothreat hangs heavy in the rhetorical atmosphere that has enveloped our daily work with the rise of violent discourse and bigoted rhetoric in the wake of the 2016 presidential election. When does someone really mean that they want to "punch his lights out?" And when is it just loud-mouthed posturing?

Statements from WPA organizations have helped us think through pseudothreats, because they name what we are feeling. Like it or not, writing program administrators work in a time where the fear of violence such as the El Paso shootings are a possibility.[4] This raises questions about what additional responsibilities we should take on in situations like the one described in scene 4. Whether it is or not, this feels like a new reality of administrative work to me. Certainly, my graduate education did not train me for *this*. How could it?

Moreover, this situation has also caused us to consider what responsibility we have for proactively addressing the acts of hate-filled violence that feel more common in the Trump era. The 2016 "Statement on Racism and the (g)WPA" from WPA-GO describes the problem from the point of view of those who have suffered the most violence recently and includes a long list of actions administrators can take to support students who are endangered as a result of the current state of affairs (WPA-GO Graduate Committee). We read these, aware that we have much work to do. Given all the weeds in our administrative space, we see this as the most serious and important task facing writing program administrators today. And, although physical violence ultimately did not happen, how could we have known? Did we leverage our agency in every ethical way possible to protect our students?

REFLECTIONS ON PROGRAMMATIC INTERVENTIONS TO VIOLENCE

These four scenes highlight our continuing engagement with recursive reflection. Our current political moment can be felt across all four scenes, such as the different moments in which Lynn and Josh first "see" the problems with Dick, or the way Lynn perceives a student's disrespectful behavior toward Lucy from her position as an administrator. Alongside the zeitgeist, we recognize our gendered, raced, and classed embodiments structuring our responses.

By acknowledging these nested complexities, we begin to intervene in their power. This acknowledgment occurs through active reflection, and we have come to realize that effective reflection can occur in short bursts: in hallway conversations, between classes, or a quick five minutes during our office hours before students arrive. In part, these are the material realities of our administrative lives. Often, these are simply the only available times for reflection and conversation, but they are vital to our capacity to intervene. Our analysis of the four scenes brought this home to us—a primary strategy and our first conclusion.

Second, in reflecting on these scenes, we note that ineffective interventions in covert and overt acts of violence depend on working institutional structures. Writing program administrators should create, cultivate, and maintain working relationships with deans, their leadership teams, and staff across various departments and support structures on campus, such as Human Resources, EEO Offices, academic advisors, and behavioral consult teams. Finding moments for reflection and conversation—moments between classes, quick conversations in the hallway—has become an essential strategy. As administrators, we need to mind the gap between actual and perceived power in each situation. Such awareness enables WPAs to create and foster relationships with those who can offer support and help them intervene when necessary.

Third, we argue that there is no WPA "bubble" outside politics, an extension of the NCTE's (2017) declaration that "there is no apolitical classroom." Nor is it an option for administrators to run programs as though they could exist in a bubble apart from the current political moment. Intervention strategies must include more than responding to these moments as they occur: we now address them in workshops such as "Composing the Civil Classroom in an Uncivil Age," "Working through Resistance," and "Power and Gender" as well as in teaching-observation discussions and informal meetings. Intervention also occurs in training sessions with instructors before an incident occurs, as well as in the moment of a challenging event.

Fourth, affect undergirds our in-the-moment responses to these scenes. We are angry to see a young female instructor bullied, furious that a male instructor attempts to suborn cooperation in eliding authority, and shaken by an outburst that teeters on the edge of violence. We fear violence in our instructors' classrooms and in our own administrative spheres in this political moment, an ever-present dread. Before the election and its aftermath, the possibility of violence seemed distant. Now, it seems always just around the corner, hunkered down in the weeds. We recognize, now, that acknowledging, writing, and talking through these affective responses lessens their power on us. Most important, the "we" in this essay allows us space to share, validate, and process our emotional responses so that we can move on.

Locating spaces for reflection, inquiry, and collaboration will always be challenging for writing program administrators, who are ever in the weeds. We find those spaces in Saturday lunch meetings, hallway conversations, text messages, regular meetings, emails, and even social media conversations. While interventions must always be local, dialogic, process-oriented, and timely, we suggest that active interrogation of perceptions of power, authority, and influence, as well as of the undeniable power of affect in violence-laden moments, remains crucial to effective interventions. More than anything, reflecting on the scenes in this essay has forced us to realize that intervening in overt and covert violences has emerged as a quotidian feature for writing program administrators in the "post-truth" era. Certainly, it has changed our calculus for how we think about training graduate students, particularly those who work with us in the FYC program. We see it as essential to make such scenes and our responses as visible as possible moving forward. In sharing these moments and our interventions, we hope they may help current and future administrators reflect usefully on the agency they wield in order to increase the range of possible responses and their potential for mowing a path through the weeds.

NOTES

1. Dick is a pseudonym.
2. Lucy is a pseudonym.
3. This refers to a mass shooting at a high school in Parkland, Florida, in February 2018. Seventeen students were killed, and another seventeen were injured by a former student.
4. This refers to a mass shooting at a Walmart in El Paso, Texas, in August 2019. Twenty-two people were killed and another twenty-four were injured by a right-wing terrorist who digitally posted an anti-immigration, white supremacist manifesto shortly before the shooting.

REFERENCES

NCTE Standing Committee Against Racism and Bias in the Teaching of English. "There Is No Apolitical Classroom: Resources for Teaching in these Times." National Council of Teachers of English, August 15, 2017. https://www2.ncte.org/blog/2017/08/there-is-no-apolitical-classroom-resources-for-teaching-in-these-times/.

WPA-GO Graduate Committee. "Statement on Racism and (g)WPA." Council of Writing Program Administrators. http://wpacouncil.org/aws/CWPA/pt/sp/wpa-go.

9

ANTIRACISM IS ANTIVIOLENCE
Utilizing Antiracist Writing Assessment Theory to Mitigate Violence in Writing Centers

Eric C. Camarillo

In my second semester as manager of the writing center, I had a conversation with a professor. He had come in to discuss plagiarism issues, specifically plagiarism committed by one of his students who had used the writing center. He'd referred (or, rather, remanded) the student to the writing center because the first draft had been "incoherent." At first, he asked a couple of probing questions about our plagiarism policy. He also stated outright, "Yeah, the tutor really dropped the ball. What's your policy on plagiarism?" We had a plagiarism policy in place, but it was geared toward treating issues of plagiarism as issues of citation—and never outright accusing a student of idea theft. Citation is something of a novel concept to most of our new students, especially first-generation ones, and we can't risk alienating a student by accusing them of something that may have been unintentional.

"You guys really need to watch out for that stuff," he said when I explained our practice to him. I realized then that this was his conception of the writing center—as either plagiarism police or formatting police. At the very least, he seemed to conceive of the writing center as a kind of surveillance unit, another set of eyes, through which he could cast his own vision. Combined with his previous account that he only referred the student to the writing center because of "incoherence," his concerns indicated that I had the opportunity to explain the mission of the writing center. This instructor clearly envisioned a center that served primarily basic or remedial writers, and I could show him how the center under my management would be different. However, I was new to my role, and I found this notion of the writing center as some kind of policing unit to be anathema, so I'm not sure what kind of expression was on my face when I quietly, but firmly, reiterated our policy about citations.

https://doi.org/10.7330/9781646422791.c009

What I do know is that the number of students we saw from that instructor decreased that semester.

To his credit, the instructor thought he was helping students at our Hispanic-Serving Institution (HSI) acquire the language of power, that he was preparing them for the world beyond the academy. For him, this preparation required that writing centers police student writing, that they serve a correcting function. In his *Labor-Based Grading Contracts: Building Equity and Inclusion in the Compassionate Writing Classroom*, Asao Inoue (2019) asserts that "writing teachers' and programs' inability to value all *habitus*—and it is an *inability* to do so—because of the way their assessment ecologies are structured, amount to one social group exerting its dominance over others. It is . . . immoral. It is racist. It is White supremacist. It is how writing teachers perpetuate White language supremacy" (43, emphasis original). This type of oppression, if left unchallenged and unquestioned, perpetuates itself.

In my second semester as manager of the writing center, I was still trying to build policies and procedures, to craft a theoretical framework, to rewrite our mission statement. In short, I was trying to reestablish the writing center, refresh it. Our writing center exclusively hires students, mostly undergraduates, so a strong training program became vital for transforming the center. While the peer writing consultants were compassionate and empathetic to students, their vision of "helping" students was related to the professor's. Their help often came in the form of correcting. While both versions of "helping" grew out of a sincere desire to see undergraduate writers at a Hispanic-Serving Institution succeed, both reflected a desire to enforce what Inoue (2019) calls "White language supremacy," leading me to ask in what ways our various visions of "help" actually harm students visiting the writing center.

It's an unnatural question for writing center folks to consider. Writing centers have developed a culture of help and assistance. Yet Nancy Grimm (2011) examines how this can be problematic: "This propensity to describe writing center work as 'helping' neutralizes the hierarchy and power of our positions within a system of advantage/disadvantage based on race. . . . If we narrate our work only in terms of what good we do ('helping'), we cannot develop a practice that challenges a racial system of privilege because we will not have the theoretical context or capacity to imagine doing harm. Without an examination of tacit theories and an articulation of explicit theories, writing center practice does have the potential to hurt (or continue hurting) people" (78). If a writing center exists to "correct" students who deviate from standard academic discourse, how much of what writing centers call "help" is really harm? Are students any less victims because they happen to be willing participants in a writing consultation? And, if those willing participants are students of color, does that make writing center practice any less racist?

Inoue's description of white language supremacy also mirrors descriptions of imperialism. In his "A Structural Theory of Imperialism," Johan Galtung (1971) asserts that imperialism promotes structural violence (rather than physical violence, for example) through the intentional perpetuation of inequality. The terminology Galtung uses casts an eerie overlay for terms used in writing centers, particularly his use of "center" (a dominant or larger country) and "periphery," (a subordinate or smaller country). Drawing from Galtung's work on imperialism, this chapter considers how an antiracist framework can mitigate the covert structural violence in writing centers. Importantly, this framework emphasizes a bird's-eye view of writing center practice, one that sees various interacting layers and conceptualizes this vision as the first step in lessening, or even eradicating, structural violence. In order to enact this kind of framework, writing centers need a praxis that connects the violence of imperialism and racism with the work of writing centers. I propose that an antiracist writing center based on an ecological model can potentially intervene in this covert structural violence by making it more visible and by encouraging students to question the expectations of dominant academic discourse.

The chapter begins with a brief description of the colonialist, imperialist nature of the writing center, before shifting into the problems to which this model gives rise. Next, the chapter links Inoue's (2015) ideal antiracist assessment to the writing center through Grimm's (2011) "Retheorizing Writing Center Work to Transform a System of Advantage Based on Race." Grimm's work demonstrates the challenges writing centers can face when attempting to remove inequities that are inherent in the system. The chapter concludes with broad strategies and specific practices enacted at the writing center of my institution, University of Houston-Victoria (UHV), and with a discussion of how and why other writing centers might adopt these practices.

WRITING CENTER AS COLONIAL/WRITING CENTER AS EMPIRE

In this section, I draw together the concepts of structural imperialism and traditional writing center practice, discussing briefly the various metaphors that are often overlaid on the writing center. Specifically, when writing centers function as empires, they treat their practices as inherently neutral, which prevents the center from accounting for issues of diversity and challenging power structures that may oppress students. Writing centers function as empires because of the regulating function they perform. As a result, many students may not feel comfortable in questioning writing center staff when it comes to working on their papers, which can be considered a type of cultural transmission. In other words, if the writing center performs a regulating, correcting function, then students visit this space in order to be corrected. What writing centers need is a way to prevent students from sublimating their agency to that of the writing center.

In "The Idea of a Writing Center," Stephen M. North (1984) remarks on how the writing center is conceptualized. He observes that the writing center is "to illiteracy what a cross between a Lourdes and a hospice would be to serious illness: one goes there hoping for miracles, but ready to face the inevitable" (435). He made this observation in 1984, but it's no less true now. If writing centers are hospitals, then the people who go there must be sick. It thus becomes the job of writing centers to "cure" those who visit, in the hopes the patients never have to come again. In order to address the issue of fixing writing, to counter the notion of the writing center as fix-it shop, North shifts attention away from the paper and to the writer, claiming that "in a writing center the object is to make sure that writers, and not necessarily their texts, are what get changed by instruction" (438). He moves the emphasis from products of writing to the process of writing.

However, the goal of changing the writer is problematic because, as Anis Bawarshi and Stephanie Pelkowski (Bawarshi and Pelkowski 1999) assert, "The shift from a product- to a process-based pedagogy becomes an invitation to interfere with not just the body of the text but also the body of the writer . . . in ways reminiscent of imperialist practices around the world" (45–46). This goal constructs the writing center as empire, doing nothing to question the inherent privilege of the dominant discourse, which marginalizes other discourses. In their "Postcolonialism and the Idea of the Writing Center," Bawarshi and Pelkowski (1999) claim that remediation is a way to "initiate under-prepared students into the ways of the university and to protect the university from the threat posed by the racial, rural, immigrant, underprivileged, under-prepared Other" (46). The writing center becomes a site of acculturation and remediation, where students who speak and write other home dialects or languages must suppress these dialects and languages in order to maximize success in academia.

The writing center as colonizer, as empire, is necessarily a site of covert structural violence. In their discussion of postcolonialism in the writing center, Bawarshi and Pelkowski (1999) use Mary Louise Pratt's (1991) idea of the contact zone as a way of conceptualizing the work that goes on there: "social spaces where cultures meet, clash, and grapple with each other, often in contexts of highly asymmetrical relations of power, such as colonialism, slavery, or their aftermaths as they are lived out in many parts of the world today" (34). As Pratt goes on to explain, in spite of, or because of, this "grappling," the subordinate subject acquires and deploys the dominant discourse to their own ends. In a similar way, writing centers can help students learn how to "describe themselves in ways that engage with representations others have made of them" (36). However, helping writers achieve this level of fluency in the dominant discourse requires reenvisioning how a writing center operates and exists. That is, if the writing center is an imperialistic force, it is an inherently violent space, however covert this linguistic violence might be.

This imperial function also assumes a race-neutral, or color-blind, approach. Because of its focus on the process of writing, on language alone, the regulating model within writing centers seems to treat every-one the same. However, this is not quite the case. Grimm (2011) notes the various assumptions that she and her writing center staff had when it came to attracting students of color to their writing center. In particu-lar, she and her staff assumed "that the literacy education offered by the university and the writing center contributed to leveling the playing field, allowing [minority students] to become like us, thus (ahem) 'bet-ter' and 'equal'" (75). This type of assumption is imperialist, despite its good intentions.

Galtung's (1971) work on imperialism provides insights into the dynamic of writing-center-as-empire that Bawarshi and Pelkowski (1999) describe and that Grimm (2011) alludes to. In his discussions of impe-rialism, Galtung (1971) focuses on structural inequality between two nations. Yet replacing the words "nations" with "people" renders his argument readily applicable to writing centers. Essentially, imperialism is "a sophisticated type of dominance relations" (81), one that doesn't rely on overt forms of violence like military occupation or aggressive conquest. Rather, "*only imperfect, amateurish imperialism needs weapons; professional imperialism is based on structural rather than direct violence*" (91, emphasis original). Maintaining imperialism requires a "divide and rule" strategy between the center nation and the periphery one. There are various elements that help maintain an imperialistic relationship between nations, but the most important one for this chapter is the transmission of cultural values from the center to the periphery.

As the periphery nation is rewarded for imitating the center nation, so too are students rewarded for imitating academic writing. Galtung (1971) argues that the "Center nations possess some superior kind of structure for others to imitate (as long as the Center's central position is not seriously challenged), and which gives a special aura of legitimacy to any idea emanating from the Center" (92). In the opening anecdote, the power to describe a student's writing as "incoherent" is reserved for the instructor; a student is not similarly empowered to critique the professor. Grimm (1996) asserts that "because power circulates in the normalized writing practices of the institution, it cannot be challenged" (7). In the imperial model of the writing center, students seek out the center in order to more closely align themselves with standard literacy practices. The writing center, and the practices it endorses, are rarely questioned. This requires, as Galtung notes, a division of labor: "some nations produce decisions, others supply obedience . . . the Center nations [process] the obedience provided by the Periphery nations into decisions that can be implemented" (92). Or, as Bawarshi and Pelkowski (1999) argue, "in accepting the service (in this case, instruction in 'good writing'), the oppressed consent to their own domination" (51). These descriptions highlight some of the experiences that consultants have with passive or uncertain writers.

Take, for example, Patty,[1] a nontraditional student who came in frequently to the UHV Writing Center in the fall of 2017. She self-identified as having a learning disability. As one consultant noted, "In attempts to reach understanding, [Patty] would allow her confusion to reach such a point of frustration that she requested I write her papers for her." The consultant felt as if she were doing the assignment for the student in order to help the student understand what was being asked. In this case, the student found it easier to submit to the decisions of the writing consultant, to the point where she did not want to make any decisions herself about her own assignment. I attribute this to the anxiety surrounding the "reward" of completing an assignment (a good grade) and the distrust Patty had of her own writing abilities. Her uncertainty made her hypercritical of her own thinking and completely uncritical of the consultant's suggestions.

All of this is essentially cultural transmission, or cultural imperialism. Galtung (1971) contends that "if the Center always provides the teachers and the definition of that worthy of being taught, and the Periphery always provides the learners, then there is a pattern which smacks of imperialism" (93). In the above anecdote, we can see how Patty wanted to place herself in the peripheral position and to center the authority of the consultant. In this subject position, Patty (the periphery) "can get much in return from a humble, culture-seeking strategy (just as it will get little but aggression if it starts teaching the Center anything)" (Galtung 1971, 93). Patty's behavior is similar to Grimm's (1996) "illustrative stories" in "The Regulatory Role of the Writing Center." Grimm notes, as she tells the experience of one female student, "As a good female student, she knew how to please and to stay out of trouble by repeating the performance required of her . . . the student—and others like her—will perform for the benefit of a grade" (10). While imitation is rewarded, difference is punished. The fear of a bad grade, of punishment, coerces students like Patty and the one described by Grimm into sublimating their own agency. Writing centers often function to reinforce the status quo, to ensure that the empire of literacy remains undisturbed, and students are rarely in positions to challenge this function.

WRITING CENTER AS ANTIRACIST ECOLOGY: AN ANTIVIOLENT INTERVENTION

In this section, I use Inoue's (2015) conception of antiracism as a way to transform the imperial writing center model, using Grimm's call for structural changes as a thread. Specifically, I challenge the neutral concept of literacy instruction that occurs in writing centers, comparing this to the way in which imperial countries may place their own values as the standard to which peripheral countries must adhere in order to avoid persecution. Grimm (2011) calls for systemic changes to the writing center itself and the way it performs its work. This strategy illuminates how writing centers can shift from locating error in students, and move away from their imperial function, to serving students more fairly.

First, I draw on Inoue's (2015) notion of assessment as a key function of writing centers. When Inoue discusses assessment, he means acts of judging, "which all begin with processes and acts of reading . . . Assessment as an act is at its core an act of reading" (119). If reading is a core activity of writing centers, then judgment is also a core feature, and this judgment is what labels students as proficient or deficient.

Writing centers as assessment instruments might also demonstrate Galtung's (1971) idea of a sophisticated "mechanism of imperialism," one that is more or less invisible because it's seen as a neutral practice. The worst thing writing centers can do is leave the expectations of dominant discourse unchallenged and unquestioned, because that acquiescence renders these imperial forces invisible and powerful. Incorporating antiracist assessment ecologies is one way to begin complicating the dominant discourse and the white racial habitus with which it is linked. Inoue (2015) asserts that an antiracist writing assessment ecology "provides for the complexity and holistic nature of assessment systems, the interconnectedness of all people and things, which includes environments, without denying or eliding linguistic, cultural, or racial diversity, and the politics inherent in all uneven social formations" (77). He posits that writing assessments are racist because they use a particular discourse belonging to a particular group as the standard for evaluation. Because the discourse is itself tied to race and is then used as a measure of assessment, the assessment itself is a racist act. He asserts that "because we live in a White dominant society, and our dominant Englishes have historical White racial roots in White racial formations in the US, coming from White racial habitus, not to value all habitus, or to punish students for not demonstrating a dominant one, is to enact racist writing assessments" (43). Antiracist writing assessment ecologies, then, are necessary for valuing other kinds of discourses and even destabilizing the dominance of conventional academic discourse.

Second, like Inoue, who wants to examine practices of assessment more closely, Grimm (2011) calls for writing center administrators to examine the assumptions upon which writing center practice itself is based. Instead of focusing on individual writers, Grimm asserts that writing centers should reconceptualize the learning that happens in writing centers in such "a way that places less emphasis on individuals and more emphasis on making changes to the social structure, particularly the social structure of the writing center itself" (76). The emphasis on structural changes is important because it prevents writing centers from evading "the responsibility to examine and challenge privileging mechanisms, including the discourse that shapes business as usual within writing centers" (79). When writing centers leave unquestioned the problematic nature of writing center work, they fail to help students, particularly students of color, in the ways that would allow them to engage with the social structures that constrain them.

Inoue's (2015) dual emphasis on writing assessment ecologies as well as Galtung's (1971) structural theory of imperialism links to Grimm's (2011) focus on these social structures. Grimm calls for a social model of learning: "it should alter our understanding of why we do the work we do; it should change the language we use to describe our work; it should shift the focus of what we aim to change away from individual students and toward the social structure" (81). This idea encapsulates her aim to bring about change on a larger, structural scale—change to the writing center itself rather than just the student who is visiting. Similarly, when

Inoue advocates for antiracism in the classroom, he says, "It is about cultivating and nurturing complex systems that are centrally about sustaining fairness and diverse complexity" (12). Both Grimm and Inoue are calling for a shift away from changing individual habits within a student and toward a more systemic, equitable change in writing centers and in composition classrooms, respectively.

Engaging with discrimination on a systemic level is necessary because the one-with-one setting only impacts individual students, laying praise and blame on single students and veiling the imperial work of the writing center in the process. Grimm (2011) asserts, "It doesn't matter whether strongly prejudiced or generous-hearted people work in writing centers, the unchallenged or common-sense mottos that guide writing center practice allow structural forms of racism to continue" (82). As Galtung (1971) notes, "Imperialism is a more general structural relationship between two collectivities, and has to be understood at a general level in order to be understood and counteracted in its more specific manifestations" (81). As writing center directors, we must understand our regulating practices on a more global scale in order to more thoughtfully enact local change and resist the covert violence the "structural relationship" between the student and writing center produces. As Grimm (2011) engages and challenges three writing center mottos, she notes that these common practices can be used to disguise discrimination and racism. Inoue (2015) mirrors this argument when he writes, "Thus it doesn't matter if teachers or readers see or read student writing with prejudice or with a preference for whiteness in their classrooms. It doesn't matter at all. What matters is that the assessment ecology produces particular results, determines (in the Marxian sense) particular products, reinforcing particular outcomes, which make racist cause and effect difficult (even impossible) to discern" (16). Neither Grimm nor Inoue means to discount the hard work that writing consultants do, but they both acknowledge that an individual consultant cannot alone turn the writing center or the writing assessment into a fair and equitable place. Both acknowledge that writing centers, writing consultants, students, and teachers all exist within a larger framework, a larger social structure, a larger ecology.

For Grimm (2011), taking this wider view of writing centers is essential for making fairer systems in writing centers, ones that don't force students of color "to identify tacit expectations and negotiate institutional hoops, all while encountering reminders that this place wasn't designed with [nondominant racial identities] in mind" (79). Inoue (2015) contends, "Racism is an assessment problem, which can only be fully solved

by changing the system of assessment" (15). While Grimm focuses specifically on writing centers, it is Inoue's notion of racist writing assessments
that connects Grimm's social model of learning to a larger ecological
context. Regardless, both assert that writing center practitioners must
focus on systems of oppression in order to accomplish real change.

Take, for example, a traditional-aged Latina student who came
to work with a UHV consultant several times over the course of the
semester. The consultant noted, "At the beginning of the semester,
she had trouble identifying the thesis of the paper that she was meant
to interpret, but, by the end of the semester, she seemed much more
confident and was able to identify the thesis and main points. What I
think helped was that I made sure to ask a lot of leading questions about
what she thought during the earlier sessions while trying to guide her
to the parts of the text where the author was explaining or alluding to
his thesis." In this case, the consultant was able to use previous consultations as scaffolding for further learning, offering individualized help for
understanding a particular aspect of academic discourse. If the student
had only come in once, it would have been impossible for us to see if
she had truly grasped how thesis statements functioned. Regular visits
to the writing center, especially for students who are unaccustomed to
academic discourse, may be a potential element for enacting antiracist
praxis in the writing center and reconceptualizing the social structure
of the writing center.

PRAXIS

This section offers a series of tactics and strategies writing center administrators could adopt in order to cultivate antiracist writing centers along
with brief descriptions of how those strategies are implemented at the
UHV Writing Center. Versatility and adaptation are the hallmarks of this
approach. Inoue (2015) calls on instructors and other users of assessment to consider their locally diverse population of students in order
to most fairly engage students in the task of writing. Writing centers can
do the same. We have to know who our students are, where they come
from, in order to maximize our effectiveness and avoid merely forcing
students to align their discourse with the dominant academic one. The
work of cultivating antiracist writing center ecologies, then, begins with
consultant training. However, not every strategy listed here may be effective, possible, or appropriate at other types of institutions.

First, begin from the top down. What I'm arguing for in this section
is to treat writing consultants, undergraduates or otherwise, as theorists

and researchers, not just practitioners. This helps redistribute the flow of power in the writing center, dispersing it from a centralized location (the director) to the entire staff. This gives writing consultants the ability to effect change and influence practice.

To help writing consultants think about complex ideas, to conceptualize power, I developed a writing center canon that consists of theorists and scholars that form the theoretical foundation for the UHV Writing Center. It consists of some of the works I include in this paper (Bawarshi and Pelkowski 1999; Grimm 1996; North 1984) and others I haven't (for example, Vershawn Young's [2010] "Should Writers Use They Own English?"). As consultants read and take notes, we discuss key takeaways and any questions they might have. I don't always have an answer to their questions, but even just discussing them is generative for them and me. This fulfills Grimm's (2011) notion that "when writers *are* newcomers to a discourse or a culture, a writing center should be a place where they can expect to find someone who knows how to make discourse and cultural expectations explicit" (77, emphasis original). Bawarshi and Pelkowski (1999) and Young (2010) allow me to shape conversations about race, discursive expectations, and hegemonic power structures. I don't expect the writing consultants to necessarily introduce these ideas to the students with whom they work, but consultants should leave our conversations with the idea that there's no *right* way to write. This will give them the versatility to work with a wide array of writers and to adjust to the various goals each writer has.

Writing consultants are also encouraged to conduct original research that can affect policies and procedures in the writing center. For example, I had one consultant who, when I offered him time off from consulting to do research, presented ideas on how writing consultants might manage stress through meditation. We are now working on getting meditation guides for all writing consultants and teaching them techniques for meditating in between their appointments. The idea here is that more relaxed consultants can more effectively respond to anxious students and make the atmosphere of the center itself more pleasant.

Next, question best practices with your staff. Writing centers must examine our practices and traditions when it comes to the consultation. The range and breadth of best practices in writing centers is extensive and covers everything from conceptualizations of our work to day-to-day office procedures. Best practices can consist of things like ensuring the writer does all the work, scheduling appointments at least twenty-four hours in advance, limiting appointments to a certain amount per week (or month or semester), emphasizing process over products, and so on. I'm not (necessarily) advocating for a total revision of these policies, but I am suggesting that writing center administrators examine the habitual practices that exist in their writing centers. Ask things like: Why is this policy in place? When was it enacted? Who benefits from it? Who is harmed by it?

Consider how these policies allow you to embrace students rather than correct them. To move away from the imperial, oppressive model of writing centers, we must conceptualize our work less as *for* them (which infantilizes them) and more as *with* them (which positions them as equals). As Paulo Freire ([1970] 2018) asserts in *Pedagogy of the Oppressed*, "Authentic education is not carried on by 'A' *for* 'B' or by 'A' *about* 'B,' but rather by 'A' *with* 'B,' mediated by the world—a world which impresses and challenges both parties, giving rise to views or opinions about it" (104). Working *with* students ensures Bawarshi and Pelkowski's (1999) vision of the contact zone in the writing center, where students can grapple with academic discourse rather than being subsumed by it.

As one example of questioning best practice, I turn to my own training as a consultant. When I was trained as a consultant, directive methods and questions were verboten. Consultants had to be nondirective and evasive in the guidance they offered to students, which sometimes resulted in students becoming frustrated with certain consultants. In this model, it can appear as if we're purposefully keeping answers from them or, worse, touting our power over them. To help avoid this tension, I encourage consultants to go back and forth between being directive and nondirective, depending on student need. Additionally, regarding grammar, I noticed that a strong majority of students who entered the writing center struggled with mechanics (commas, specifically). To that end, we adopted a more holistic approach to the paper, one that includes addressing student concerns, whether that concern is about sentence-level questions or issues related to the paper as a whole. My point here is that the policies we have in place should serve our students; our students shouldn't serve our policies. More importantly, it's okay to bring students into the consultation process, to be transparent about how the session should work and seek feedback on that process. The most important aspect of questioning best practices is the removal of the assumption that we have all the answers when it comes to effective writing.

In this vein, most of our policies are dictated by how students actually use the writing center. We have offered writing consultations in three modalities for about five years now: in-person, synchronous online, and asynchronous online. We find these modalities necessary in order to best serve our diverse student body, both our large online programs and our growing on-site student population. While each mode necessitates slightly different rules about usage, there are some polices across the board: students may make one appointment per assignment per class every twenty-four hours; appointments are made in thirty-minute or sixty-minute increments only; students should make appointments (but we occasionally take walk-ins when it's slow); students should bring helpful materials with them to their appointments; students should refrain from using their cell phones while the consultation is happening; students are encouraged to discuss their writing at any point in the writing or revision process. We find these policies useful in helping students find agency for themselves, for engaging in meaningful revision, and for managing their time. As we move forward, the UHV Writing Center will also be adding 24/7 writing tutoring through a third-party vendor in order to make academic support even more accessible. However, I'd like to add that just because something is a long-established best practice doesn't mean it needs to be abandoned completely. Best practices should be questioned, examined. And, if it turns out this practice does serve the locally diverse student population, then it should be kept.

Third, encourage consultants to examine how they read. If assessment is an act of reading, as Inoue says (2015), then reading is also an act of assessment. To become anti-imperial agents, we must change the way that we read. As Inoue notes, "The myth of linguistic homogeneity really boils down to how we read and judge writing of locally diverse students. A writing pedagogy that doesn't assume a unidirectional monolingualism is one that assesses writing and writing students by considering more than a single dominant English" (69). Deviation from a standard does not denote a deficit—something about which we have to be careful to remind ourselves and our students. To engage critically with how we read and to shift the way we think of deficit, we must necessarily engage in reflective activities, which may help to expose and reveal potential biases in our approaches to reading. To this end, the writing center at UHV draws heavily on the work of Romeo Garcia (2017), specifically his "Unmaking Gringo-Centers." This article is part of the UHV Writing Center's canon, and it informs much of our practice, perhaps more so than the other texts. Where scholars like Grimm (1996; 2011) and Bawarshi and Pelkowski (1999) engage heavily with the theoretical aspects of writing center management and offer high-level, abstracted solutions, Garcia's ideas are concrete and practical. Also important is the inclusion of his own personal narrative in his approach to writing center administration and consultant training.

Garcia (2017) claims, "We cannot just accommodate difference nor should we approach differences as that to be solved" (49). To this end, consultants must engage in more reflective activities. As Garcia asserts, "Tutors need to engage in reflection and reflexivity. I suggest tutors become researchers of their everyday experiences and researchers of the everyday of writing centers" (50). This is something I'm still trying to build at UHV. Consultants do reflect on their experiences in the center, but that typically takes place at the end of the academic year, which is likely not often enough. Garcia recommends a portfolio and "describing the everyday thickly, accounting for the ways in which power, issues of race, and social relations play out" (50). This type of reflection takes time, though, and allowing that kind of time, especially in the busiest parts of the semester, is challenging. I could ask the consultants to reflect and create these portfolios on their own time, but that feels somewhat exploitative since all of the consultants at UHV are part-time undergraduates. At any rate, I'd posit that any kind of reflective activity is better than nothing and can help the consultants reach a clearer understanding of their reading practices and how they engage with students.

In lieu of written reflections, I meet with the consultants on a regular basis, both in scheduled biweekly meetings and in unscheduled "walk-in" meetings. In the former, I send out a calendar invite to the consultants, and I may provide them with a text I want them to read or a topic I want them to think about beforehand. We then discuss the text or idea for about half an hour. In these meetings, the consultants come to me. In the walk-in meetings, I go to them. I try to wait for a lull in appointments before approaching and checking in on them. These meetings don't have a set agenda. We might discuss our weekends, interesting shows we're watching, funny memes we saw recently, or frustrations or accomplishments consultants experience from their work in the center or from some other area of their academic life. I find these types of meetings essential to my work, because the meetings humanize us to each other, and I'm able to decentralize how power flows in the center.

CONCLUSION

I'd like to return to the anecdote that opened this chapter. In reflecting on that moment, I can now see the ways in which the instructor sought, unconsciously, to maintain the status quo, to act as an agent of imperialism. I proposed an alternative view of writing, of reading, of the center, but this alternative was not welcome. Galtung (1971) asserts that education can function as a tool of cultural transmission: "For in accepting cultural transmission the Periphery also, implicitly, validates for the Center the culture developed in the center. . . . This serves to reinforce the Center as a center, for it will then continue to develop culture along with transmitting it, thus creating lasting demand for the latest innovations" (93). In my case and the professor's, though, it was more like two agents of the center trying to reinforce two different conceptions of the "latest innovations." To stretch this metaphor slightly, I was an emissary of the writing center meeting with an ambassador of the university and putting forth an idea that the ambassador may have found alarming. I see why he would. In the imperialist writing center, in a writing center that regulates and norms, and as the leader of this center, I should have been more than happy to surveil the students who entered, to change them—to fix them.

Yet there are ways to move beyond this traditional approach, beyond the assessment and imperialistic functions. By incorporating antiracist writing assessment ideology into writing center praxis, we can begin to mitigate the complicity of writing centers in the racism inherent in larger systems. We can, as Grimm (2011) says, begin to understand writing centers "as the social structures designed to facilitate deeper learning and fuller participation in the academic community rather than as places for students who 'need help'" (90). We can begin to see beyond the individual and toward the larger forces that bend and shape writing center work. Once the ecologies are no longer veiled, once racism is no longer able to hide behind the cloak of neutrality and thus enabling the structural violence of imperialism, writing centers can begin to make deep changes both with students and with institutions. Students themselves may be able to participate in these systemic changes, the periphery moving to the center and the center becoming more peripheral.

NOTE

1.   Pseudonyms are used to protect identities.

REFERENCES

Bawarshi, Anis, and Stephanie Pelkowski. 1999. "Postcolonialism and the Idea of a Writing Center." *The Writing Center Journal* 19, no. 2: 41–58. JSTOR.
Freire, Paulo. (1970) 2018. *Pedagogy of the Oppressed.* Translated by Myra Bergman Ramos. Reprint, New York: Bloomsbury.
Galtung, Johan. 1971. "A Structural Theory of Imperialism." *Journal of Peace Research* 8, no. 2: 81–117. JSTOR.

Garcia, Romeo. 2017. "Unmaking Gringo-Centers." *The Writing Center Journal* 36, no. 1: 29–60. JSTOR.

Grimm, Nancy. 2011. "Retheorizing Writing Center Work to Transform A System of Advantage Based on Race." In *Writing Centers and the New Racism: A Call for Sustainable Change and Dialogue*, edited by Laura Greenfield and Karen Rowan, 75–99. Logan: Utah State University Press.

Grimm, Nancy. 1996. "The Regulatory Role of the Writing Center: Coming to Terms with a Loss of Innocence." *The Writing Center Journal* 17, no. 1: 5–25. MLA International Bibliography (2001700091).

Inoue, Asao. 2019. *Labor-Based Grading Contracts: Building Equity and Inclusion in the Compassionate Writing Classroom.* Fort Collins: WAC Clearinghouse.

Inoue, Asao. 2015. *Antiracist Writing Assessment Ecologies: Teaching and Assessing Writing for a Socially Just Future.* Fort Collins: WAC Clearinghouse.

North, Stephen. 1984. "The Idea of a Writing Center." *College English* 46, no. 5: 433–46. JSTOR.

Pratt, Mary Louise. 1991. "Arts of the Contact Zone." *Profession*: 33–40. JSTOR.

Young, Vershawn. 2010. "Should Writers Use They Own English?" *Iowa Journal of Cultural Studies* 12, no. 1: 110–18. Iowa Research Online. https://ir.uiowa.edu/cgi/viewcontent.cgi?article=1095&context=ijcs.

10

CULTIVATING RESPONSE TO HATE SPEECH IN THE DIGITAL CLASSROOM

Elizabeth Chilbert Powers

A TROLL IN THE ONLINE CLASSROOM

This is a story of a troll in one online undergraduate public writing and rhetoric class. It is a story of a teacher's frustration and her students' unease, all held captive by the university-supported free speech of an individual assailing members of the LGBTQ+ community and other vulnerable populations. It is a story of the violence that animates such hate speech, and, finally, it is a story about "rhetorical looking," one pedagogical strategy for responding to hate speech to diminish its power.

The story is set in a familiar institutional context: an open-admissions, regionally serving public university. Most programs can be completed entirely online, and many students take a mix of online, video synchronous, and on-site courses from faculty across two campuses and a handful of centers based in rural communities. The online public writing and rhetoric course draws majors across disciplines, as it satisfies an upper-level humanities requirement. The course is set up in weekly modules, each including a mix of reviewing and responding to texts and peers, individual and collaborative activities, and reflection. Most of this work is visible to all students, including the forums and activities to which the troll posted misogynist and antiqueer statements.

The troll's speech regularly invoked historical and contemporary violent oppression of women and minorities that was disconnected from assignments and class conversations. His work in the course was disruptive and unsettling, constructing a hostile environment for women and trans students. His statements clearly exemplified hate speech, for his words were "deliberately abusive and/or insulting and/or threatening and/or demeaning directed at members of vulnerable minorities, calculated to stir up hatred against them" (Waldron 2012, 8–9). His posts, through hateful metaphor, slogans, and professed worldview, participated in the cultural violence of internet troll culture. In Johan

Galtung's (1996) peace framework, cultural violence is defined as "those aspects of culture, the symbolic sphere of our existence—exemplified by religion and ideology, language and art, empirical science and formal science (logic, mathematics)–that can be used to justify or legitimize direct or structural violence" (196). The troll was not the only purveyor of violence in this context: institutional policy and strategy that protect dehumanizing hate speech legitimized the posts as acceptable contributions to the course, acceptance of violence being a central element of cultural violence (196).

Considering hate speech in the online classroom as a form of cultural violence, disruptive to human dignity, provides avenues toward redress, in pedagogy and practice if not policy. Throughout the semester, I worked to untangle the complexities of policy and pedagogy at play: how can faculty at a public institution foster inclusive online learning environments while complying with campus policies protecting students' free speech? In order to work through these competing needs, I had to reframe my assumptions about the instructor's role in the classroom, as well as my understanding of and response to hate speech. That process began early in the class.

It was only the second week of the semester when I spotted the work of the troll in a discussion forum on which students were provided a set of questions for thinking through the NCTE Definition of Twenty-First Century Literacies (2013). This student had posted disparaging claims about women, interwoven with religious undertones, in extra-large hot pink font.[1] A solitary peer comment was restrained and on point: "What does this have to do with the reading?" The troll hadn't responded. I clicked through the week's work to see if there were any other antagonizing comments. In a collaborative wiki activity on literacies, the same student had uploaded an image macro of human silhouettes superimposed into a bonfire. The all-caps Impact font read, "Transsexuals are Satan's lie to the world." While the misogynist comment was annoying, the fire and bodies image and accompanying text were frightening. It was January 2017, and recent federal steps toward ensuring LGBT+ student rights were at risk. I consulted with an upper-level administrator at the institution about the troll, and they responded that nothing seemed actionable. The student hadn't made any direct threats, so his ideas were protected free speech. Not only could I not remove the posts, the administrator told me, but any reply I posted viewable to the class could not insinuate what type of score the student would receive on the assignment or hint towards evaluation because of FERPA. Since many of my rubrics include an item like "fully addressed assignment prompt," I could not even echo the peer's reminder to connect to the assignment prompt, at least not directly in the troll's thread. I resigned myself to posting announcements, such as sweeping reminders to stay on topic, and to act civilly.

I regretted seeking the administrator's advice, feeling I might have been able to better strategize on my own, but I complied with their instructions. My suggestion to review our civility policy, my encouragement to engage with the material of the course, my offer to talk with the troll via video conference, phone, or in person, all took place within Blackboard private message and assignment rubrics. The troll never responded to my attempts to reach out, and the pattern of behavior continued. I sought advice from another university administrator, who confirmed that the advice I previously received was policy. The troll's posts weren't directly targeted threats to specific individuals, I was told, along with other points of rationale for inaction, including the position of the troll's posts (always in new threads, not as responses to peers' posts) and the unconventional sentence structures that clouded meaning at times. The posts had to remain in the digital classroom, untethered by any evaluative comments from me. I tried to continue my one-sided conversation in the grading notes and in Blackboard messages: "I'm confused by your disconnect from the subject matter of the course," "How do you see this class fitting in with your academic goals?," "You still have time to re-do this assignment for credit, if you'd like to delete your current submission and re-submit something in line with the tasks at hand," and "Please let me know what questions you have about this assignment. The current post seems to indicate a lack of understanding of the stated goals." He continued to ignore these notes and also ignored the occasional frustrated peer comments and questions. Whatever his purpose for being in the course, it appeared not to include engaging in dialogue as a member of the course community.

Many of the projects in the course were recursive, and, thus, we revisited the same spaces again and again, which meant we experienced his harmful posts again and again. They were a permanent, unmovable fixture of our digital classroom, fitting within Jeremy Waldron's (2012) description of contemporary hate speech on the internet as "expressions that become a permanent or semi-permanent part of the visible environment in which our lives, and the lives of vulnerable minorities, have to be lived" (37). While Blackboard was private and the site could be closed after the semester, the troll's posts were an unavoidable constant in our classroom, the environment in which we had to live our academic lives for the duration of the course.

Other students reached out to me, concerned about the troll. The troll seemed paranoid, unstable, and, as indicated by the doomsday rhetoric and conspiracy theory threaded throughout his posts, perhaps caught up in a cult-like organization. These concerns led me back to campus administrators. They reached out to the student's local advisor, who assessed him as neither dangerous nor in danger, just "an odd duck."

By week five, I was resigned to accepting the off-the-wall, stuck-forever-to-the-wall comments. At this point in the course, students were conferencing with me in person as well as in synchronous online meetings for their midterm projects (the troll did not sign up for a conference). Unprompted, several students aired frustration, discomfort, and fear about the troll's vitriolic presence in the class. Additionally, I observed that students' misgivings about online education seemed confirmed by my lack of response to the troll's statements, based on the questions they directed to me—"Have you seen these posts?" "Do you read all the discussions?" My individual feedback to each student and the conversational questions, additions, and clarifications I posted in discussions and group projects were not enough to meet their expectations of an instructor's role—I wasn't present where it mattered, where intervention seemed necessary.

"Students are concerned. Please let me address the troll," said one student. I asked administrators, and they instructed me to tell concerned students, individually, simply not to read the troll's contributions to the course—the statements were not creating a hostile environment, they said, because they were easily avoidable. This proposed solution of avoiding harassing speech online is common. In general, online harassment is not seen as severe or pervasive enough to require action, and women and racial minorities (who are most often targets of online hate speech and harassment) are expected to scroll by or unplug if they find attacking and harassing statements to be bothersome (Poland 2016). University administrators saw the constraints of the online classroom as protection enough, based on the idea that learning management systems are secure and private because they generally lack anonymity and are not permanently accessible. The disruptive remarks of one student did not constitute a hostile environment for women and LGBT+ students, I was told. Concerned students could avoid or ignore the distracting student.

These instructions paused my struggle against university policy and shifted my focus to the problem of online pedagogy: how could I tell students to ignore a classmate, tell them his statements don't need to bother them or affect them? What would it mean to tell a student that another student's participation doesn't matter, can be easily ignored and dismissed outright? Not only would such direction restrict students' course experience and hinder their agency in navigation, but it would also carry the message that they, too, can be ignored, that their contributions are not pivotal to the course. The policy was impossible to implement pedagogically. An online classroom gains "an emergent identity, a gestalt of transacting elements that cannot be reduced to a sum of its parts" (Fleckenstein 2005, 150). Cohesiveness and connection across the areas of an online course means that one cannot expect students to put on hate-blinders and continue to engage with the class as an open forum for an audience-aware, sincere academic discussion. Narrowing opportunities for students to engage in course material and interact with peers could not be productive pedagogically. Because I couldn't conscionably offer the suggestion of avoidance, I offered the unsatisfactory but unavoidable truth of the situation to students who contacted me about the troll: "I am not able to comment on other students' work or performance in the course because of FERPA. Campus administrators maintain an absolutist position on student free speech rights and consider the comments in question protected speech. While I am not able to comment on the posts, you are welcome to respond to them if you wish. You might find the Engaging in Controversial Discussions guide in Blackboard helpful. I truly appreciate your concern and I am sorry for this distraction in our course." Students continued to try to engage the troll in discussion, but he never indicated reading any of his peers' notes, just continued posting hateful statements and doomsday numerology.

By the end of the semester, the troll was still there, though several other students—some who had raised concerns with me about his behavior and some who had not—had dropped out or faded away. I don't know with any degree of certainty why the students left, but I would speculate that the presence of the troll and my lack of visible response to the troll had not reassured them of the value of online education or fostered any sense of safety or trust in the process. My public silence in the face of hate speech had been acceptance of hate by way of inaction. I was complicit, allowing the hate speech to contribute to the violence. I felt acutely my failure to act.

Having such a consistent, motivated hate-speaker in an online class might be rare, but conflict between official university policy on free speech and individual pedagogy is less so. I needed to be better informed. I needed a better plan. In what follows, I consider free speech in the current US university context and then explore and adopt the strategy of rhetorical looking to mitigate the effects of hate speech in the digital writing classroom.

EXPLORING HATE SPEECH POLICY AND DIGITAL PEDAGOGY IN THE US PUBLIC UNIVERSITY

More than two hundred universities in the United States have civility codes that disallow hate speech (Delgado and Stefancic 2014). These codes are aspirational rather than practical, at least from a legal perspective. The Supreme Court has not ruled on college speech codes, and a majority of lower court rulings have delegitimized campus speech codes as infringements on first amendment rights (Chemerinsky and Gillman 2017). Because universities are held as cultural champions of free speech, there is strong legal precedent against policies for being vague, overbroad, or unduly invasive of viewpoint (Delgado and Stefancic 2017). Therefore, most universities, especially underresourced ones, formally discourage hate speech but do not take action that might lead to litigation. Including civility codes in syllabi can set expectations for respectful exchange, but the codes cannot be relied upon to defend action taken against hate speech. Until US courts recognize the civil rights violations inherent in much hate speech, nonlegal strategies outside of official university and course policy are essential.

Addressing hate speech in the online classroom is necessary for fostering inclusive educational environments. Richard Delgado and Jean Stefancic (Delgado and Stefancic 2017) argue that, without equality, the first amendment cannot function. To realize free speech, there must first be an assurance of variety in speakers and viewpoints, which cannot happen in a campus atmosphere where not all contributors feel safe. Interpreting occurrences of hate speech as a free speech issue precludes the rights of others to pursue educational opportunities in a nonhostile environment. Sara Ahmed (2015) explains, "The freedom of some rests on the restriction of the freedom of others. So much harassment is justified and reproduced by framing the very language of harassment as an imposition on freedom." The prioritization of hate-speakers' free speech rights over safe, nonhostile environments for others is not limited to school-based online contexts, of course. Women experience more online harassment than men, and marginalized women even more so: "What is beyond dispute is that being a woman raises one's risk of cyber harassment, and for lesbian, transgender, or bisexual women and women of color, the risk may be higher" (Citron 2014, 14). The online classroom, privileging absolutist free speech rights for bigoted ideas, becomes a reflection of what women, people of color, and LGBT+ communities experience elsewhere online. The gendered and labor-based promises so prevalent in the contemporary online education marketing ("Go to school while raising kids"; "Get a degree while working full time") dissolve in online classrooms that cannot combat the hostility that meets marginalized students when they attempt to pursue their educational goals online. Educators who believe in online education's value to provide inclusive access may not easily succeed in shifting law or institutional policy, but they can seek out pedagogical strategies to ensure more equitable access to online learning.

A cursory glance at pedagogical texts hints toward disconnect between policy and pedagogy. Some recent work in digital pedagogy, like Beth Hewett and Kevin DePew's (Hewett and DePew 2015) *Foundational Practices of Online Writing Instruction*, does not address situations of conflict and harassment in the digital classroom. Other texts, like Brian Van Brunt and W. Scott Lewis's (Van Brunt and Lewis 2014) *A Faculty Guide to Addressing Disruptive and Dangerous Behavior*, provide suggestions for online classrooms that could be in conflict with institutional policy, like removing student posts (106). Angela Laflen (2016) addresses the complexities of negotiating tense moments in the classroom, offering empirical methods for gauging emotion in asynchronous online discussions and effective strategies for intervention when things turn hostile. Her chapter is helpful for new and seasoned online writing instructors alike, providing practical strategies for encouraging students to engage in and reflect on their contributions and roles in online forums. Like Van Brunt and Lewis, Laflen sees the instructor role as intervener: "though it may be necessary to accept that online writing is simply more negative than face-to-face discussion, it is also important to be able to recognize when intervention is warranted and what steps to take in order to keep a discussion fluid and not simply moving toward less neutrality" (115–16). These texts' emphases on respect, mutual understanding, and listening are valuable elements of an inclusive pedagogy, but none alleviate concerns regarding the potential violence of protected free speech in the classroom. Laflen and others illustrate how discussions can grow in intensity and misunderstanding and culminate in an outburst, a different problem from trolling.

Invitation to dialogue is limited in the face of hate speech. In my class, the troll had not exposed his hostility in an emotional crescendo of a heated debate. He was not interested in engaging in discussion with me, nor was he interested in responding to peers' questions. My misplaced emphasis on fostering dialogue was an idealized interpretation of rhetoric's goal to remedy misunderstanding (Richards 1965). Delgado and Stefancic (2004) posit that "hate speech is rarely an invitation to a dialogue; it is like a slap in the face" (207). They describe a hate speaker's actions as "uttering a performative—a word that enacts its own message without the need of decoding. The idea that talking back to the aggressor is wise, sensible, or even safe lacks a sense of reality" (207). Safety might be interpreted differently in an online context, but the root of the sentiment remains: attempting dialogue is not usually an effective response to hate speech. My dissatisfaction with the suggested strategy of silence and growing awareness of the ineffectuality of engaging with the hate speech perpetrator prompted me to reconceptualize hate speech in the online classroom. Rather than seeing hate speech as a possibility for dialogue across difference, I shifted to approach it as an obstruction, a significant interruption better addressed through contemplative analysis than attempts to engage the perpetrator.

APPROACHING HATE SPEECH AS VISUAL INTERRUPTION

Interruptive hate speech is not meant to engage discourse but rather provoke emotion and shut down discourse, creating need for an extra-discursive approach. Considering the visual/textual interplay of the asynchronous online classroom, I decided to integrate the visual rhetorical framework of rhetorical looking (Fleckenstein, Gage, and Bridgman 2017) into my next online course, a different 300-level writing course. As conceptualized by Kristie S. Fleckenstein, Scott Gage, and Katherine Bridgman (Fleckenstein, Gage, and Bridgman 2017), rhetorical looking is a means of slowing down the interpretive process when confronting atrocity images, defined as "photographs depicting human-against-human violence" (12). Rhetorical looking as an analytical framework includes four recursive tactics—looking-through, looking-at, looking-with, and looking-into—which help promote thoughtful, responsible, and responsive action to atrocity images. The authors articulate the goal of rhetorical looking as "undermining violence through visual engagement" (12). Adopting this pedagogical tool to combat hate speech in the digital classroom requires conscientious understanding of the alignment and misalignment between hate speech and atrocity images. Even in the form of image macros that allude to violence, trolling hate speech is generally an insinuation of potential violence rather than a documented scene of what Galtung (1996) refers to as direct violence. Yet hate speech indicates the cultural violence from which direct violence (and photographs documenting that violence) also emerges, so the two are not disconnected.[2] Some conventions of online trolling, like the inclusion of crude images and stylized text, create a visual experience, and therefore focusing on the experience of seeing, as emphasized in rhetorical looking, can broaden possibilities of response. Rhetorical looking, with its "invitation to take the what and how of seeing violence as a means to discover the what and how of ameliorating violence," positions students as agents imbued with ethical responsibility (14). The four tactics of rhetorical looking offer ways for students to broaden and deepen their perspectives and ideas of action, expansion that could help students like those in my digital writing and rhetoric course who reported feeling stuck. Rhetorical looking could offer opportunity for thoughtful and agentive response, not to the hate-speaker but to the classroom community.

To experiment with rhetorical looking in the context of hate speech before introducing it in the classroom, I returned to an early post from the previous year's troll: the macro with the flames and silhouettes and anti-trans message. I began the recursive process with looking-at, the tactic meant to help in "uncovering the belief systems contributing to any act of perception" (Fleckenstein, Gage, and Bridgman 2017, 25). A clash of ideologies, between me as the viewer and the creator of the macro, was certainly at play here. Through looking-at, I considered the evangelicalism the macro connected to its anti-trans message, the textual reference to Satan, and the visual allusion to hellfire; I also considered my own feminist-humanistic ideological position, from which I saw the macro as counterproductive to coming to a shared understanding, to gaining new knowledge, or to working toward equality. The ideological opposition created a barrier between the viewer and the image macro and between the viewer and creator of the macro. In other words, we'd have a hard time finding common ground.

I continued the process of slow looking by looking-with, which places emphasis on point of view and the role of "viewer as civic participant, one who engages with an atrocity image as a means to alter the conditions giving rise to both the violence depicted and the violence stemming from the production and circulation of the atrocity image itself" (27). I viewed the image macro within an internet search displayed in a browser window, within the encompassing frame of my computer screen, on the desk in my office. There were layers of distance between me and the macro, which itself was layered, a combination of multiple images and text. The layers and frames created distance between us, which had informed my original reaction to the macro. I was viewing the piece through teacherly frames (Blackboard window, computer screen, office desk) that habitually lead to assessing, taking action in the form of grading. Through looking-with, I saw how my initial reaction to the macro—attempting official university sanction—had come up framed in this instructor context.

I moved on to looking-through, the rhetorical looking tactic focused on constructing perception and unsettling notions of perception as transparent, through the action of moving back and forth from image details to description applied (Fleckenstein, Gage, Bridgman 2017, 23–24). I described what I saw: crudely edited overlaid images of bonfire and human silhouettes, writhing or dancing; outdated noun, *trans-sexuals*; suggested violence through pairing written statement with fire image. Reviewing these jotted lines, I saw my critique of the creator's digital composing skills, the value judgment about the student's skills in an area that was connected to our course outcomes. I saw the ambiguity present in "writhing or dancing" that indicated a possibility that the silhouettes clipped and placed over the flames were not functioning in the way intended. I had also evaluated, rather than described, his use of terms, based on an understanding of contemporary LGBT+ identification language. Looking-through the image macro illustrated how my perception of the piece was shaped through discrediting the competence of the creator detail by detail, tracing naiveté about technology and about gender and sexuality.

I proceeded to the fourth tactic, looking-into, which "helps viewers determine *answerable action*, in which action exists not as a discrete operation, isolated in space and time, but instead, as part of a 'conversation' of deed" (Fleckenstein, Gage, and Bridgman 2017, 29, emphasis original). I had previously felt powerless to respond to the image macro, frozen by interpretations of policy. Looking-into guided me to consider response more broadly. The image-macro was one of many hateful memes against LGBT+ communities created by trolls in online spaces. The image macro as a digital genre comes from trolling culture, though it has since been adopted by the larger digital public (Phillips 2015). Why not, I wondered, follow that pattern and adopt a response corresponding to the genre? Under the hate speech macro, I could have posted a pride meme, something positive to celebrate trans identity, to stand in solidarity with the vulnerable community targeted. Such a response seemed appropriate in the larger cultural context and even permissible from the point of view of the administration, because of its nonevaluative nature. Later, I also continued looking-into the situation by developing a student-facing overview of free speech and community membership.[3]

To fully engage in the recursive process of rhetorical looking, I returned to looking-with. I had reflected on the structure of my own point of view but had not considered the others I was looking-with. I imagined other students in the course, figuring their way into assignments, checking out what others had done before posting their own. Coming across the troll's image macro, without any notes of context or responses from the instructor, could cause angst, anger, fear, or confusion. Since I wasn't able to make any evaluative comments, my response macro would have stood alone without comment, as far-flung from the prompt as the troll's post, perhaps adding to students' confusion about the goal of the assignment. Still, considering the peer reactions to the text (confusion along with fear and anger) when there was no instructor response, a transpositive macro seems a fitting response. Through the process of rhetorical looking, I discovered, evaluated, and prepared to take responsibility for what had transpired, including the responsibility to clarify the assignment for any confused students. This trial exercise signaled that, in addition to a pedagogical tool for approaching atrocity images, rhetorical looking carries potential for strategizing response to hate speech in the classroom.

Rhetorical looking offered me avenues to see what I might have done differently as an instructor to give pause to and call out the troll's violent hate speech, to cultivate a path forward. While rhetorical looking is image-focused by design, the method may be adapted and employed effectively with nonphotographic, discursive texts participating in cultural violence, especially in cases where members of a shared community (like a classroom) find themselves searching for a means of response other than attempting dialogue with the violence perpetrator. Examining the troll's post as a visual object instead of a contribution to discussion helped me generate ideas for response. In retrospect, I could have set up clearer parameters for student coursework and clarified different strategies of response toward context-specific goals, facilitating more examination of the texts and their impact, all through the practice of rhetorical looking. The students may have benefited from guidelines responding to a text in an exchange of ideas as well as responding to a text as an object of analysis. If students had both conversation and analysis in mind as appropriate approaches to discussion board posts, we could have better addressed the troll's posts in a way that did not depend on his continued engagement or violate free speech.

As a result of my experiment, I offered rhetorical looking as one strategy toward mitigating the effects of hate speech the next semester. We began the semester with an in-depth discussion of community expectations, individual agency, and roles, comparing our assumptions to university policy. In the discussion, multiple students brought forward assumptions that, if something "inappropriate" was posted, I would take it down (an assumption aided by the sheriff's badge icon next to each of my posts in Blackboard, connoting policing and control). Along with introductions to critical reading and conversation strategies, I presented rhetorical looking as a strategy "concerned with undermining violence through visual engagement," one that might equip students to confront hateful speech outside the boundaries of conversation (Fleckenstein, Gage, and Bridgman 2017, 12). The course centered on digital writing and online community, so introducing the concept of rhetorical looking did not overtly indicate that I assumed students would attack each other. Instead, in conferences and discussion board posts, students reported that the strategy could be usable beyond the classroom, as they negotiate hate-laced discourse they perceive as characteristic of contemporary internet spaces. Subsequently, I prepared a short guide to circulate in the event of an occurrence of hate speech in the classroom.

Along with students' new understanding that school policy that meant to preserve student free speech also limited censorship of hate speech, rhetorical looking expanded students' approach to the classroom, as their own perceptions of agency in the online classroom increased. Early in the semester, I focused the course activities on reading, creating, and collaboratively selecting and debating definitions of concepts key to the digital classroom, including civility, respect, cyberharassment, free speech, and hate speech. Hate speech was discussed in digital contexts, which students found especially applicable to social media contexts. There was no requirement that students seek out hate speech, but rhetorical looking was presented to students interested in working against the hate speech they found outside of class. I saw traces of rhetorical looking across the semester, as students worked to understand the prevalence of trending videos and social media posts that deride and threaten vulnerable identities and communities, taking up a range of points of view and offering answerable action. More so than in previous semesters, students took time to call out the hate speech they found online, slowing down to provide context-based analyses that considered perception, values, and context at play. Orientation toward rhetorical looking may also have supported interaction within the boundaries of the classroom community. There was no trolling, but hostile, racist comments showed up in reading responses and activity reflections. Each time, peers approached the comment by reporting what they saw on the page, why they felt that way, and what social systems and cultural values might be implicated. For example, several students became practiced at looking-through inflammatory posts by pointing out how they had come to interpret the words as harmful before articulating their response. Students also positioned their perspectives among others, looking-with classmates whose experiences and readings of challenging posts varied. There were no faux-conversational questions asking the writers to engage in a dialogue that wouldn't take place. The students were different, the course was different, and the semester was different, so no concrete comparative assessment can be made, but I am encouraged by the possibility that rhetorical looking can help a class move beyond attempts at reforming a troll and instead find moments of purposeful critique and individual and community action and accountability.

Trolling and its effects in the online classroom cannot be predicted; responses cannot be planned. Yet, in this era where politicians, universities, and software companies promote online education as a haven of progress and access, along with legal precedent prioritizing unrestricted free speech over civil rights, trolling in the online classroom will continue. Addressing hate speech is imperative for building nonviolent, inclusive learning communities online, and rhetorical looking is one way to generate meaningful response, to move beyond failed attempts of dialogue and into responsive and responsible action.

NOTES

1. Many internet harassment experts, like Whitney Phillips (2015), warn against replicating the language of trolls as we study it; such reproduction can normalize their antagonisms. Here, I offer one example, an approximation that fits with the troll's themes, to illustrate method of response.
2. See Appendix B: Classroom Overview of Free Speech and Community Membership.
3. See Appendix B: Classroom Overview of Free Speech and Community Membership.

REFERENCES

Ahmed, Sara. 2015. "Against Students." *The New Inquiry*, June 29, 2015. https://thenew inquiry.com/against-students/.

Chemerinsky, Erwein, and Howard Gillman. 2017. *Free Speech on Campus*. New Haven: Yale University Press. doi: 10.2307/j.ctv1bvnfnb.

Citron, Danielle Keats. 2014. *Hate Crimes in Cyberspace*. Cambridge, MA: Harvard University Press.

Delgado, Richard, and Jean Stefancic. 2017. "Four Ironies of Campus Climate." *Minnesota Law Review* 101, no. 5: 1919–41. Nexis Uni (0026-5535).

Delgado, Richard, and Jean Stefancic. 2014. "Hate Speech in Cyberspace." *Wake Forest Law Review* 49, no. 2: 319–43. Nexis Uni (0043.003X).

Delgado, Richard, and Jean Stefancic. 2004. *Understanding Words that Wound*. Boulder: Westview Press.

Fleckenstein, Kristie S. 2005. "Faceless Students, Virtual Places: Emergence and Communal Accountability in Online Classrooms." *Computers and Composition* 22, no. 2: 149–76. doi:10.1016/j.compcon.2005.02.003.

Fleckenstein, Kristie S., Scott Gage, and Katherine Bridgman. 2017. "A Pedagogy of Rhetorical Looking: Atrocity Images at the Intersection of Vision and Violence." *College English* 80 (1): 11–34. MLA International Bibliography (2017873679).

Galtung, Johan. 1996. "Cultural Violence." *Peace by Peaceful Means: Peace and Conflict, Development and Civilization*, 196–210. London: SAGE Publications.

Hewett, Beth L., and Kevin Eric DePew. 2015. *Foundational Practices of Online Writing Instruction*. Fort Collins: The WAC Clearinghouse and Parlor Press.

Laflen, Angela. 2016. "Taking the Temperature of the (Virtual) Room." In *Applied Pedagogies: Strategies for Online Writing Instruction*, edited by Daniel Ruefman and Abigail G. Scheg, 106–20. Logan: Utah State University Press.

"The NCTE Definition of 21st Century Literacies." NCTE Position Statement. National Council of Teachers of English. http://www.ncte.org/positions/statements/21stcentdefinition%20.

Phillips, Whitney. 2015. *This Is Why We Can't Have Nice Things: Mapping the Relationship between Online Trolling and Mainstream Culture*. Cambridge, MA: MIT Press.

Poland, Bailey. 2016. *Haters: Harassment, Abuse, and Violence Online*. Lincoln: Potomac Books, University of Nebraska Press.

Richards, I. A. 1965. *The Philosophy of Rhetoric*. New York: Oxford University Press.

Van Brunt, Brian, and W. Scott Lewis. 2014. *A Faculty Guide to Addressing Disruptive and Dangerous Behavior*. New York: Routledge.

Waldron, Jeremy. 2012. *The Harm in Hate Speech*. Cambridge, MA: Harvard University Press.

11

RHETORICAL IN(TER)VENTION
Teacher Guides for Responding to Covert Violence in Student Writing

Thomas Sura and Ellen Skirvin

Writing teachers encounter all manner of ill-formed arguments. Some lack citations. Others simply reiterate deep-seated beliefs. Still more neglect to argue a point, favoring instead to present "the facts" in order to let the reader decide. Mixed in with these tenuous rhetorical pursuits is another, even more dangerous, ill-formed argument. These arguments are the ones we can begin to identify as covertly violent. That is to say that even though they are not explicit, overt calls to physical violence, they inflict harm on others in less visible ways, and they threaten to perpetuate that harm. On top of that, without a clear definition of violence, they can be hard to identify as violent and even harder to respond to. This is especially true for new and developing teachers with little experience grappling with covert violence in student writing and even less guidance on how they might do so. In response to these challenges, this chapter presents three lines of argument for writing program administrators. The first line of argument is that Sonja K. Foss and Cindy L. Griffin's (Foss and Griffin 1995) conceptualization of invitational rhetoric as an alternative to traditional argumentation offers a usable means of identifying student writing that can be classified as *covert violence*—a form of "cultural violence" that is "deeply intertwined within the fabric of a culture's, and an individual's, existence" and not openly shown (Fleckenstein, Gage, and Bridgman 2017, 17). The second line of argument is that education on writing pedagogy must make room for training writing teachers to identify and respond to covert violence in student writing. Third, Foss and Griffin's invitational rhetoric provides a usable foundation for addressing covert violence in student writing through nonviolent means. Responding to covertly violent student writing through nonviolent means is especially important because, if writing programs and

https://doi.org/10.7330/9781646422791.c011

teachers neglect doing so, they both run the risk of perpetuating the very violence they wish to squelch.

The exigence for this chapter bloomed from a desire to synthesize experiences as a writing program administrator, existing composition scholarship, and program lore into something more tangible, usable, and shareable. As a writing program administrator, I have had important conversations with my institution's Office of Diversity, Equity, and Inclusion as well as other faculty and students to discuss and develop strategies for balancing institutional priorities like safe learning environments and free speech. In that work, I've learned about thresholds for appropriate, or at least "nonactionable," speech contingent upon equally ambiguous terms like severity, duration, and repetition. By "nonactionable" in this context, I mean student writing that would not pass a threshold for a university sanction of some kind, though, from a teacher's perspective, all student writing is actionable in the sense that teachers have the expectation and responsibility to act through response. It is in this action, and this approach to response, that this chapter seeks to offer a blueprint for guiding, or at the very least prompting, discussion about how writing programs and writing teachers might develop an informed and explicit practice of rhetorical in(ter)ventions when grappling with covert violence in student writing. This is especially vital because, without careful consideration of their principles, methods, and outcomes, writing teachers and writing programs may be susceptible to responding in kind to covertly violent writing—perpetuating the very ills that they see themselves eradicating.

DIVISIVENESS AND COVERT VIOLENCE IN STUDENT WRITING

Though related, divisive writing and covert violence in writing are two separate phenomena worth untangling. Divisive writing can be classified as any writing with polarized perspectives like political writing, writing on "hot-button" issues, or simply writing that elicits strong, opposing emotional reactions. By this definition, any subject has the potential to be divisive depending on how invested the discourse participants are. For example, in describing his pedagogy in the context of a history course, David Pace (2003) writes that "in the face of an issue that elicited powerful emotions [students] began to assume uncharacteristically extreme positions, and conflicts within the class threatened to poison interactions for the remainder of the course" (42). Divisive writing is marked by what scholar Deborah Tannen (2013) identifies as *agonism*— "taking a warlike stance in contexts that are not literally war—[which]

pervades our public and private discourse, leading us to approach issues and each other in an adversarial spirit" (177). Even though *agonism* exists in divisive writing, it does not necessarily make the writing covertly violent. Writing may be divisive but not covertly violent.

What, then, constitutes covert violence in writing? Writing teachers and writing programs must work to clarify when writing is divisive and when it is violent. This is not to say that anyone needs help identifying overt violence, in the sense of writing that might call explicitly for bodily harm to another, but instead refers to the ways that writing and rhetoric may demonstrate covert violence: a form of violence that is not so easily seen. Feminist scholar Sally Miller Gearhart (1979), for example, views "any intent to persuade as an act of violence" (195). Although this perspective has value, argues Susan C. Jarratt (1991), it may lead composition teachers to avoid conflict all together in favor of creating a supportive classroom climate (106). The danger in doing so, she contends, is in allowing oppressive perspectives to flourish unchecked. While each of these viewpoints provides valuable angles on discussions of student writing and classroom discourse, they do not quite provide the clarity needed for understanding the covert ways that violence may manifest itself in student writing or even in instructor response.

Invitational rhetoric, as described by Foss and Griffin (1995), provides a useful framework for writing teachers and writing programs to identify what can be classified as covert violence in writing. In their earliest conception of invitational rhetoric, Foss and Griffin identify three feminist principles undergirding the theory: equality, immanent value, and self-determination (4). The key to understanding covert violence in writing resides with the second principle Foss and Griffin describe: immanent value. By their definition, "the essence of this principle is that every being is a unique and necessary part of the pattern of the universe and thus has value" (4). I argue that covert violence occurs in writing when the writing, implicitly or explicitly, either rejects or positions others as having less value than the author. To borrow Tannen's language, writing that rejects immanent value aligns with an "agonistic" stance, one that sees "others as 'dumb' and therefore different from and opposed to oneself" (177). Real-world examples include the following:

- A white male student writes an essay arguing that Islam is inherently more violent than any other religion.
- A white female student writes an editorial arguing that the Confederate flag is only a symbol of Southern heritage.
- A male student writes a fictional narrative about a female teacher's private relationships.

- A heterosexual, cisgender student argues that homosexuals do not have the same legal right to marry as other people.
- A writing teacher who simply denigrates a student's writing as ignorant, uninformed, or wrong.

Any writing—or response, for that matter—that argues that an individual or group of people has any less value than others can be classified as covertly violent for three reasons. First, the writing rejects the principle of immanent value—the belief that the person is a necessary and valuable part of the universe. Second, the rejection of immanent value creates inequality, because it creates separation in terms of value between the author and the person or people identified in the writing. Whereas the author's humanity and value are assumed, the other's humanity and value are called into question. Third, by rejecting the principle of immanent value and creating inequality, the writing is covertly violent in that it does harm to another person or group. As rhetorical scholars Kristie Fleckenstein, Scott Gage, and Katherine Bridgman (Fleckenstein, Gage, and Bridgman 2017) suggest, "violence occurs when people are influenced in such a way that the current status of their physical and mental health is less than the promise of both their physical and mental potential" (17). To elaborate on one of the above examples plucked from the classroom, a writing teacher may encounter a student paper that uses cherry-picked quotations from a sacred text to argue that Islam is a violent religion. Though an argument like this is rife with logical fallacies and inadequate research, it can be classified as covertly violent because the argument creates separation between the author and the other—in this case, Muslims. It calls into question the value and humanity of the other. In sum, divisive writing does not automatically contain covert violence, but it may become covertly violent when it denies the immanent value of others. Furthermore, covertly violent writing—depending on the context—may not even be divisive, which cuts to the core of its insidiousness. Without explicit awareness of the concept of immanent value, the violence done in writing may slip past teachers and students alike while still perpetuating real harm. The principle of immanent value enables writing programs and teachers to name this writing for what it is.

By using the concept of immanent value, it becomes easier to distinguish covertly violent student writing from other student writing issues that may be related though not the same. Covert violence in writing is not simply writing that adopts a particular political ideology. Nor is covert violence in writing something that simply elicits a strong emotional response. It is something that denies the immanent value of others.

INVITATIONAL RHETORIC AS A FRAMEWORK FOR
NONVIOLENCE IN WRITING PROGRAMS

Developing tools and methods for helping teachers grapple with covert violence in writing must take a more prominent place in how we prepare teachers for the classroom. For evidence of this need, one might quickly look to the charged political and cultural climate in the United States. Movements like #BlackLivesMatter and #MeToo all point to groups continuing to fight for equality and recognition of their immanent value. The first-year writing classroom is one context where these issues can be explored and scrutinized. Though not prevalent, I've encountered the argument that first-year students should not write about provocative or controversial topics, because they cannot yet do so with the wisdom and sensitivity required. I can also recall my own hesitance and uncertainty when trying to grapple with provocative, divisive, and covertly violent writing as a graduate teacher. Moreover, recent scholarship suggests that even though the field grapples with subjects like race, individual programs must seek "curricular innovations" and "pedagogical interventions" to address the issue (Sanchez and Brannon 2016, 19). As rhetoric scholar Genevieve Garcia de Müeller (2016) suggests, simply "including texts by diverse authors is a political move but not a big enough one" (37). Taken together, the evidence suggests that writing programs cannot ignore the need for tools for engaging covertly violent writing. Because of their roles, writing program administrators can begin to change curriculum and pedagogy through the many administrative genres they create—from mission statements to writing exercises (McLeod 2007, 18). Using invitational rhetoric as a foundation, writing program administrators can develop the curricular innovations and pedagogical interventions that will help instructors grapple with contentious topics in the classroom while diminishing the possibility that divisive writing turns into covertly violent writing. They will also be better prepared to identify and contend with the covert violence that might otherwise escape notice.

By rooting the challenges of identifying and responding to covert violence in writing, the principles of invitational rhetoric also position invitational rhetoric as a means for addressing these challenges. As previously mentioned, Foss and Griffin (1995) describe invitational rhetoric from the outset as an alternative to traditional persuasion, understood as a form of domination. In their original articulation of the concept, they explain that "as far back as the Western discipline of rhetoric has been explored, rhetoric has been defined as the conscious intent to change others" and that "embedded in efforts to change others is a desire for control and domination, for the act of changing another establishes the power of the change agent over that other" (2). They argue that this traditional conception of rhetoric and the notion of "self-worth derived from and measured by the power exerted over others" contributes to the devaluing of the "life worlds of others" (3–4). To challenge, if not counteract, this violence, Foss and Griffin propose invitational rhetoric as a rhetoric based on three principles: equality, immanent value, and self-determination (3–4). Equality, they argue, is centered on intimacy, mutuality, and camaraderie rather than alienation, competition, and dehumanization. Immanent value, as described above, suggests that all people have value and are necessary. Finally, the third principle, self-determination, "allows individuals to make their own decisions about how they wish to live their lives." Through these principles, invitational rhetoric is identified by "the openness with which rhetors are able to approach their audiences," and, while change is possible through invitational rhetoric, what sets the approach apart from traditional conceptions of rhetoric is that change is not its explicit and intended purpose (4).

Invitational rhetoric cultivates nonviolence based on the premise that aggressive attacks or counterattacks don't actually change people's minds. Instead, they re-entrench the attitudes of others (Kroll 2008, 466). In other words, people don't change their minds; they just come to realize that they are in a context where their ideas are not shared. However, it is also possible that, by consciously eliminating attempts to dominate, invitational rhetoric can work to make space for growth and understanding. A common misperception of invitational rhetoric is that, without an explicit effort to change someone else's mind, invitational rhetoric also removes agency. Yet, as Jennifer Erling Bone, Cindy L. Griffin, and T. M. Linda Scholz (Bone, Griffin, and Scholz 2008) explain, "in invitational rhetoric, the agency or the means to act includes establishing an invitational environment built on the principles of safety (others have a right to their own views), value (views different than one's own are worthy), and freedom (people have the right to make choices that work for them)" (445). In this way, invitational rhetoric can make room to both welcome and challenge divisive rhetoric that is also covertly violent rhetoric, because that violence can be drawn out into the open, analyzed, and discussed.

For the WPA supporting teachers who wish to create writing assignments that foster engagement with controversial rhetoric—rhetoric that, while divisive, is not covertly violent—three principles that comprise invitational rhetoric are important, especially the concept and value of self-determination. It is axiomatic that within institutions there are hierarchies of power and privilege. While instructors occupy positions of power in their classrooms, often they do not benefit from the same power and privilege institutionally. This is especially true for instructors who are graduate students or adjunct faculty. In these frequently less privileged institutional roles, which also happen to comprise a large and growing number of writing instructors, instructors may find that explicitly identifying and practicing invitational rhetoric is a valuable approach to grappling with divisive and covertly violent writing—particularly as political tensions run high and debates swirl regarding free speech in educational contexts. By invoking self-determinacy, instructors can avoid the burden of changing a student's ideology while risking professional repercussions. Students remain in control of their own writing. Likewise, instructors remain in control of their own response. They choose what method of response is appropriate, to the degree that they are comfortable with. By explicitly invoking invitational rhetoric, writing programs, too, can support their instructors by explicitly introducing and enacting invitational rhetoric as a useful framework for thinking about and responding to divisive and covertly violent rhetoric, while leaving decisions about how and when to implement the framework in the hands of instructors. We sought to do exactly this in the revision of our instructor manual.

SHAPING PROGRAM DISCOURSE THROUGH PROGRAM DOCUMENTS

In addition to pedagogies and assignments for the classroom, writing programs can utilize documents meant to communicate policies and practices as sites to also foster the knowledge, skills, and attitudes necessary to achieve nonviolence. For example, I began to use my institution's instructor manual as a site to host a brief tool entitled "A Concise Guide for Responding to Divisive Student Writing."[1]

To adequately demonstrate conceptions of invitational rhetoric, the document we created had to do more than explain the concept. It had to demonstrate it. In other words, the document needed to move in function from manual to mentoring text in the same way that a teacher might present a well-crafted narrative to students as a loose guide to help them craft their own. Therefore, the drafting of this new section began with the complex question of how equality, immanent value, and self-determinacy could be reflected in document design.

These principles are demonstrated first and foremost through the document's medium and structure. The guide exists as a shared document with permissions that can be set so that anyone with the link and the appropriate account may view, comment, or edit it. The guide itself consists of six components:

- Why is Understanding Divisive Writing Important?
- How Do You Identify Divisive Writing?
- What are Key Principles for Responding?
- What Response Options are There?
- What Else Do Teachers Want to Know?

Each component contributes to the audience's experience by framing subjects as questions. In doing so, the document simultaneously aims to provide answers while also cultivating a dialogic *ethos* through its heuristic qualities, honoring the sharing of perspectives so integral to invitational rhetoric. The audience can take up the response offered or consider their own responses to the questions. To take this a step further, the structure of the document as well as the medium it is being presented in means that these sections are set up for growth and development. They are prompts for spurring conversation rather than dominating or ending it. For example, the section describing response options currently identifies offering, performing neutrality, and re-sourcement, yet it can just as easily include tactics like "turning to stand alongside one's opponent" described by composition scholar Barry Kroll (2008, 463). In this way, the document's medium and structure avoid domination by any one approach, offering instead multiple means of thinking about and practicing nonviolence in the writing classroom. Rather than prescribing a "correct" approach, it invites the instructors to accept, reject, or experiment with different approaches, deciding for themselves what to do.

As a preliminary test of the document's effectiveness, I shared this work and the guide itself with a graduate teacher, Ellen, in the undergraduate writing program. Ellen had been working within the undergraduate writing program to develop her own expertise on divisive and covertly violent writing, so she was already a valuable collaborator on the subject. As a type of pilot study, we recorded some of Ellen's responses to the document as a process of what Foss and Griffin (1995) describe as "offering"—"the giving of expression to a perspective without advocating its support or seeking its acceptance" (7). According to Foss and Griffin, "in offering, rhetors tell what they currently know or understand; they present their vision of the world and show how it looks or works for them" (1995, 7). Through offering, Ellen and I were able to create a dialogue on the design and outcomes of the guide as an example of invitational rhetoric—specifically in terms of how it does and does not achieve the goals of equality, immanent value, and self-determination. Importantly for other writing programs and writing teachers, offering as a practice is informal and conversational. It exists outside of conventional scholarly methodologies that demand high-stakes assessment or rigorous empirical protocols for "proving" something to be true. In this case, I offered the guide to Ellen, and Ellen offered her reading of it.

One of the salient themes that emerged from Ellen's offering was the openness and elimination of domination that invitational rhetoric aims to achieve. She writes,

> The most helpful aspect about the guide is that it lays out options for instructors rather than a strict code or steps to follow. From talking with fellow instructors, I find that we all have very different styles of instruction and levels of comfortability when dealing with student writing that challenges us, and there never seems to be a clear right or wrong approach.

This excerpt demonstrates the potential for invitational rhetoric for both sharing and modeling its precepts. Whereas writing program administration may often involve policy-writing that "establishes the power of the change agent over [the] other" (Foss and Griffin 1995, 3), the guide avoids that level of domination and encourages the audience to retain agency. Ellen continues,

> In addition, offering options rather than commands makes me feel trusted and supported by my colleagues at the university. It shows me that they recognize the diversity of experiences, perspectives, and techniques among instructors, and provides us the flexibility to decide the best approach for our classroom.

This sentiment resonates strongly with what Foss and Griffin (1995) articulate about equality. Quoting bell hooks (1984), they argue that "efforts to dominate and gain power over others cannot be used to develop relationships of equality, so feminists seek to replace the 'alienation, competition, and dehumanization' that characterize relationships of domination with 'intimacy, mutuality, and camaraderie'" (4). To emphasize, I am no more advocating that writing program administrators replace all policies with suggestions than Foss and Griffin were suggesting that all argument should be supplanted by invitational rhetoric. Rather, the takeaway for writing program administrators is that there are alternatives to policies of domination that support instructor agency and equality within a writing program.

Like the document's structure, the style also works rhetorically to demonstrate the principles of invitational rhetoric. To further promote equality, it was important for the document to eliminate lexical elements of dominance, power, and elitism. In their discussion of offering, Foss and Griffin (1995) argue that discursive forms make a difference. "Offering," they contend, "also is marked by discursive forms such as 'I tried this solution when that happened to me; I thought it worked well' or 'What would happen if we introduced the idea of _____ into this problem?' rather than statements with forms such as 'You really ought to do _____' or 'Your idea is flawed because you failed to take into account _____' " (8). Therefore, I sought to remove language that reinforced perceived power structures, deleting or revising words like *should, ought,* and *must* wherever possible, for example. This move was important because, from a programmatic standpoint, one of the ways that WPAs assert their power and authority is through policies that *require.* Likewise, over seven years and 150-plus teaching observations, I have witnessed the ways writing teachers reinforce their own power and authority by making decisions for students. Whether it is the number of sources for a project or the arrangement of a writing portfolio, I have often heard writing teachers (myself included) begin statements with phrases like "I want . . ." and "You have to. . . ." In this way, they often unnecessarily reinforce the already existing power differential in the classroom. By presenting options instead of making choices, this document rhetorically shifts power to the instructors and embodies the principle of self-determination. Likewise, writing teachers may begin to make more conscious or unconscious efforts to do the same in their classrooms by reducing the number of decisions they make for the students and increasing the number of options they present.

One notable exception to this approach involves student writing that threatens overt physical violence, or any writing that identifies Title IX issues such as sexual assault, sexual harassment, and stalking. Ethically and institutionally, writing teachers must report these concerns, and, while it is possible to imagine an audience suggesting that these exceptions enervate the salience of invitational rhetoric, it is also necessary to point out that safety, too, is a necessary external condition for invitational rhetoric. These exceptions do not weaken invitational rhetoric but rather enhance and ensure a safe environment in which the approach, and the critical thinking it enables, might thrive. Offering strategies for nonviolence does not mean that responses cannot be direct or even forceful when necessary.

In addition to equality, the document works to promote self-determinacy through the heuristic used to define divisive writing and covert violence. It also promotes this principle through the subsequent section on response options. As evident in Ellen's offering, consensus for responding to divisive and violent writing is not easy to come by:

> Recently, a fellow instructor and I helped lead a discussion with other instructors on the topic of "Having Difficult Conversations with Students." Although we had some shared techniques on this topic, we also found it difficult to come to a consensus on the most productive way to have a difficult conversation.

There is a substantial body of scholarly work addressing how instructors can respond to writing on provocative subjects, divisive issues, and covert violence (Sura 2017; Abraham 2011; Lynch 2009, Kopelson 2003; Pace 2003). To help address this concern, the guide presents condensed versions of some of these approaches along with citations—like so many bread crumbs—to help instructors read more deeply about the approaches. Ellen's offering helps to affirm the value in this approach for several reasons, even when instructors may ultimately reject one possibility:

> One of the options that the guide recommends is Kopelson's suggested method of "performing neutrality." After reading more on the subject and reflecting on my own experiences, I found that I had automatically attempted this approach as a new instructor. I feared my students might not trust or respect my point of view, so I consciously concealed my beliefs. While I feel this approach may have provided a sense of trust with my students, the performance of neutrality at times felt too dishonest or inauthentic. I often agonized over whether rhetorical samples I provided for my class, such as op-eds or political cartoons, leaned too politically in a certain direction or did not provide a fair balance. The guide does not explore this dichotomy in depth, but it does reference other readings that might help instructors think about the best approach for their classroom when performing neutrality.

In sharing the options for responding to divisive and covertly violent writing, instructors have a framework of possibilities. What is especially interesting in Ellen's offering is both the identification of performing neutrality as something attempted and the analysis of how it worked for her in her own experience. As an outcome, it is less important for an instructor to once and for all choose an approach than it is to encounter multiple valid possibilities and—through reflective practice—arrive at their own conclusions.

Ellen's offering provides a specific example of this process of choice and reflection. First, Ellen expresses some discomfort with the strategy of performing neutrality, writing, "My anxieties about performing neutrality made me reflect on some of my early experiences teaching and how I might have stopped a student's 'thinking' when encountering divisive rhetoric." Second, she gives an example from her own teaching:

> For example, during one of my classes, we discussed possible research topics as a class to garner some ideas for research papers. One of my students mentioned that "welfare" would be an interesting topic, particularly because they personally knew people who "game" the system and live lavishly off of their benefits. Another one of my students, visibly upset, said that the people they knew on welfare were hardworking people who received very few benefits. I felt uncomfortable responding to the students' disagreement, especially in front of the full class, because I did not want the class to think I was "picking sides." My performance of neutrality paralyzed me as an instructor.

Next, Ellen describes her resolution of the issue in the moment:

> To diffuse the situation, I told the students that they could both choose to write a paper about ways to improve welfare programs, such as eliminating loopholes or increasing benefits. This tactic allowed me to lend credibility to both arguments without revealing my own beliefs. I ended the conversation in order to avoid conflict and remain neutral.

Finally, Ellen reflects on what she might have done differently:

> However, after reflecting on that moment and reading the guide, I feel like I missed an opportunity. I stopped my students' "thinking" about the topic during a crucial moment of conflict and divisiveness. Reflecting back on the experience, I would have liked to have used the thermostatic method to challenge the students' use of rhetoric, open their perspectives, and strengthen their arguments. For example, I might ask them whether they believe relying on personal experience or observations would be enough credible evidence to support their arguments about welfare programs.

At this point, it is important to note that Ellen's initial reaction wasn't wrong and in need of correction. Quite the contrary. The issue revealed in Ellen's offering is her feeling of dissatisfaction with the original outcome and the identification of another possibility. As rhetorical in(ter)vention, the guide helps to facilitate the invention of other possibilities generated by the individual instructor's experience. Just as Foss and Griffin position invitational rhetoric as an alternative to the paternalistic bias in traditional conceptions of rhetoric, here, as Ellen's responses indicate, the guide offers alternatives for responding to student writing that is divisive and/or covertly violent and, in doing so, creates opportunities for reflection on action while leaving agency and choice in the hands of the instructor. This dynamic reinforces the principle of self-determinacy by creating space for instructors to develop their own solutions based on their own experiences and to decide for themselves how to deploy them.

Finally, in the spirit of invitational rhetoric, Ellen's offering extends the work of the guide presented here in three meaningful ways. First, Ellen questions the very foundation of what the guide is supposed to do:

> While the guide focuses on responding to divisive writing, I think that it should also focus on anticipating divisive writing before it happens. Should we instruct our students in a way that avoids divisive writing? Or should we invite divisive writing in order to respond to it?

The questions Ellen poses are vital to continued development and expert understanding of how instructors respond to divisive and covertly violent writing. Remaining true to invitational rhetoric, however, requires instructors and writing program administrators to avoid, or at least remain skeptical of, dominating answers to these questions because answers may vary from person to person and place to place.

Next, Ellen begins to theorize a pedagogy in the vein of critical cultural studies that more fully engages with equality, immanent value, and self-determinacy, which in the later work of Bone, Griffin, and Scholz (2008) are refined as safety, value, and freedom.

> The discussion on comparing "writing" to "thinking" begins to explore this idea, but I think more options to address this would be helpful. For example, one option might focus on instructing students to think about rhetoric as broadening an audience's perspective rather than winning an argument, as Sonja Foss and Cindy Griffin suggest. Defining rhetoric as an empathetic act rather than a zero-sum game might avoid divisive rhetoric before it starts.

Finally, Ellen argues for more information. There is a distinct sense that the guide merely scratches the surface and more information will be useful for continued development.

> Overall, I would like to see more options to choose from within the guide that represent a range of methods, theories, and techniques. Other options might include Paul Lynch's thermostatic method, Barry Kroll's method of rhetorical aikido, or Arthur Brooks' study on anger versus contempt. While I understand too many options may seem overwhelming, I think a working list of options to continually expand upon will give instructors the agency and comfortability to find the method that works best for them in a given situation. A broader menu of options also highlights the diversity of perspectives and definitions of divisive rhetoric across all instructors.

While Ellen argues for more, her offering also demonstrates an awareness that more can at some point become too much. Nonetheless, because of the relatively easy refinement of the document as a digital artifact, there is nothing that prevents the brief guide from remaining brief while also linking to another, richer resource (like an annotated bibliography) that instructors can use to delve even deeper into the subject.

CONCLUSION

Divisive and covertly violent writing are enduring challenges in writing instruction. Although ample scholarship aims to address these issues case by case and classroom by classroom, writing programs must make greater strides in weaving our knowledge of divisive and covertly violent writing into the very fabric of our programs. Invitational rhetoric provides a useful and positive foundation for writing programs as well as for new and developing teachers because of its commitment to reducing and eliminating the patriarchal bias inherent in argumentation. It challenges WPAs and instructors to seek equality, to recognize value, and to promote freedom in their programs and classrooms. Moreover, strategies such as offering, as a rhetorical form rooted in sharing what one knows, extending one another's ideas, and coming to a new understanding of a subject, provide a blueprint for spurring these discussions and the insights they can bring.

I recognize that some may find an invitational rhetoric framework unsatisfying or insufficient when each day brings new examples of the overt and covert violence plaguing our nation and world. Yet, true to the rhetorical form I offer here, such a rejection is perfectly acceptable. The intent is not to dominate other approaches to contending with students' writing on divisive subjects. It is, rather, to continue to revise and improve, and I hope that other writing programs may choose to build on or extend this offering in new and thought-provoking ways. While domination and superiority are not the goals of invitational rhetoric, it is not powerless. Foss and Griffin (1995) conclude their original article on the subject by suggesting that "invitational rhetoric . . . may transform an oppressive system precisely because it does not engage that system on its own terms, using arguments developed from the system's framework and orientation" (17). It is a simple logic: if writing teachers aim to reduce, diminish, and ultimately change the "agonistic" discourse that Tannen (2013) decries, then they must practice, teach, and model an alternative.

Acknowledgments. The author would like to extend a special thanks to Lexi Brown, an undergraduate researcher, for her contributions to early work on this chapter. Ms. Brown was a participant in West Virginia University's Research Apprenticeship Program (RAP).

NOTES

1.   For a full copy of the document, contact the authors at sura@hope.edu.

REFERENCES

Abraham, Matthew. 2011. "Response to Paul Lynch's 'Composition as a Thermostatic Activity.' " *College Composition and Communication* 62, no. 4: 739–42.

Bone, Jennifer Erling, Cindy L. Griffin, and T. M. Linda Scholz. 2008. "Beyond Traditional Conceptualizations of Rhetoric: Invitational Rhetoric and a Move Toward Civility." *Western Journal of Communication* 72, no. 4: 434–62. doi.org/10.1080/10570310802446098.

Fleckenstein, Kristie S., Scott Gage, and Katherine Bridgman. 2017. "A Pedagogy of Rhetorical Looking: Atrocity Images at the Intersection of Vision and Violence." *College English* 80, no. 1: 11–34. https://search-proquestcom.www.libproxy.wvu.edu/docview/1935730238?accountid=2837.

Foss, Sonja K., and Cindy L. Griffin. 1995. "Beyond Persuasion: A Proposal for an Invitational Rhetoric." *Communication Monographs* 62, no. 1: 2–18. doi:10.1080/03637759509376345.

García de Müeller, Genevieve. 2016. "WPA and the New Civil Rights Movement." *WPA: Writing Program Administration* 39, no. 2: 36–42.

Gearhart, Sally Miller. 1979. "The Womanization of Rhetoric." *Women's Studies International Quarterly* 2, no. 2: 195–201. doi.org/10.1016/S0148-0685(79)91809-8.

hooks, bell. 1984. *Feminist Theory: From Margin to Center.* Boston: South End.

Jarratt, Susan C. 1991. "Feminism and Composition: The Case for Conflict." In *Contending with Words: Composition and Rhetoric in a Postmodern Age,* edited by Patricia Harken and John Schilb, 105–23. New York: Modern Language Association of America.

Kopelson, Karen. 2003. "Rhetoric on the Edge of Cunning; Or, the Performance of Neutrality (Re)Considered as a Composition Pedagogy for Student Resistance." *College Composition and Communication* 55, no. 1: 115–46.

Kroll, Barry. 2008. "Arguing with Adversaries: Aikido, Rhetoric, and the Art of Peace." *College Composition and Communication* 59, no. 3: 451–72.

Lynch, Paul. 2009. "Composition as a Thermostatic Activity." *College Composition and Communication* 60, no. 4: 728–45.

McLeod, Susan H. 2007. *Writing Program Administration.* West Lafayette: Parlor Press.

Pace, David. 2003. "Controlled Fission: Teaching Supercharged Subjects." *College Teaching* 51, no. 2 (Spring): 42–45. http://www.jstor.org/stable/27559130.

Sanchez, James Chase, and Tyler S. Brannon. 2016. "The Role of Composition Programs in De-Normalizing Whiteness in the University: Programmatic Approaches to Anti-Racist Pedagogies." *WPA: Writing Program Administration* 39, no. 2: 47–52.

Sura, Thomas. 2017. "What Counts as Inclusive?: Articulating Writing Program Stances on Divisive Student Writing." *Present Tense* 6, no. 2. https://www.presenttensejournal.org/volume-6/what-counts-as-inclusive-articulating-writing-program-stances-on-divisive-studentwriting/.

Tannen, Deborah. 2013. "The Argument Culture: Agonism and the Common Good," *Daedalus* 142, no. 2: 177–84. doi.org/10.1162/DAED_a_00211.

12

TRAINING TUTORS TO RESPOND
The Potential Violence of Addressing Sexual Violence Disclosures in the Writing Center

Krista Speicher Sarraf

In October 2017, the #MeToo hashtag on Twitter focused worldwide attention on sexual violence. As evidenced by the stories of sexual violence that poured out in the following months, the #MeToo hashtag inspired many survivors of sexual violence to disclose their experiences in writing via the #MeToo hashtag. In the wake of #MeToo, tutors at my writing center, where I was the assistant director, voiced their concerns about an increase in the number of sexual violence disclosures shared during tutorials. Tutors' concerns led to a subsequent study about sexual violence disclosures in the writing center, in which sixty percent of tutors who participated reported having tutored a student for a paper about sexual violence.[1] With more than half of the participants confronting such disclosures in our writing center, we could no longer ignore the potential for exacerbating survivors' experiences of sexual violence in writing center consultations.

In this chapter, I argue that writing centers must develop strategies for preparing tutors to address sexual violence disclosures during consultations. Writing about sexual violence may involve extreme emotional and physiological responses, which, if mishandled, can lead to traumatization of both tutees and tutors. To intervene in the potential violence caused by conversations during writing tutorials about sexual violence, tutors need to know how to have supportive conversations, how to enforce their own boundaries, and how to care for themselves during this emotional work. In this post-#MeToo world, it is not supplemental work to prepare tutors for the range of writing they might encounter; it is imperative work. This chapter responds to that imperative, addressing incidents of sexual violence disclosures in my writing center and offering strategies to prepare tutors to respond with minimal harm. First, I discuss the intersecting forms of violence in sexual violence disclosures

https://doi.org/10.7330/9781646422807.c012

in the writing center present in university mandates, tutorials, and tutor trainings. Then, I articulate an intervention for addressing sexual violence in writing center work, detailing my approach to tutor preparation in my writing center. The chapter ends with a focus on how other writing centers can design and implement tutor training to intervene in the potential violence of such disclosures.

UNRAVELING THE WEB OF VIOLENCE

To understand how to prepare tutors to address sexual violence disclosures in the writing center, we must unravel the intersecting forms of violence involved in such disclosures. After all, sexual violence disclosures in the writing center are enormously complex, as the potential for violence in tutorials is layered and intersecting. When a student discloses sexual violence to a tutor, both the student and the tutor must navigate university mandates that may require the tutor to report the disclosure to the Title IX Office. Moreover, the conversation within the tutorial itself could retraumatize the student who is disclosing, as well as tutors who are survivors of sexual violence but must negotiate such disclosures. A third complexity enters the equation when writing centers consider approaches to tutor preparation for responding to sexual violence: tutor training about sexual violence is a necessary step toward intervening in the potential violence of disclosures in the writing center; yet tutor training may retraumatize tutors who are survivors of sexual violence. In this section, I review the intersecting forms of violence in university mandates, tutorials, and trainings, and I connect each form of violence to the work of writing center tutors.

University Mandates

Designed to protect students, university mandates such as Title IX, a regulation that outlines processes for handling sexual assault and harassment cases on federally-funded United States college campuses, can enact violence by potentially eroding survivors' agency, defined as the degree of control an individual has over their own behavior or body (Duranti 2004). University mandates undermine that agency in four main ways. First, the discourse of university mandates paints survivors as complainants of alleged crimes rather than as survivors with agency. Consider this excerpt from Indiana University of Pennsylvania's (2018) policy on "Sexual Harassment and Sexual Violence": "Complainants may want to consider carefully whether they share personally identifiable details with non-confidential employees, as those details must be shared by the employee with the Title IX Coordinator" (1). The word "complainants" in the above policy withholds survivorship status, discursively shaping perceptions of the survivor. Critical Discourse Analysis (CDA) reminds us that words like "complainant" are not ideology-free. CDA focuses on the "ideological nature of language" (Fairclough 1989, 3), in which language is not merely referential, but formative, especially in terms of a culture's belief systems. Language reflects ideology, and ideology shapes how societies view who should (or should not) have power (2). Although my goal here is not to conduct a full analysis of IUP's (2018) policy, a concordance of the policy in AntConc[2] reveals patterns in the discourse: the top content words include *sexual, complaint, violence, IX, University,* and *alleged.* The word "student" (rank forty-one, frequency sixteen) is a lower-ranked and less frequent word, as is "victim" (rank sixty-one, frequency nine), and the word "survivor" does not appear at all. In this way, the language in this document focuses on the "alleged" "complaint," reminding survivors of the tentativeness of their reality and their lack of power in the legal process.

Second, because Title IX designates mandatory reporters, the survivors' agency is compromised as they lose control over the terms and situation of disclosure. The policy (2018) states, "Failure of employees to report an incident or incidents of Misconduct of which they become aware, may be a violation of University policy subject to disciplinary action" (1). Because employees who do not comply with Title IX may be "subject to disciplinary action" (1), employees, including writing center tutors, are incentivized to comply with the university mandate. Although such mandates might intend to protect the campus community by helping the university to maintain records and reports of misconduct, these mandates may constitute a form of violence by taking away the survivor's control over the terms and situation of disclosure. Consider this excerpt from the policy: "If a complainant does not wish for their name to be shared, does not wish for an investigation to take place, or does not want a formal resolution to be pursued, the complainant may make such a request to the Title IX Coordinator, who will evaluate that request in light of the duty to ensure the safety of the campus and comply with federal law. In cases indicating pattern, predation, threat, weapons and/ or violence, IUP may be unable to honor the complainant's request for confidentiality, investigation or pursuit of formal resolution" (2). Here, survivors are informed that, although they may request confidentiality, the Title IX Coordinator may disregard the survivor's request in the name of campus safety and compliance. I do not mean to suggest that the safety of the campus and compliance with the law are unimportant. My concern is that the discourse in the above excerpt ascribes agency to the institution while potentially stripping the survivor's control over the terms and conditions of disclosure. Those survivors who wish to remain confidential and who do not wish to pursue an investigation may not have a choice once the Title IX Coordinator learns of the misconduct. Because Title IX training requires tutors to report any disclosures concerning sexual violence and obligates them to share this fact to students who may disclose, survivors are presented with a choice: either share their experience in an attempt at human connection with a tutor and have their story reported to Title IX—or remain silent.

Third, university mandates erode survivor agency through silencing, for survivors, concerned that that they will lose control of the disclosure if they write about or talk about sexual violence, may lack the space to share their stories and seek the support that they need. Survivors may shy away from writing about sexual violence for fear of a tutor reporting them to the Title IX Coordinator. Specifically, university mandates may encourage students to produce writing that includes limited details about the sexual assault. The policy (2018) warns survivors against sharing personally identifiable details with non-confidential employees: "Complainants may want to consider carefully whether they share personally identifiable details with non-confidential employees, as those details must be shared by the employee with the Title IX Coordinator." This language highlights potentially negative consequences of disclosure. Thus, university mandates may deny survivors' agency by inadvertently discouraging survivors from sharing details in their writing for fear those details will be shared with the Title IX Coordinator. This second erosion of agency is particularly troubling because writing about the experience of sexual violence is potentially healing. As John MacDevitt (2013) points out, students tend to write about trauma because "they want to air their pain" (145). Thus, writing is an important outlet for traumatized students, and the writing center needs to ensure that students can write freely. However, documents like the "IUP Sexual Harassment and Sexual Violence Policy" curtail these students' voices and violate survivors' agency to speak and write about trauma in ways that invite healing.

Fourth, university mandates like Title IX also erode tutor agency and, thus, the ability for tutors to adequately help survivors or offer a supportive conversation. Because tutors must comply with Title IX, they are presented with several challenges. For one, tutors must become familiar with Title IX regulations, which are rather nebulous, so that tutors will know when to report incidents to the Title IX Coordinator. One tutor, Bobby, highlights the anomalous nature of the mandate. For example, he described an incident in which he tutored a student who shared with him a paper about her experience with ongoing sexual abuse while she was in high school. According to Title IX, Bobby must report any incidents of abuse of minors, even if the disclosure of abuse appears in writing. However, the student's paper did not mention her age at the time of the abuse; although she delineated that the incident happened when she was in high school, she may have been eighteen or over at the time. In this moment, Bobby was required to understand Title IX guidelines well enough to know the nuances of reporting abuse of minors, even when the disclosure is in a paper and even though writing tutors normally are only required to disclose verbal disclosures of sexual violence. And yet, without being certain about the student's age at the time of the abuse, Bobby was exempt from reporting. Thus, the first challenge to tutor agency is the abstruse constraints posed by the complex landscape of Title IX documents. This burden further erodes tutor agency in that, while Bobby may wish to focus on empathizing with the student, he must juggle Title IX's overly complex regulations.

Not only does the complex nature of Title IX regulations potentially erode tutors' control over how they respond to students who write about trauma, but Title IX regulations require tutors to prioritize reporting over other potentially more appropriate responses, like listening and empathizing. In Bobby's case, he was able to exercise some control over his response to the student. Instead of probing the student for details about her age, which might require him to report, Bobby prioritized empathizing with the student by acknowledging to her that he felt "sadness for the student." It is unclear whether Bobby offered empathy instead of reporting because he was uncertain about when to report or because he wanted to respect the student's control over the conversation. Regardless of Bobby's reason for prioritizing empathy, what is clear is that university mandates impact the work of tutors like Bobby by presenting a challenging situation in which the tutor must choose how to navigate compliance with the Title IX Office while offering empathy and respecting the student's agency.

Furthermore, Title IX regulations compromise tutor agency by limiting their choices in determining how deeply to engage with content that triggers their own past traumas. In other words, because tutors are mandatory reporters, tutors may not be able to walk away from triggering conversations about sexual violence or reduce their exposure to retraumatizing details of assault. Since Title IX does not attend to the fact that mandatory reporters like tutors may be survivors themselves, it potentially erodes tutors' agency to control how to navigate their own survivorship. Title IX mandates may do more harm than good to tutors, in terms of both how tutors can respond to students who write about or disclose trauma and how tutors can enforce boundaries to attend to their own mental health.

Tutorials

In addition to the problem posed by Title IX mandates to survivor and tutor agency, tutorials themselves can become sites of potential violence. Tutors' responses and approaches to sexual violence disclosures within consultations may participate in a larger complex web of violence. During writing center tutorials involving disclosures of sexual violence, tutors must carefully choose the language they use when speaking with students who write about trauma to mitigate the potential of retraumatization. As tutors navigate these sessions, there is risk of both student and tutor experiencing retraumatization. Such experiences can exacerbate the initial violence of the sexual assault, since talking about trauma with someone who lacks knowledge of the appropriate language to use with survivors may create a physical, visceral sense of revisiting the initial trauma. Writing center tutorials may evoke the memories of the original sexual violence and cause additional harm as survivors interact with tutors who may buy into cultural rape myths or who may be unversed in the problematic nature of discourses about sexual violence.

A lack of tutor training about how to interact with and talk with traumatized students is an issue, as tutors may subscribe to dominant discourses about sexual violence that give rise to inappropriate and potentially damaging responses to writing about sexual violence. These discourses and narratives derive from social norms and may be circulated by mass media. As Wendy Hesford (1999) writes, "the American mass media tend to focus on victims and perpetrators' psychological states rather than on the sociological, political, and material forces that facilitate and sustain violence" (196). Tutors may be unaware of problematic ideologies and social norms, such as the belief that modest dress or avoiding alcohol can protect someone from sexual violence. Thus, tutoring sessions may be potential sites of violence if tutors lack an understanding of sexual violence and talk about sexual violence in potentially damaging ways.

Specifically, tutors may use language that could disenfranchise students who disclose their experiences with sexual violence. One such language choice that tutors might make is whether to use the term "victim" or "survivor" when conversing with students who write about sexual violence. This word choice may not be without consequence. In Michael Papendick and Gerd Bohner's (Papendick and Bohner 2017) study of the effects of the label "survivor" versus the effects of the label "victim," they found that "overall, 'survivor' was associated with positive valence, activity, strength, and optimism, whereas 'victim' was associated more with negative valence, passivity, weakness, and helplessness" (16). Even though their study's participants held more positive associations with the term "survivor," those who have experienced sexual violence may have different preferences. To some, the word "victim" might allow the individual to view the experience as a crime, which could be empowering. Thus, tutors in writing tutorials must carefully choose their language and discern (or ask) the tutee's preference when talking about the student's experience with sexual violence.

Since the conversations about sexual violence during tutorials can constitute a form of violence, it is important that tutors are prepared for these conversations.[3] In my interviews with tutors, participants noted the challenges that language posed during tutorials with students who disclose sexual violence experiences. Specifically, tutors pointed to the challenge of speaking to students about the content of their writing that relates to sexual violence without upsetting or triggering the student. Bobby said, "I want to pick my words very carefully because I don't know if I say something it's going to trigger [the tutee] and if she's going to fall apart." Another tutor, Elizabeth, said, "You don't want to put the [tutee] in the spotlight, like did you do this? Did this happen to you? You don't want to make them feel uncomfortable." In both cases, tutors were concerned about their word choice during tutorials and were aware that a poor choice of words could cause issues for the traumatized student. Thus, tutoring sessions with papers about sexual violence impact the work of writing tutors as tutors navigate their word choice during these tutorials.

A tutor responding to a student who has disclosed sexual violence may also experience secondary trauma, which occurs when tutors experience symptoms of PTSD because of exposure to stories of sexual violence (Harrison and Westwood 2009). As readers of student writing, tutors "witness" trauma, and their automatic responses may resemble those of someone with firsthand trauma. Therefore, tutorials are potential sites for violence, because reading student writing about sexual violence can traumatize tutors. This traumatization can be exacerbated if tutors have their own traumatic experiences with sexual violence.

Tutors who are survivors of sexual violence themselves may be impacted by consultations with students who disclose, in both beneficial and detrimental ways.[4] On one hand, Elizabeth illustrates how a tutor with personal experience of sexual violence may be well equipped to navigate these sessions. In my interview with Elizabeth, she noted that "this stuff doesn't really phase me because I've kind of been there done that in terms of those grey areas, those kinds of things have happened to me." Elizabeth said her background can be an asset during tutoring, as she connects with people on a deep level when she talks to them and knows when to stop. Because of Elizabeth's own background with sexual violence, she understands boundaries, such as not wanting others to ask many questions, and she applies those boundaries to tutorials. Elizabeth later conceded, "I know it can be tough to write about [sexual violence], too. I get triggered when I write about it." Tutors like Elizabeth who are also survivors of sexual violence may be well prepared for these tutorials.

Conversely, tutoring a student who writes about sexual violence could be challenging and even retraumatizing for other tutors. Although tutors who are survivors of sexual violence may use their experiences to navigate tutoring sessions on these topics, these tutors may also be reminded of their own traumas when they read papers about sexual violence. Bobby pointed to the concern for retraumatization "if there is a tutor who has experience with sexual assault reading stuff like that where it may trigger not only them but the tutee who is experiencing it." Whereas students who bring writing about sexual violence to the writing center do so voluntarily and may be more prepared to disclose, tutors who encounter this writing may not be prepared for the emotional labor of being reminded of their own traumas. As a result, tutors who are survivors themselves need options for managing or even opting out of working conditions at the writing center that may negatively impact their mental health.

Trainings

As we consider the impact of writing about sexual violence in the writing center, we must also consider the potential violence of trainings aimed at preparing students to address this kind of writing. For tutors with firsthand experience of sexual violence or other traumas, a mandatory tutor training may create an unhealthy work environment in which the writing center requires the tutor to endure a retraumatizing experience in the name of helping other traumatized students.[5] Thus, the challenge that writing centers face is to be mindful of tutors' traumas while preparing tutors with responses and approaches useful for these consultations. Below, I describe one such tutor preparation that I designed with the aim of equipping tutors with the skills to navigate tutorials about sexual violence.

TUTOR PREPARATION

Because sexual violence impacts the work of writing tutors, it is imperative that writing centers prepare tutors to respond to students and to practice self-care. Here, I describe my writing center's work to prepare tutors for these interactions. At our writing center's Fall 2018 staff meeting, I delivered a workshop titled "When Students Write about Trauma: Techniques for Tutoring." The training focused on discussing trauma and PTSD broadly, with some specific conversations of sexual violence. Below, I describe this training and how the study I conducted to understand sexual violence disclosures in my writing center guided my choices in design.

The workshop presented what I call trauma-informed tutoring, or tutoring that draws on the knowledge and practice of trauma-informed education (Tang 2011, 304), which emphasizes making trauma education less harmful for participants. Trauma-informed educational practices support the training of educators in academic settings to respond to psychological trauma. As Catherine Tang (2011) writes, trauma-informed training includes two goals: (1) to train educators, counselors, and others to understand trauma psychology and to protect against misapplications of knowledge about trauma, and (2) to design trauma education to "prevent students from feeling overwhelmed by the traumatic material" (310). I applied Tang's (2011) goals for trauma-informed training to the writing center context to prepare tutors to understand trauma, to respond to student writing about trauma, and to manage their exposure to traumatic material, including student papers and the writing center training itself.

The workshop I describe here was delivered for twenty-five tutors and writing center staff-members, including our director and secretary, during a writing center all-staff meeting on September 9, 2018. Throughout this ninety-minute workshop, I talked about trauma rather than only sexual violence so that tutors could apply the content to a range of scenarios and so that tutors with experiences of sexual violence may feel more comfortable in the workshop. Also, I established several guidelines for the workshop:

- You are free to step out for a break at any point.
- You are free to avert your gaze from materials.
- Conversations will focus on fictional scenarios. If you wish to talk about scenarios, please pose them as hypotheticals or in the third person.
- Respect the privacy of tutees and others you know who have experienced trauma. You may share examples of tutorials you've encountered, but please exclude identifying information.

I explained that these guidelines were in place to remind participants of their agency to decide how they approach the workshop, an important first step before delving into any triggering content. I then shared our study's results to encourage buy-in from tutors about the workshop's importance and relevance to their work as tutors, before sharing the workshop's objectives:

- Tutors will learn about trauma, PTSD, and sexual violence so they have key knowledge needed to support survivors who disclose in the writing center.
- Tutors will learn supportive responses to students who write about trauma.
- Tutors will learn ways to set boundaries and care for themselves as tutors.

After we established learning objectives, two representatives from an on-campus organization, the Haven Project, shared their thirty-minute lecture-style presentation, which aimed to build tutors' knowledge of sexual violence, including identifying physical and emotional effects of trauma, responding to someone who has been traumatized, using strategies for coping, and developing awareness of additional resources. To improve tutors' knowledge of the prevalence of sexual violence, this presentation opened with statistics about the pervasiveness of sexual violence to ensure a shared understanding of the topic.[6] After sharing facts, the presenters then described the physical and emotional effects of trauma, including symptoms such as survivors experiencing changes in sleep patterns and feeling panicked or out of control. Because we acknowledge that workshop participants may have experienced these symptoms, this section of the workshop lasted only five minutes to mitigate the potentially triggering nature of this content. Then, the presentation focused on how to respond to someone who shows symptoms of trauma. Suggested responses included believing the person and being ready for a range of emotions. Because we wanted to build tutors' repertoires for supportive responses, this presentation then suggested that tutors can offer helpful coping strategies, such as writing about the experience and mobilizing a support team if survivors express interest in this kind of help. The presentation concluded with additional resources, including campus and community hotlines for survivors.

Once participants developed a shared knowledge of trauma and a sense of the resources on campus, the second portion of the training began: I led a sixty-minute interactive workshop focused on techniques for tutoring. In Part 2, entitled, "When Students Write about Trauma: Techniques for Tutoring," the discussion focused on three skills for handling tutorials focusing on writing about trauma: (1) empathetic listening, (2) assertiveness, and (3) coping and self-care. In this highly interactive session, characterized by open-ended questions and hands-on activities focused on the nitty-gritty of communication, tutors were encouraged to think broadly about how to apply these three techniques and to imagine sessions where the student has written not only about trauma but also about other emotionally trying sessions, such as those in which the student felt upset about a grade or seemed apathetic about their paper.

First, participants learned about empathetic listening, a choice guided by our study's interview data that reflected different comfort levels with empathetic listening. To illustrate, Elizabeth reported a high level of empathy, explaining that she uses her facial expression to connect with the student and to communicate, "Oh, I'm so sorry this happened." Through her expression of empathy, she and the tutee discuss "how things kind of are and how to deal with them." When I asked Elizabeth for an example, she described talking about sexual violence as a societal issue and discussing with tutees how people react when sexual violence comes up in conversation. Conversely, Bobby described his discomfort in responding to a student who disclosed: "There was a sense of uncomfortableness when I wanted to ask her specific questions about the story, but then I withheld it."[7] Bobby's comment suggests that tutors may stick to matters of writing because they do not know how to offer empathy or address the sexual violence disclosure. Thus, during the tutor training, participants discussed definitions of empathy and their prior experiences with giving and receiving empathy, watched a short YouTube video that offers a definition of empathy, and practiced empathetic nonverbal communication and verbal communication with a partner. These activities helped participants to develop a shared definition of empathetic listening as listening to hear the other person's feelings, needs, and requests without trying to fix things, a definition adapted from Marshall B. Rosenberg's (2003) *Nonviolent Communication*. The role-playing activity encouraged participants to practice the techniques of empathetic listening and to reflect on how it feels to be empathetically listened to. Participants then debriefed with a large-group discussion of their role-playing experience, including the techniques they used and how those techniques could be useful in real tutoring sessions. To express empathy, tutors must not only feel empathetic toward students but also articulate that feeling. Since sexual violence can be a taboo subject, tutors may hesitate to express empathy.[8] To do so, they may need to learn how to voice their empathy despite their discomfort. This led to the next focus in the training: assertiveness.

The next section of Part 2 focused on assertiveness as a technique that helps tutors to navigate tutorials with writing about trauma. After defining assertiveness as communication that respects both the interlocutor's needs and other people's needs, participants learned the difference between passive communication (which violates the interlocutor's needs and gives other people's needs priority), assertive communication (which respects both interlocutor's needs and other people's needs), and aggressive communication (which violates the rights of other people as the interlocutor's needs take priority). Participants learned assertiveness techniques, such as the "basic assertion" statement to express one's needs (e.g., "I need to run down the hall and get a drink of water," or "I need to find another tutor for you to work with"); the "sharing assertion" statement to share personal feelings with a simple statement (e.g., "I don't feel well right now"); and an expression of empathy (e.g., "I appreciate how vulnerable you've been in this piece"). Further, participants learned nonverbal communication techniques: keeping one's voice normal and one's pace even, keeping good eye contact, and keeping one's physical tension low. Participants practiced assertiveness through a Think-Pair-Share activity with two scenarios:

- **Scenario 1:** You are in a tutoring session and the student has written a paper with detailed descriptions of abuse. This is triggering to you, and you decide to end the session. Write down what you would say. Then, practice saying it to a partner.
- **Scenario 2:** A tutee wrote a narrative about suddenly losing a loved one. You want to tell the student that you're moved by their story. Write down what you would say to share your emotional reaction to the writing. Then, practice saying it to a partner. You and your partner should take turns so you each get to try responding as a tutor.

These scenarios allowed participants to practice assertiveness techniques that relate both to the tutors' self-care and to express empathy to the student. After a large-group debriefing discussion, participants learned the third technique: coping/self-care.

Since some tutors may relate the topic of sexual violence to their own experience, the workshop then helped tutors to practice coping strategies and self-care strategies. Because tutoring sessions about sexual violence may be uncomfortable or stressful, in particular for tutors who can relate the topic of sexual violence to their own experience, tutors need to have coping strategies that help them to manage their discomfort.[9] The section on coping techniques taught participants to deal with stress as soon as they feel it, like during a tutoring session; the section on self-care techniques taught participants to care for themselves beyond tutoring sessions so that they can be as resilient as possible when stressful sessions arise. I explained self-care using the metaphor of a gas tank: self-care is like filling up your car's gas tank on your way home from school with the knowledge that you'll need to drive back to campus tomorrow. In other words, when we practice self-care, we anticipate and prepare for the future. In this part of the workshop, I drew on my own experience as a certified stress management coach to teach participants 4-7-8 breathing, a technique that helps to slow breathing and relax the body during anxious moments. As a large group, participants practiced breathing in for four seconds, holding the breath for seven seconds, and exhaling for eight seconds. Then, participants learned progressive muscle relaxation, a technique that releases tension in muscles. I guided participants through the following prompt:

> Tense up each muscle group for 2–3 seconds, then release the tension. Begin with your hands by balling them into fists. Squeeze for an inhale. Release for an exhale. Now, move to your shoulders. Squeeze your shoulders back or up for an inhale. Release for an exhale. Continue with your forehead, eyes, jaw, shoulders, arms, low back, legs, feet.

Finally, participants practiced a "grounding" exercise. Grounding exercises help refocus and calm anxious thoughts and reaffirm the present moment, and they are particularly useful for people with PTSD who experience flashbacks. I guided participants through a grounding exercise using the following prompt:

> Place your feet on the floor. Sit up straight and feel the chair support you. Notice the physical, material reality of the chair and the floor. Now, look around you. Identify and name the things you see, smell, hear, and feel. Silently name these things to yourself (for example, water bottle, the hum of the computer, someone coughing, couch). Consciously take deep breaths as you name things.

After the grounding exercise, the coping and self-care portion of the workshop concluded with another Think-Pair-Share activity using the following discussion questions:

- Which of the three techniques did you like the most? Why?
- It may seem tricky at first to try these techniques during a session. What are some ideas you have for modifying the techniques?
- Let's imagine that you just don't feel comfortable trying these during a session. How can you pause before, during, and/or after a tutoring session for some 4-7-8 breathing, progressive muscle relaxation, or grounding?

These questions were designed to help tutors connect the coping and self-care strategies to their work as writing center tutors. Further, we integrated self-care throughout the workshop by offering participants opportunities to disengage from the material, inviting participants to take a break, and incorporating deep breathing exercises at the beginning, middle, and end of the training session.

The workshop concluded by revisiting the main question that guided the ninety minutes: How can tutors appropriately respond in emotionally heightened sessions (such as those about trauma)? Tutors shared their responses to the question using Mentimeter, a website which allows participants to vote or offer responses to a question in real time and projects answers on a screen. This allowed tutors to anonymously share the takeaways and review the material. By ending the workshop with the Mentimeter and a final discussion about how to apply the knowledge and skills to writing center work, participants engaged in the kind of reflection that fosters metacognition and transfer of the learned material to other situations relevant to their lives as students and tutors.

Through the training, twenty-five writing center tutors learned about trauma and practiced three techniques for tutoring. Tutors' comments after the workshop were positive, with several tutors noting that they felt more prepared for tutorials in which students disclose experiences with sexual violence. After the workshop, the PowerPoints and activities were posted on our Writing Center Tutor Training site on our universities' learning management system, D2L. The D2L site allows tutors to engage in ongoing training beyond the biannual staff meetings and to reference staff meeting materials. "Trauma-Informed Tutoring" is now a module on the D2L site, and tutors participated in an online discussion in that module a month after the training to continue the discussion about coping strategies and the relevance of self-care for writing center work. With a digital repository for materials and ongoing discussion in our center, tutors can continue to engage in preparation for emotionally challenging sessions, including those about sexual violence.

CONCLUSION

As disclosures of sexual violence become more common in student writing brought to the writing center, it is imperative to prepare tutors to respond to these situations. Without such preparation, the violence and trauma of the sexual violence itself may be exacerbated, as conversations between tutor and student may lead to secondary traumatization or retraumatization. Using an approach like the one described in this chapter, writing centers can prepare tutors with knowledge about sexual violence and with tools to practice empathetic listening, assertiveness, and coping and self-care. Such training can prepare tutors to respond to sexual violence disclosures in the writing center while diminishing the potential for harm to themselves and to the survivors.

NOTES

1. To better understand the issues related to sexual violence disclosures in the writing center, I worked with two undergraduate tutors and our writing center director to design and implement an IRB-approved mixed-method study (Log #: 18–084). Throughout this chapter, I draw on interview data from this project to demonstrate the problem of mandatory reporting for disclosures in the writing center. All participant names included in this chapter are pseudonyms.

2. AntConc, a computer program used in corpus linguistics, reveals patterns in language. Users of AntConc upload a document to the program, and AntConc generates a concordance, or a list of words present in a text and calculates how frequently each word appears.

3. Through our online survey using Qualtrics ($n = 15$), we learned that 89 percent of participants reported that they felt they know what to say and what not to say in a tutoring session if the topic of sexual violence comes up.

4. From our survey, we learned that 44 percent of participants reported being able to relate the topic of sexual violence in a student's paper to their own experience. Thus, disclosures of sexual violence in tutorials impact the work of tutors who are survivors of sexual violence or trauma themselves. Two survey participants disclosed that they are survivors of trauma and reported that they sometimes share their own experience with students who disclose, but sometimes feel more comfortable sticking to matters of writing.

5. Of the survey participants, 40 percent reported that they would like to see the topic of sexual violence made a part of a regular writing center staff meeting, and 44 percent reported being extremely likely to attend a training in the writing center on sexual violence, while 56 percent of participants reported being only somewhat likely to attend. These numbers are not for tutors' lack of desire to learn more about sexual violence, as 78 percent of survey participants reported that they would like to learn more about sexual violence.

6. Of the tutors who participated in the study, 50 percent reported prior participation in educational or advocacy efforts related to sexual violence, so our writing center's training sought to increase tutors' previous understandings of sexual violence.

7. Survey results indicated that tutors may not know how to offer empathy, as 35 percent of survey participants reported that they "stick to matters of writing" when

students in the writing center write or talk about sexual violence, making this the most common response from tutors.

8. Survey participants reported feeling self-aware during tutoring sessions about sexual violence, as 89 percent of survey participants reported that they are slightly, very, or extremely aware of their body language when the topic of sexual violence comes up.

9. Since 44 percent of survey participants reported that they related the topic of sexual violence to their own experience, it became clear that an important aspect of the training would be to prepare tutors with coping and self-care strategies for tutorials about sexual violence.

REFERENCES

Duranti, Alessandro. 2004. *A Companion to Linguistic Anthropology*. Oxford: Blackwell.

Fairclough, Norman. 1989. *Language and Power*. New York: Longman.

Hesford, Wendy S. 1999. "Reading Rape Stories: Material Rhetoric and the Trauma of Representation." *College English* 58, no. 2: 192–221.

Indiana University of Pennsylvania. 2018. "IUP Sexual Harassment and Sexual Violence Policy." Office of Social Equity and Title IX, Indiana University of Pennsylvania. https://www.iup.edu/socialequity/policies/title-ix/.

MacDevitt, John. 2013. "Responding to Student Traumatic Writing: A Psychologist's View." *Teaching English in the Two-Year College* 41, no. 2: 135–48.

Papendick, Michael, and Gerd Bohner. 2017. "'Passive Victim—Strong Survivor'? Perceived Meaning of Labels Supplied to Women Who Were Raped." *PloS One* 12, no. 5: 1–21.

Harrison, Richard L., and Marvin J. Westwood. 2009. "Preventing Vicarious Traumatization of Mental Health Therapists: Identifying Protective Practices," *Psychotherapy (Chic)* 46, no. 2: 203–19. doi: 10.1037/a0016081.

Rosenberg, Marshall B. 2003. *Nonviolent Communication: A Language of Life*. Encinitas: Puddledancer Press.

Tang, Catherine S. 2011. "Education for Life Adversities and Challenges: Mainstreaming Trauma Training in University and Professional Training Curriculum." In *Healing Trauma: A Professional Guide*, edited by Kitty K. Wu, Catherine S. Tang, and Eugenie Y. Leung, 295–312. Hong Kong: Hong Kong University Press, 2011.

PART 3

Ameliorating

13

VIGILANT AMELIORATION THROUGH CRITICAL LOVE
Lessons My Students Taught Me

Kristie S. Fleckenstein

Violence, Willem de Haan (2008) warns, is "notoriously difficult to define because as a phenomenon it is multifaceted, socially constructed and highly ambivalent" (27). Nonviolence, a concept that only exists in the negative—the "not violence"—is equally "impossible to define" (Johansen 2007, 143). Amelioration, defined as the complex process of nonviolent peacemaking through intervention or the equally complex process of nonviolent peacebuilding through prevention of violence (Barnett et al. 2007), suffers from the same confusion. For, if we cannot know what either violence or nonviolence is, how do we enact the latter to redress or circumvent the former? Nowhere is the amorphous, slippery nature of violence, nonviolence, and amelioration more apparent than in the classroom.

Initially, in my teens during the turbulent 1960s, I envisioned education as the sine qua non of nonviolent transformation, the ideal way to palliate violence, both physical and social. Like others of my generation, emboldened by the clarion call to affect our environments—to shape a world less riven by human-to-human aggression, ecological havoc, and deeply entrenched injustices—I found in the call of teaching a way to make my personal political, a way to bridge "the gulf between practice and profession, between doing and saying" (King 2010, 32). Rich with talk—exploratory, dialogic, celebratory, freewheeling, or carefully structured—the classroom constituted a key tool for effecting social justice, a crucial method and mode of transmuting "swords into ploughshares" and "spears into pruning hooks" (Isaiah 2:3), for adapting "atoms to the arts of peace" (Eisenhower 1953). So inspired, by my junior year in college, I added secondary education certification to my double major of journalism and English. The classroom, not the public sphere, would be the alembic through which I, with my students, would distill peaceful change.

https://doi.org/10.7330/9781646422807.c013

However, the intervening five decades spent in three high schools, one community college, and five universities have taught me that the separation between violence and peace, as de Haan (2008) warns, is fluid at best and specious at worse. In retrospect, I see that too many of my choices and actions as a teacher, administrator, and scholar emerged from, enacted, and sustained violence, rather than ameliorated it. Without knowing, I courted violence in microaggressions that manifested whenever I chose which student to speak (or not speak), privileged beliefs or creeds over others, selected texts by dismissing others, mandated unilateral change, worshipped rationality and avoided emotion, favored one body over another, and, perhaps most egregious, neutralized controversial conversations. As the previous chapters in this collection underscore, the educational spaces of school—our classrooms and writing programs, our studios and centers, our outcomes and assessment practices—are no safer from violence than the public streets or the private home. Education, too, is a site and a source for multifaceted violence, where quotidian pedagogical and programmatic decisions all too frequently replicate rather than redress injury, reify rather than amend the status quo. And, in so doing, these spaces transform amelioration into another act of violence, undermining the idealistic goals that called so many of us to teach in the first place.

In the face of this truth, it would be easy to surrender to a species of despair, to yield to "some sort of intellectual and moral capitulation" that undermines action, including the action of teaching (Galtung 1969, 186). Martin Luther King Jr. (2010) offers me both censure and hope. Yes, he confirms, my good intentions, my sincerely held principles, are not enough. People of integrity, such as white Southerners, he points out, acted in accordance with their core beliefs about the stability of the social order when they opposed racial equality in the 1960s. But their integrity led them astray, blinding them to their own unjust actions. Thus, King tells me, more than my integrity, more than my good intentions, is necessary to act in ways that amend violence, whether it harms the body, the mind, or the soul, the individual or the collective. But, even as he admonishes me, he also encourages me to believe that I can be an agent for amelioration. What is necessary, King shares, is not integrity alone but *enlightened* integrity, an integrity with insight into the ways in which principles can be anchored in honor as well as in dishonor, in rectitude as well as betrayal (36).

King's (2010) belief in enlightened integrity reaffirms my faith in the possibilities of my classroom and of my teaching. However, left unanswered by King is the form that enlightened integrity might take for me and others like me who wish to prevent or amend violence in educational spaces. What does enlightened integrity look like, how might it operate, for a compositionist who teaches, administrates, and researches in the twenty-first century? Inspired by my students, I offer *critical love* as one answer to that question, one means of navigating the intricacies of violence and nonviolence so that I might strive to do the work of composition with enlightened integrity. Such critical love dances on the cusp between violence and nonviolence, leading not to amelioration but, instead, to *vigilant amelioration*: a contingent, situationally sensitive response to violence that requires continual monitoring and adjustments to ensure it remains ameliorative. In what follows, I offer one example of critical love and vigilant amelioration in action, and my story begins with Lennie, who exposes the complexity of violence and thereby exposes the limits of an amelioration premised on a stark binary between violence and nonviolence.

VIOLENCE ALL THE WAY DOWN

In his penultimate paper for my upper-division course focusing on rhetoric and (non)violence, Lennie destabilizes any easy separations between violence and nonviolence, troubling the traditional stark boundary between the two, destabilizing as well any easy disjuncture between harm and help, hero and villain.[1] In so doing, he challenges my understanding of amelioration and myself as its agent. Tying violence to anything human generated "that directly or systematically threatens or results in harm," Lennie in his "This I Believe" paper draws the widest possible circumference around violence. Extending insights he rehearsed in previous assignments, Lennie contends that violence consists of everything from physical harm to any effort to influence, even casually, another person's "free flowing thought and action process." Thus, for Lennie, violence, like the mythical recursive turtles holding up the world, goes all the way down. The scope and the complexity of violence that Lennie delineates initially dismayed me: "But, Lennie," I wrote in a comment box, "if violence is everything, isn't it also nothing? How can we change it if change itself is violent?" Then, as I continued reading Lennie's unapologetic embrace and amplification of what Vittorio Bufacchi (2005) calls a "comprehensive concept of violence" (197)—a theory that defines the scope of violence as any exercise of nonconsensual physical force *and* any violation of a human right—I began to confront the degree to which teaching may similarly be violence all the way down.

The scope and complexity of violence fused together for me in Lennie's categorization of talk—all talk, not just abusive talk—as violent. For, as Lennie argues, even a classmate—who, in an innocuous, casual conversation recommends a particular class that might prepare Lennie for law school—commits a violent act by seeking to alter the flow of Lennie's thoughts. Echoing Sonja K. Foss and Cindy L. Griffin (Foss and Griffin 1995), who likewise see such acts as coercive (3), Lennie's position extends the parameters of violence to include all words, even ostensibly kind ones. Nor is Lennie alone in elucidating the dangers intrinsic to language as a symbol system and as a performance. Scholars across a variety of disciplines emphasize the necessity of including words within, rather than excluding them from, the scope of violence. Daniel Silva (2017) notes the importance of this agenda, insisting that "comprehending the complex entanglements between violence, signification and social life" requires comprehending the relationship between language and violence. However, such a project further requires recognition of "non-Western sensibilities" that operate outside the "idealized Eurocentric models of languages and speakers," because the models themselves injure by erasing those situated in the peripheries (2). Johan Galtung (1990) reinforces Silva's insight, identifying language itself as a form of cultural violence through its construction as a system that privileges some and subordinates others; in addition, language as a system constitutes a symbolic sphere that provides the tools to justify and warrant violence through its performance (291). Thus, violence is woven into the very nature and use of language, all too frequently becoming a "violence that works on the soul" (Galtung 1969, 169). Neil L. Whitehead (2004) goes even further, contending that, as violence weaves in and out of a culture's creation of sociality, it itself becomes a "discursive practice, whose symbols and rituals are as relevant to its enactments as its instrumental aspects" (5). Jeremy Engels (2013) hones that generalization by illuminating the pattern of violence in one ritualistic performance of language: political rhetoric. He contends that such public discourse exists not in an antithetical relationship to violence but in a symbiotic one, each essential to the life of the other. As a result, Engels rightly insists on the importance of attending to the "violence of rhetoric," not merely the "rhetoric of violence" (180). In addition, and perhaps even more troubling, the intersection of violence and talk embraces, as Lennie insists, everyday talk, including everyday classroom talk, as well as public discourse. Teun A. van Dijk (1995) details in concrete terms exactly the threat posed by our common talk, pointing out that people "*do* things with words," and that *doing* frequently includes verbal aggressions that are "sometimes more disastrous than those of physical assault" (307, emphasis original). From language as a system to language as a performance, talk carries with it both the seeds and the fruits of violence, a fact that calls into question my belief in "teaching talk" as ameliorative.

The idea that talk is the opposite of violence, the tool of tools for amending violence, formed the heart of my commitment to teaching and a tenet of my life. From dinner-table debates with my father to lines written on flimsy paper shipped to a young man deployed to a South Asian country almost eight thousand miles away, from antiwar college-wide discussions to continuous feminist sharing, from student-teacher conferences and parent-teacher meetings to program policy decisions, words anchored me in nonviolence during and after my stormy teen years. But, in folding talk into violence, Lennie forced me to reconsider the binary separation of violent and nonviolent talk. I had to acknowledge that for me, as a compositionist, violence "covers a huge and frequently changing range of heterogeneous physical and emotional behaviors, situations and victim-offender relationships" (Levi and Maguire 2002, quoted in de Haan 2008, 27), infiltrating my work in composition through the words constituting Lennie's manifesto, the words shaping my syllabus, the words defining the infrastructures sup-porting our department majors, the words comprising disciplinary best practices, and the words animating the day-to-day decisions I make on the fly in my classroom. Thus, my tool of tools that can turn swords into ploughshares, spears into pruning hooks, and atoms into peace can turn them right back again. But, while the scope of violence is dismay-ing, it is the complexity of violence— especially, again, as manifested in talk—that is daunting, a complexity that renders amelioration even more problematic. Lennie gestures to this complexity.

Lennie's attention to complexity arises implicitly from his example of the classmate who offers him well-meaning advice about prepping for law school that only adds to, rather than palliates, Lennie's inner turmoil. Good intentions and goodwill yield not good ends but harmful ones, he contends. Such unintended consequences result from the com-plexity of violence, whereby the intricate interrelationships comprising violence transmute amelioration into injury. Unlike Newton's third law of motion, in which every action yields an equal but opposite reaction in a linear cause-effect chain, violent and nonviolent actions unfold according to a nonlinear logic in which small causes can have outsized effects or in which causes—violent or nonviolent—can have opposite effects. Good words hurt; aggressive words heal. Even Galtung (1969), considered a key figure in the emergence of peace studies, acknowl-edges the convoluted weave of violence and nonviolence in ameliora-tion. He warns that a side effect of eradicating one type of violence through a nonviolent action can be another kind of violence. "Absence of one type of violence," he cautions, "is bought at the expense of the threat of the other" (180). Thus, efforts to prevent physical violence, such as school shootings, terrorist attacks, or intimate partner violence, can easily result in a different kind of violence, such as a violation of human rights. Michael Barnett, Hunjoon Kim, Madalene O'Donnell, and Laura Sitea (Barnett et al. 2007) note this very conundrum. In the aftermath of violence, do stakeholders seek to maintain peace by committing resources to create a military that might eliminate threats stemming from the "root causes of conflict" (42)? Or do they address the root causes themselves by rectifying the social, economic, and humanitarian inequities that contributed to the conflict in the first place (44)? The choices stakeholders make in their drive to build and sustain peace can all too frequently become a subsequent source of additional violence. Paul Duncum (2006) articulates this potential in even more vivid terms: how can people of goodwill differentiate between violence and nonviolence when "even despicable acts can be viewed favorably if one harbors the desire to breaks norms experienced as repressive" (2). After all, one country's terrorists are another country's freedom fighters.

The insights initiated by Lennie's manifesto leave a compositionist like me mired in what F. Scott Fitzgerald (1936a) calls a "a real dark night of the soul," marked by a "disintegration of one's own personality" (35). During my three a.m. moments, I remember course evaluations, obsessing about students' narrative comments, such as one which pil-loried me for my "brutal teaching," seeing me as "a monster" lacking any "human sympathy," a force of violence rather than a proponent of nonviolence. It is an indictment that recycles in my moments "of solitary pillow-hugging" (Fitzgerald 1936b, 41). If, in fact, Lennie is right, and it is violence all the way down, dragging amelioration with it, then how could I teach, write, and administrate without becoming *always* that heartless creature my past student(s) experienced? One answer for me lies in critical love.

CRITICAL LOVE AS ENLIGHTENED INTEGRITY

Paradoxically comprised of compassion and dispassion, tenderness and teeth, critical love provides a matrix from which I might shape vigilant amelioration, conceding that, while *being* nonviolent as a stable state is beyond reach, always *becoming* nonviolent might be within grasp. Although the concept of *critical* love is a bit of an outlier in composition studies, love is no stranger to the field. A key figure in twentieth-century rhetorical theory, Kenneth Burke (1950) cites love—embodied in unity through identification—and strife—embodied in fragmentation through division—as the two ultimate motives "propelling the ongoing and definitive activity of *Homo Dialecticus*" (Kastely 2013, 175). While Burke sees love and strife as jointly powering human activity and integral to justice, Jim W. Corder (1985) "insists" on their union in rhetoric: rhetoric—evoked in moments of strife when the narratives of our lives bump up against the seemingly incongruent narratives of someone else's life—"must begin, proceed, and end in love," he claims (28). Even more radical, he contends that "rhetoric is love, and it must speak a commodious language" so that it "will hold our diversities" (31), thereby diminishing our strife. Furthermore, situated firmly in the composition classroom, Catherine E. Lamb (1991) operationalizes love by advocating a feminist form of argumentation based on maternal caring, which, committed to "attentive love, loving attention" (Ruddick 1989, quoted in Lamb 16), operates like empathy, "the ability to think or feel as the other" (16). However, although love has a role in the disciplinary drama, it is a secondary one at best.

Despite explicit and implicit emphases on the crucial importance of various faces of love, love may well be the Other in our discipline and in the academy at large. Under the dominance of a Eurowestern epistemology where the doctrine of rationality holds sway, academics, including compositionists, tend to be conflicted about love. While we might honor it as the "white light of emotion" (Ackerman 1995, xvii), "a positive force that ennobles the one feeling it" (xviii), we are still, especially those of us within postsecondary institutions, "embarrassed by love" (xix). As Diane Ackerman (1995) points out in *A Natural History of Love*, while it is the "most important thing in our lives," we are reluctant to linger over its name except in private, intimate settings (xix). Timothy P. Jackson (2003) notes as much, admitting that "the ideal of love is largely alien to our elites and their public discourse" (2), including composition's elites and academic discourse. For evidence, Jackson points to critics who excoriate love, especially the charitable, unconditional outpouring of *agape*, as soft, private, dangerous, irrational, and suspect, leading only to "social impotence" (3). King (2010) concurs, contending that many foes of nonviolent resistance condemn love as a strategy suitable only for "the weak and the cowardly and not for the strong and courageous" (43). Ellen W. Gorsevski (2004) extends that imbalance to rhetoric as well, noting that "vast analyses and knowledge exist concerning hate rhetoric and war rhetoric, but there are comparatively few studies of nonviolent rhetoric and rhetorics of peacemakers" (xxii). Gorsevski ascribes the denigration of peaceful rhetorics to the perception of non-violence as "a tactic of choice among wimps while violence is taken to be, without question, 'the strongest and most effective means available to resist injustice, destroy an oppressive system, or counteract a violent attack'" (Sharp 1995, quoted in Gorsevski 9). Yet, despite academic marginalization, love emerges as a crucial element for enlightened integrity, one that might help ameliorate violence in my daily life as well as in my policies, procedures, and mindset as a compositionist.

Love is especially vital for those seeking to redress violence embedded within and erupting from systems of domination, such as racism, sexism, ableism, and classism, among others. Resonating with Paulo Freire's (1985) contention that "true revolutionaries must perceive the revolution, because of its creative and liberating nature, as an act of love" (77n4), bell hooks (1989) underscores the necessity of love in any struggle to eradicate oppression: such a struggle is, she says, "a gesture of love" (26). Proponents of nonviolent activism and action agree, seeing love as central to their agenda. As King (2010) affirms, "love is the most durable power in the world"; it is "the most potent instrument available in mankind's quest for peace and security" (51), because "nonviolence is a weapon fabricated of love. It is a sword that heals" (1965, 349–50). Mohandas Gandhi (2007) adds weight to King's fervent avowal of the power of love, noting that "the sword of satyagraha [truth-force] is love, and the unshakable firmness comes from it" (42). Even Galtung (1990) speaks of the "virtuous triangle" of "cooperation, friendliness, and love" as a counter to the "vicious" collaboration of direct, structural, and cultural violence (302). In addition, love is an implicit pillar of nonviolent rhetoric, with its key "themes and orientations toward community, collectivity, mutual responsibility, and a pointed use of cooperation or noncooperation" (Gorsevski 2004, 3). Finally, while Foss and Griffin (1995) never use the term *love* in their depiction of invitational rhetoric—a rhetoric of sharing rather than changing—it, too, serves as the source of and sustenance for nonviolence, the embodiment of what Galtung (1969) calls "positive peace" (183).

Love, then, constitutes a fundamental force animating ameliorative change. But, given the scope and complexity of violence, that fundamental force is not just love per se—not the *eros* of romantic love or the *philia* of friendship between equals or the *storge* of familial bonds or even the *agape* of unconditional charitable love. Rather, it is *critical* love, a love that combines elements of *eros, philia, storge,* and *agape* while integrating the cutting edge of rationality. Such a love defies the deceptive binary between violence and nonviolence to conjoin heart and head, emotion and reason. In fact, the very paradoxical quality of critical love might be what is required to ameliorate violence in the work of composition. King (2010) suggests as much, advocating a love that balances "tough mind and tender heart" (3). He cautions his parishioners that "love is something deeper than emotional bosh," counseling them that adherents of nonviolence cannot afford to be confused by love as "sentimental outpouring" (8). Instead, those seeking to amend social inequity through nonviolent means "must combine the toughness of the serpent with the softness of the dove" (3). For to possess only serpent-like qualities devoid of dovelike qualities is to be passionless, mean, and selfish. And to have dove-like qualities only is to be mawkish, anemic, and aimless (6).

Here, then, is the core of critical love, a contradictory nature that moves me out of the binary logic of violence and nonviolence—out of what Keith Lloyd (2016) calls the *dichotonegativity* of false dichotomies—and into the realm of fuzzy logic, or multivalent thinking where we reason "*in the spaces between* true and false" (87, emphasis original). In other words, the paradox of serpent and dove in critical love provides the means by which I might conceive of and work not toward amelioration, with all its deceptive, shining utopian hope, but toward *vigilant* amelioration, a process that requires hard decisions as well as care-full responsiveness to the twists and turns even a nonviolent intention can take as it cycles its way through the complicated movements of thought, expression, practice, and response.

VIGILANT AMELIORATION THROUGH CRITICAL LOVE

Combining the tenderness of love with the teeth of dispassion, embracing not love or violence but an unstable region blending the two, critical love neither demonizes violence nor deifies nonviolence, for, in human sociality, they intricately intertwine with each other. Rather, it aims to provide a source of and parameters for a vigilant amelioration that, despite its imperfections, offers "renewable hopes" for our present and future flourishing (Haraway 2003, 5). Born of critical love, vigilant amelioration constitutes what Donna J. Haraway (2003) calls an emergent practice: "vulnerable, on-the-ground work that cobbles together non-harmonious agencies and ways of living that are accountable both to their disparate inherited histories and to their barely possible but absolutely necessary joint futures" (7). But, while reliant on vulnerability, that emergent practice is equally reliant on calculability: knowing when, with whom, and under what conditions to be vulnerable. To illustrate the dynamic of vigilant amelioration, I begin with Elena's enthusiastic positive response to a class activity which I used as icebreaker on the first day, one that began in amelioration only to morph into violence.

Love, Amelioration, and Vulnerability

Two hours after completing the last day of my summer course on rhetoric and (non)violence, I sit browsing through my students' manifestos when Elena, within her first paragraph, propels me from the last to the first day of class. Contrary to my typical opening-day protocol, I had instead begun with what I called the "memory activity." Handing out mini-notecards, I instructed the strangers before me to "think about a past experience, one you would prefer to keep private, one that might even haunt you." Despite resistant body language, I continued: "Write it down and put it in your pocket or keep it face down in your hand." I will do the same, I promised them. I then proceeded with my typical first-day rituals: describing the focus of the class, hitting the high points of the syllabus, pointing out key policies, and describing grading procedures—all while holding my memory in my hand. Finally, I looked across the room, across the hidden memories, met each gaze, and asked: "does this activity constitute an act of violence?"

Like most activities that teachers employ, this strategy attempted to serve a variety of masters: it aimed to break the ice, to initiate a lively discussion, and to create a common ground among strangers. But, perhaps, above all, I wanted it to combat what King (2010) calls the "paralysis of analysis" (quoted in Coretta Scott King 2010, xiv): the point at which studying—intellectualizing—a problem becomes more important than the problem itself. The threat posed by the paralysis of analysis is a very real danger in a class like mine, where violence and rhetoric, the focus of academic inquiry, become not something that harms and, thus, requires amelioration but instead something to be atomized, dissected, and cobbled back together. The paralysis of analysis shifts attention away from the visceral nature of violence and nonviolence, substituting, instead, discussions akin to debating the number of angels that can dance on the head of a pin. Thus, the memory activity sought to highlight the degree to which we are all vulnerable to violence, all invested on an embodied level with nonviolence. Elena's response underscores the degree to which vigilant amelioration requires, first and foremost, the dove: tenderness and openness to the other.

In her manifesto, Elena makes vividly present the extent to which the success of the memory activity relied on her willingness to risk vulnerability's bite. As she writes in her first paragraph, "I could feel my eyes begin to widen, my legs begin to move around with anxiety, and my heart begin to race" in response to my invitation to remember. Her intense flight response highlights the degree to which any form of an amelioration guided by love depends on the courage to be vulnerable, defined as a person's perceived precarity, their susceptibility to physical, emotional, social, or even economic harm. Without a willingness to risk harm, we cannot "emerge toward the other" in an "untiring stretch toward the other" (Corder 1985, 26), a prerequisite for conceiving of amelioration in the first place. In addition, without connecting with one another, we cannot act together to redress—or prevent recurrences of—violence. This openness to the other becomes increasingly risky in direct ratio to the degree to which the other is unknown, separated from us by competing agendas, agencies, histories, and life experiences. To bridge those separations and cohere, "we have to see each other, to know each other, to be present to each other, to embrace each other" (23). But, to see, know, be present to, and embrace, we must be willing to shed our protective shells and expose our soft parts: we must be vulnerable. In their advocacy of invitational rhetoric Foss and Griffin (1995) make a similar point. The heart of invitational rhetoric—the communicative strategy of offering perspectives—relies on opening one's self up to someone else who, in fact, may espouse an alternative view contrary, perhaps even antagonistic, to one's own (5–6). Elena's manifesto spells out the parameters of vulnerability, its costs, and its rewards.

As Elena details, she experiences all the physiological reactions of fear because she is twice vulnerable—in the past with her terror and helplessness as well as in the current evocation of that past—something she indirectly states: "I don't think I've ever actually wrote it down before. I don't think it ever made sense to me, my truth, my vulnerability." In addition to the threat posed by the intensely personal revelation, to self and other, Elena also teeters on the edge of risk because she confronts past and present within an environment where trust—in me and her classmates—is initially nominal at best. But, regardless of her fear and confusion, she, in an immense act of courage, proceeds, impelled forward by the novelty "of a professor asking this question." Thus, even as her "This I Believe" essay records her past and present fears, her paper also testifies to her bravery in accepting that vulnerability as, on the first day of class, she literally writes down on her mini-notecard the traumatic event. Then she returns to it on the last day of class, articulating it and sharing it in her manifesto with the teacher she describes as "this crazy lady." Finally, the courage to embrace vulnerability shines through in her willingness to permit me to share her memory with an audience of unknown others through this chapter. As she and I both discovered, harrowing as it is, without vulnerability there can be no dove, no tenderness toward self and other, no fledgling move to amelioration. With the risks, though, come rewards, as Elena demonstrates: significant otherness.

Although resistant to quantification, the richest payoff for a loving amelioration's vulnerability resides in the promise of what Haraway (2003) calls *significant otherness* (6, emphasis original), an essential criterion of any effort to palliate violence individually or collectively. Haraway explains: "The partners do not precede their relating; all that is, is the fruit of becoming with" (2008, 17), emphasizing the degree to which critical love—an ongoing process of trust extended and returned in kind—comes to be in the doing. Only when we are vulnerable to each other can we reciprocally relate, becoming in that moment not one apart but two together, respectful partners who constitute a new identity that they work jointly to maintain (19). Elena's account of the memory activity highlights the initial tendrils of relating. First, Elena tentatively becomes with the strangers around her as she furtively "searched for responses . . . to see if they would express those same [fear] reactions" that wracked her, finding in that search reassurance that she "wasn't alone" in her panic. Second, she became with me, finding solace in my confession that I would "also be participating in this activity" and, thus, we would be jointly vulnerable; furthermore, she found safety and agency in my assurance that students could choose to opt out, to leave their mini-notecard blank. In those small incremental connections, those fragile exchanges, Elena, her classmates, and I forged our "precarious partnerships" (Fleckenstein and Worm 2019, 42), becoming "significantly other to each other, in specific difference," a tentative process signifying "the nasty developmental infection called love" (Haraway 2003, 3; see, also, Fleckenstein and Worm, 2019). Vulnerability in love's amelioration binds all participants in the same risk, enabling us to recognize together, to face together, and to work together to change realities, tasks from which we might otherwise flinch. That significant otherness enabled Elena to "let a deep breath go" and begin to "make sense" of her "truth, her vulnerability"; she found strength and power in becoming with. As a result, she empowers herself to ameliorate violence—past, present, and future—because becoming with, a pillar of love, provides the grounds for healing action.

Love anchors amelioration; thus, a key dynamic intrinsic to any effort to rectify or prevent violence depends on—emerges from—becoming with. bell hooks (2015) emphasizes this in her insistence on *relational love* (35) as the necessary foundation for the "hope and struggle" of activism (36). Derived from the "sweet communion" of her childhood in a Black agrarian community, relational love for hooks—"the care we had towards one another" (35)—supports the "strong sense of solidarity" needed for collective survival and activism. This "way of being that can be consciously practiced" (39) is essential for amelioration, including that intended by my memory activity, with its goal of undermining the effect of paralysis by analysis. Vulnerability risks harm for the opportunity "to become with those with whom we are not yet" in the hope of "opening to what is not yet" (Haraway 2008, 93). It is also an opening to craft an amelioration for a reality that is not yet. But love is not enough for amelioration, as Richard J. Bernstein (2013) makes clear. "The task (*Aufgabe*) of opposing violence is an ongoing vigilant task," he says (11). That love needs to be critical, that amelioration vigilant. Thus, opposing violence requires calculability. Jonas makes painfully clear to me my need not for love or amelioration through vulnerability but for *critical* love and *vigilant* amelioration through calculability as, in a new semester and new class, the memory activity goes badly awry, harming rather than helping.

Critical Love, Vigilant Amelioration, and Calculability

Jonas brought home the limits of an amelioration based solely on love and vulnerability at the very beginning of the fall semester. Following the first day of class, I rode a wave of exhilaration. In my advanced rhetoric class, the memory activity and subsequent student buy-in had generated visions of a semester in which the students seemingly taught themselves, carrying me along in their wake. Then, still high on elation, I checked my email before the second day of class and found Jonas's message: "Something that happened in class on Tuesday that gave me quite a bit of anxiety," Jonas wrote, "and I'd like to share that with you." Could we find a time to meet, he asks, something that "would mean a lot to" him. Worried rather than exhilarated, I reply, "of course," and we arrange to meet in private after class that same day.

A smart, sensitive, and high-performing student I had the pleasure of teaching in a previous spring semester, Jonas opened our late afternoon conversation by repeating how much he looked forward to working with me again. But, he shared, as if confessing an unforgivable transgression, he found the first-day's memory activity emotionally devasting to the extent that he considered dropping the class. Nothing but gentle and respectful, Jonas reminded me that some people have memories that they are just not ready to confront; the mere thought of them is terrifying. He does not mean to dictate my pedagogy or criticize my choices, he assured me; he just wants to share his distress so that I could better judge the hidden impact of this teaching strategy.[2] Designed as a nonviolent means to a nonviolent end, the memory activity thus twists from a benefit—a panacea for the paralysis of analysis—to a bane. Harkening back to Lennie and the complexity of violence, my good intentions resulted not in good ends but in drastically bad ends, ones that hurt my students.

Caught between Elena's enthusiastic embrace of the memory activity and Jonas's visceral rejection of it, how do I move forward in the face of competing "goods" and "bads"? Critical love offers me calculability, or the analytical "intervention of speculative thought and the practice of remembering, of rearticulating bodies to bodies" (Haraway 2008, 85). A process that balances the tenderness of the dove with the toughness of the serpent, calculability matches emotions with good reasons. Together vulnerability and calculability animate critical love, dictating the need for both rationality and love in any ameliorative activity I conceive and enact, whether as teacher, administrator, mentor, or scholar.

While perhaps counterintuitive, calculability is essential for critical love, the matrix from which vigilant amelioration emerges. While love calls for vulnerability, *critical* love calls for an *informed* vulnerability, "not an ideal love, not an obedient love, but one that might even recognize the noncompliant multiplicity of insects. And the taste of blood" (Haraway 2008, 85). King (2010) underscores this essential unity of caution with the openness of vulnerability. The tough mind, "characterized by incisive thinking, realistic appraisal, and decisive judgment" (3), is needed "to judge critically and to discern the true from the false" (2), to judge and discern the moments when the risk of openness exceeds its potential benefits. Haraway (2003) concurs, noting that the story of significant otherness, of vulnerability, is fraught with "misunderstandings, achievements, crimes" (5). Thus, citing, as a rubric, the slogan of the canine sport *Schutzhund* "Run fast; bite hard" (5), Haraway warns that significant otherness binds partners to making the hard decisions about which relatings to pursue, which partnerships to forge. Corder (1985) agrees, conceding that some "conflicts will not be resolved in time and love—(there's always that captain of the guard from Dachau)" (27), resonating with Deborah Tannen's (2013) warning that not all perspectives—such as Holocaust denial—are equal. Thus, openness to alternative perspectives must have its limits, or we end up warranting the unwarrantable (182). So, while Gandhi (2007) repeatedly insists that nonviolence is a quality of the heart rather than the result of "an appeal to the brain" (39), an appeal to the brain is exactly what critical love dictates, or, more specifically, an appeal to good reasons for our decisions about whom we bite, when, and how hard, as well as how fast we run—if at all.

The memory activity—its good intentions and ill effects—demonstrates both reliance on and continual need for calculability in critical love. From the perspective of the serpent, vulnerability operates not as a Kierkegaardian leap of faith wherein we jump into relatings with the blind belief that the unknown other will be able or even inclined to catch us. Instead, it operates with information—the depth of the abyss, the speed of the impact, the character of person at the bottom waiting to cushion our arrival—and reasons—what makes leaping better than rappelling down the cliff or not leaping at all? Who benefits and in what way? What's the cost (monetary, emotion, and physical) of those benefits? And who's footing the bill? Guided by informed vulnerability, we use such information and reasons to determine if, when, and how to make the leap. Calculability, then, bids me to query the extent to which the memory activity Elena embraced and Jonas repudiated supported both informed vulnerability and the ability to act on its assessment. Holly's "This I Believe" essay points to ways I can systematically calculate an answer this question.

In her manifesto, Holly, like Lennie from my summer class, offers a broad view of violence to ensure that we are able to see the ways in which violence—such as the inequitable distribution of resources—lurks within nonviolence. Her mechanism for recognizing systemic violence consists of scale, or the intersecting levels of violence. Scale, she says, helps us take "into account what aspects of the scenario we consider violent, even if the overall situation does not seem intimidating or dangerous." Her insights also provide a mechanism for considering the scales at work in the memory activity and the impact of those scales on students' informed vulnerability, as well as on my perception of that vulnerability. Two intersecting scales—the macro-, or institutional, level of the class itself and the micro-level, or the on-the-ground enactment of the memory activity—help me add, subtract, and divide to reach a dismaying indictment of my pedagogical strategy.

First, the institutional scale of the class curtailed students' ability to refuse my invitation, even in the face of my permission to leave their mini-cards blank. After all, this was a class that these students needed in order to complete their program of study in their major; in fact, for many of them, this was the last class before graduation. The institutional, or macro-, scale of the class, then, predisposed them to comply with whatever I wanted them to do—write down a painful memory—rather than what I'd permit them to do—leave a blank. The risk of not complying outweighed the risk of complying, a risk I inadvertently reinforced by introducing myself as "Dr. Fleckenstein," thereby establishing my authority as a senior faculty member and a representative of the institution. Thus, any common ground I might have wanted to establish via shared vulnerability—by writing down my own painful memory—was at least partially illusory because of power I wielded as an extension of the university. Students' vulnerability, then, was definitely informed, but not in the ways I had intended.

Second, the micro-scale was even more injurious, in that the quotidian actions comprising the first day of a class undermined students' informed vulnerability, or, rather, my actions informed vulnerability in ways that eroded students' ability to act on their own calculations. To illustrate, I sandwiched the memory activity between the university-mandated attendance (by which I automatically dropped from my course any student not in attendance) and a discussion of the course policies, both points underscoring my position of power. For example, as students held their memories in their hands, I reviewed my absence policy (two only—anything after that affected their grade), assignments (must be completed, must be original with the class, must be this, must be that), and, of course, grades. All these small actions accreted to reinforce the control I had and the limits of the control they had, including over their own memories. Even more damning, as a prelude to the memory activity, I had asked students to fill out a mini-notecard with the following information: institutional name, preferred name, preferred pronoun, concerns about the class, and trigger warnings. Then, immediately after collecting these, I initiated an activity that might have very well triggered past trauma. Thus, the nature of the placement of the activity within the micro-scale of the day itself reflected my failure to calculate carefully students' informed vulnerability, a mistake that, as Jonas underscores, can all too easily harm. Calculability provides insight into that violation and the need for vigilance in loving critically. It provides a similar value for amelioration.

Just as calculability provides a key pillar of critical love, so does it also provide a key pillar of amelioration, ensuring a *vigilant* amelioration. The first move in vigilant amelioration consists of accepting the reality of contingency, a reminder that any amelioration is an emergent practice, dependent on the dynamic of the moment and situation. To think that "reforms will settle the matter," Haraway (2008) warns, "is a failure of affective and effective thinking and a denial of responsibility" (90). In other words, affective and effective thinking recognizes that one size or one shape of amelioration does not fit all; and, even if it fits all at one time, it will not necessarily—or even probably—fit all at all times (or any at any time). Amelioration is contingent. The virtue of contingency is that it allows for a flexible response; the deficit is that it requires continual monitoring of any strategy of intervention and prevention. Calculability demands that, as I make the hard decisions based on what seem to be good reasons (the memory activity), I audit the impact of those decisions (the radical differences between Elena's and Jonas's reactions) and adjust carefully. But calculability works not only on the past in the present (retrospective calculation) but also on the future in the present (projective calculation).

The same rigorous inquiry into the memory assignment gestures to the second value of calculability in vigilant amelioration: working toward a future. Even as vigilant amelioration embraces its own contingency—chary of nomothetic solutions—it also embraces the long view, what I call *futurability*: acting in ways that secure the resilience, the long-term flourishing, of life, including the life of the classroom. Without a future orientation to balance contingency—vigilant amelioration in the moment—I risk rendering violence the rule and amelioration the (occasional) exception, a Band-Aid for a hemorrhage. Speaking from her position as a transitioning transgender woman in her "This I Believe" paper, Liane exposes the need for amelioration not only in moments but also in a concatenation of moments that collectively shape a future and stem the hemorrhage. She situates that insight within her own struggles with transitioning. Deeply troubled and hurt by familial and peer resistance to her reclaimed gender identity, Liane writes, "In the face of these structural hierarchies, which are overwhelmingly asserted against minorities and those who are minoritized, repression and exploitation present a constant existential threat." Echoing Corder's (1985) plea that we must "teach the world to want . . . time for care" (31) to secure a rhetoric of love, Liane implores us to attend to our "rhetorical decisions," our everyday and civic use of language, to ensure that, moment by moment, word by word, we act with "consideration and sensitivity to those who may be harmed." The endgame for her is "a gentler and less oppressive future" as each of us accumulates moments that, eventually, become greater than the sum of their parts, a habitual way of acting that reflects "more humane hierarchies." Thus, emergent vigilant amelioration can operate within and across moments; it can be futurable.

Through calculation, the serpent aids in ensuring a vigilant ameliora-tion that, while sensitive to contingency, also seeks to configure Liane's gentler and less oppressive future. Thus does the serpent lead me back to the memory activity, encouraging me to ask if and how I might revise it so that "significant others might flourish" (Haraway 2008, 92), not just today in my class but tomorrow in someone else's class, and next year in lives beyond the classroom. For example, might I better serve futurability by transforming the memory activity into a group rather than an individual action? Would significant otherness flourish in small groups where participants could each contribute a specific event, action, statement, artifact, position—current or historical, high culture or pop culture, personal or public—that troubles them? This would allow them to choose what or how much to disclose, what and how personal that disclosure can be. Then, the group might decide which one contribu-tion to share with the class, calculating why they, as a group, chose it, why it perturbs them, how they might respond to it in a positive manner, and what might be gained—personally and communally—from such an action. If I not only revise but continually revise the memory activ-ity in ways responsive to new situations, might I then build, moment by moment, to a point, to a reality, in which we can hold our vulnerabilities in our hands and find a significant otherness that edges us closer to Liane's "gentler and less oppressive" future?

ENLIGHTENED INTEGRITY: IMPERFECTLY
LOVING, IMPERFECTLY AMELIORATING

"There will never be an army of perfectly non-violent people. It will be formed of those who will honestly endeavor to observe non-violence," Gandhi (2007) notes (40). I extend that insight, accepting that, along with the army of imperfect nonviolent people there will only ever be imperfect love, imperfect amelioration. Perhaps that is the benefit and bane of enlightened integrity: no perfect choices. The vexing combination of the scope and complexity of violence complicates efforts to prevent, intervene in, or, in many cases, even recognize harm. Furthermore, the porous relationship between violence and nonviolence makes it impos-sible to identify a single root cause of violence that we might then match to a single ameliorative solution. Furthermore, we cannot even predict with any certainty that a nonviolent solution will secure a nonviolent end without transmuting itself into violence. Thus is amelioration ren-dered suspect, difficult to define, envision, and enact with any certainty of a favorable outcome. But, for me, accepting this imperfection is the beginning of enlightened integrity; it is the beginning of a commitment to aligning—and realigning—words and practice in classroom, program, major, infrastructures, and discipline through critical love, which, as it works "to heighten our awareness, deepen our compassion, intensify our course, and strengthen our commitment," simultaneously works to heighten, deepen, and intensify our vigilant amelioration (King 2010, 193).

Here, within critical love and vigilant amelioration, I hope to find my way to acting with enlightened integrity and to accepting the inevitable failures of such acting. For, just as there will never be perfectly nonviolent people, so, too, will I only ever be an imperfectly nonviolent teacher. I accept that—as a compositionist, as a human being—I will make decisions that will inevitably disadvantage some people, including my students, while privileging others. I will allocate resources that serve the needs of some while inevitably shortchanging others; I will select texts for my syllabus that emphasize one set of ideas over others; I will disappoint some students while serving others. But I can try to make decisions, allocate resources, select texts, and disappoint students in a way that is guided by the hope of vigilant amelioration through critical love, aware that my "debt is just opening up to speculative and so possible material, affective, practical reworlding in the concrete detailed situation of *here*. . . . not everywhere all the time" (Haraway 2008, 93, emphasis original). Reworlding in the here means that, to help shape Liane's hopeful future where she is no longer terrorized by the threat of daily violence, to honor Elena's epiphanies and Jonas's anguish, I must teach within the shadow of my students'—and my own—vulnerabilities. And, when, tripped by my own imperfectability, I inevitably fall into the violence that Lennie describes and Holly analyzes, I must re-calculate, re-ameliorate, and re-risk. Reworlding in the here means that I try to teach with words that listen more than speak, so that I might shape good reasons even as I acknowledge the limits of those reasons, the limits of reason itself. In imperfectly doing so, perhaps, I and my students will "come to flourish together," even if only sporadically, because we have learned to care about each other in "nonanthropomorphic, nonmimetic, painstaking detail" (Haraway 2008, 93)—with both heart and head, dove and serpent. This I believe.

NOTES

1. Students' names have been anonymized and their unedited work used with permission. The students were participants in an upper-division rhetorical theory and practice course at Florida State University. The assignment eliciting the essays from which I quote in this chapter consists of a modification of National Public

Radio's "This I Believe" project (see "Celebrating"). For my version, also called their *manifesto*, I asked students, as the penultimate requirement of the course, to articulate what they believed about the intersection of rhetoric and violence and/or nonviolence.

2.   Nor was Jonas alone in his response, as Barry revealed in his final project. Here he ably argued that icebreakers operated as violent rhetoric. Although Barry did not mention the memory activity by name, his concern with and experience of the adverse impact of the memory activity were devastatingly clear.

REFERENCES

Ackerman, Diane. 1995. *A Natural History of Love*. New York: Vintage.
Barnett, Michael, Hunjoon Kim, Madalene O'Donnell, and Laura Sitea. 2007. "Peacebuilding: What Is in a Name?" *Global Governance* 13, no. 1: 35–38. JSTOR.
Bernstein, Richard J. 2013. *Violence: Thinking without Banisters*. Cambridge, UK: Polity.
Bufacchi, Vittorio. 2005. "Two Concepts of Violence." *Political Studies Review* 3, no. 2: 193–204. doi:10.1111/j.1478-9299.2005.00023.
Burke, Kenneth. 1950. *A Rhetoric of Motives*. Berkeley: University of California Press.
"Celebrating Four Years of 'This I Believe.'" *National Public Radio*. April 27, 2009. https://www.npr.org/templates/story/story.php?storyId=103427272.
Corder, Jim W. 1985. "Argument as Emergence, Rhetoric as Love." *Rhetoric Review* 4, no. 1: 16–32. JSTOR.
De Haan, Willem. 2008. "Violence as an Essentially Contested Concept." In *Violence in Europe: Historical and Contemporary Perspectives*, edited by Sophie Body-Gendrot and Pieter Spierenburg, 27–40. New York: Springer.
Duncum, Paul. 2006. "Attraction to Violence and the Limits of Education." *The Journal of Aesthetic Education* 40, no. 4: 21–38. JSTOR.
Eisenhower, Dwight D. "Atoms for Peace." Address by Mr. Dwight D. Eisenhower, President of the United States of America, to the 470th Plenary Meeting of the United Nations General Assembly, December 8, 1953. IAEA: International Atomic Energy Agency. https://www.iaea.org/about/history/atoms-for-peace-speech.
Engels, Jeremy. 2013. "Forum: The Violence of Rhetoric." *Quarterly Journal of Speech* 99, no. 2: 180–81. doi: 10.1080/00335630.2013.775707/.
Fitzgerald, F. Scott. 1936a. "Pasting It Together." *Esquire: The Magazine for Men*. February 1, 1936: 41, 161. https://classic.esquire.com/article/1936/2/1/the-crack-up.
Fitzgerald, F. Scott. 1936b. "The Crack-Up." *Esquire: The Magazine for Men*. March 1, 1936: 35, 182–83. https://classic.esquire.com/article/1936/3/1/pasting-it-together.
Fleckenstein, Kristie S., and Anna M. Worm. 2019. "Unity and Difference: Figurations for a Future Rhetoric." In *Rhetorical Speculations: The Future of Rhetoric, Writing, and Technology*, edited by Scott Sundvall, 25–44. Logan: Utah State University Press.
Freire, Paulo. 1985. *Pedagogy of the Oppressed*. Translated by Myra Bergman Ramos. New York: Continuum.
Foss, Sonja K., and Cindy L. Griffin. 1995. "Beyond Persuasion: A Proposal for an Invitational Rhetoric." *Communication Monographs* 62, no 1: 2–18. doi:10.1080/036377595 0937636345.
Galtung, Johan. 1990. "Cultural Violence." *Journal of Peace Research* 27, no. 3: 291–305. doi: 10.1177/0022343390027003005.
Galtung, Johan. 1969. "Violence, Peace, and Peace Research." *Journal of Peace Research* 6, no. 3: 167–91. doi: 10.1177/002234336900600301.
Gandhi, Mohandas K. 2007. *Gandhi on Non-Violence*, edited by Thomas Merton. New York: New Directions.

Gorsevski, Ellen W. 2004. *Peaceful Persuasion: The Geopolitics of Nonviolent Rhetoric.* New York: SUNY Press.

Haraway, Donna. 2008. *When Species Meet.* Minneapolis: University of Minneapolis Press.

Haraway, Donna J. 2003. *The Companion Species Manifesto: Dogs, People, and Significant Otherness.* Chicago: Prickly Paradigm Press.

hooks, bell. 2015. "The Chitlin Circuit: On Black Community." In *Yearning: Race, Gender, and Cultural Politics.* New York: Routledge.

hooks, bell. 1989. "Feminism: A Transformational Politics." In *Talking Back: Thinking Feminist, Thinking Black.* Boston: South End Press.

Jackson, Timothy P. 2003. *The Priority of Love: Christian Charity and Social Justice.* Princeton: Princeton University Press.

Johansen, Jørgen. 2007. "Nonviolence: More than the Absence of Violence." In *Handbook of Peace and Conflict Studies,* edited by Charles Webel and Johan Galtung, 143–59. London: Routledge.

Kastely, James L. 2013. "Love and Strife: Ultimate Motives in Burke's *A Rhetoric of Motives.*" *Rhetorica: A Journal of the History of Rhetoric* 31, no. 2: 172–98. JSTOR.

King, Martin Luther, Jr. 2010. *Strength to Love.* Minneapolis: Fortress Press.

King, Martin Luther, Jr. 2003. *A Testament of Hope: The Essential Writings of Martin Luther King.* Edited by James M. Washington. Reprint edition. New York: HarperOne.

King, Coretta Scott. 2010. Foreword to King, *Strength to Love,* ix–xii. Minneapolis: Fortress Press.

Lamb, Catherine E. 1991. "Beyond Argument in Feminist Composition." *College Composition and Communication* 42, no. 1, 1991: 11–24. JSTOR.

Lloyd, Keith. 2016. "Beyond 'Dichotonegative' Rhetoric: Interpreting Field Reactions to Feminist Critiques of Academic Rhetoric through an Alternate Multivalent Rhetoric." *Rhetorica* 34, no. 1: 78–105. doi:10.1525/4h.2016.34.1.78.

Silva, Daniel. 2017. "Investigating Violence in Language: An Introduction." In *Language and Violence: Pragmatic Perspectives,* edited by Daniel Silva, 1–29. Amsterdam: John Benjamins Publishing. E-book. doi: 10.1074/pbns.279.

Tannen, Deborah. 2013. "The Argument Culture: Agonism and the Common Good." *Daedalus* 142, no. 2: 177–84. JSTOR.

Van Dijk, Teun A. 1995. "Editorial: The Violence of Text and Talk." *Discourse & Society* 6, no. 3: 307–8. doi: 10.1177/0957926595006003001.

Whitehead, Neil L. 2004. "Introduction: Cultures, Conflicts, and the Poetics of Violent Practices." In *Violence,* edited by Neil L. Whitehead, 3–24. Oxford: James Currey.

APPENDIX A

INTERVIEW QUESTIONS

1. What comes to mind when you think of "writing as healing?"

2. When you've written about personal life events, personal feelings, or personal issues for school assignments, what led you to include these things in your writing?

3. After you included personal life events, personal feelings, or personal issues in your school writing projects, what was the result?

4. In your general experience, what do writing teachers value in student texts?

5. Have you ever shared more than you would ordinarily share in your day-to-day life about your personal life events, personal feelings, or personal issues with your peers and/or with your instructor in a course?

6. Has writing about personal life events, personal feelings, or personal issues ever impacted your relationships outside of school?

https://doi.org/10.7330/9781646422807.c014

APPENDIX B

CLASSROOM OVERVIEW OF FREE SPEECH AND COMMUNITY MEMBERSHIP

This is a course built through interaction. To study the language of social media, we will collaborate on activities, share ideas, and engage in discussion throughout the semester.

Often, discussion on aspects of contemporary life is not easy. This course asks that we take up the hard work of such conversations in order to (1) fully think through and articulate our own observations, insights, and questions, (2) listen openly and respond compassionately to others, and (3) participate in the social process of meaning-making in order to apply new knowledge in our lives.

It is likely that you will not always agree with others in the course: this can be good. Talking across difference (of experience, of opinion, of identity) is a valuable practice that aligns with our institution's general education outcomes, including cultural diversity goals of "an understanding of the scope and limitations of one's own cultural perspective," and "critical inquiry into the problems, challenges and possibilities inherent in a diverse society," (follow this link to our GenEd outcomes). This works best when all members of our course community follow the university's conduct policy, which states "all members of the University community should act toward each other with civility, mutual respect, integrity, and reason" (follow this link to our Civility Policy).

In the rare but not impossible instance of a class member disrupting our online learning community by posting original or copied content that demeans, ridicules, or directs threatening hostility toward people based on their identity (sometimes referred to as hate speech), it is helpful to be aware of institutional policies and classroom practices related to free speech and community intervention.

POLICY AND INSTRUCTOR PRACTICE

At this time, the institution does not permit faculty to remove any student posts in our course Blackboard site. This ensures all students can exercise their free speech rights within the public university. In the case of hostile speech, however, faculty's inability to remove harmful content can be troubling. If I see a post that could be construed as hate speech, I contact the writer individually, explain how the post may be harmful to our course community, and ask them to consider removing the post. If the post violates UMA community expectations, I contact appropriate channels: the Dean of Students Office [link] and/or the C.A.R.E. Team [link]. Direct threats are not tolerated and are reported to law enforcement. These actions take place out of the public space of the classroom so that I do not violate student right to privacy as outlined by FERPA [link].

POLICY AND STUDENT PRACTICE

As a student in the classroom, you are encouraged to address situations of hate speech should you feel drawn to do so. The online classroom is your community learning space, and you have a meaningful role in shaping this learning space. Most often, engaging in discourse across difference means honing our skills in listening, empathy and considering positionality as we wade through ideas that conflict. However, in cases of hate speech, you do not need to directly engage with the perpetrator to speak out against its inappropriateness and harm to our shared classroom. In fact, "hate speech is rarely an invitation to a dialogue; it is like a slap in the face" (Delgado and Stefancic 2004, 207). Rather than attempt to interact with the perpetrator, you might approach hate speech as a visual object (or obstruction) in the course to examine its impact on our learning space and connections to broader social context.

"Is this really my task?" you might ask. Initiating commentary on posts containing hate speech is challenging work. Students whose own identities were attacked, demeaned, or ridiculed in the hostile post need not be the students who respond to the post, and should not shoulder the responsibility of response. Addressing hate speech that doesn't directly involve you is important ally work, since silence can function as passive endorsement of the hate speech and compound the hostility in the atmosphere.

If you encounter hate speech in an interactive section of our online classroom, you might choose to provide a short, straightforward comment such as "I see this as hate speech and don't appreciate it in our classroom." Such a statement situates you as a community member who has differentiated their beliefs from the hateful remarks posted in our space.

If you perceive the hate speech as a significant violation of our classroom community and want to unpack the post and its presence, you might try out the process of rhetorical looking, a way to consciously examine how you're interpreting the hate speech as you encounter it. Developed by writing scholars Fleckenstein, Gage, and Bridgman (2017) as a strategy for considering atrocity images in a classroom, this model of engagement encourages slowing down one's visual labor, taking time to look *at*, look *with*, look *through*, and look *into* an atrocity image. Encountering hate speech can make one feel stuck, forced into conversational exchange with an aggressor. Rhetorical looking offers a different opportunity, a way to approach classroom hate speech as something to observe, acknowledge, and analyze with the broader class community. Rhetorical looking encourages thoughtful, non-linear movement through a process comprising four tactics. The tactics might be taken up in any order, and each tactic may be revisited at any point in the process.

Four Tactics of Rhetorical Looking:

Looking at: As you look at the post, consider what has brought you to see it the way you do. What belief system (or, ideology) do you bring to your view of the post, and how do those beliefs factor into how you understand the post?

Looking with: As you look at the post, consider your point of view—how does the post situate you as a viewer and how are you situated to view the post? What other points of view exist, and how might considering such points of view inform your understanding and response in the online classroom context?

Looking through: How do you describe the post in words? What assumptions do you make as you move between describing what is observable in the post and your interpretation of that content? How do the language choices you make frame your interpretation of the post?

Looking into: To what larger social discourse and action is this instance of hate speech connected? What role(s) can you occupy in the larger conversation, and what does action look like in this role? Consider who is accountable to whom, and in what ways?

You may post rhetorical looking activities in their entirety or excerpt ideas as comments on perpetrator's initial post or add a new thread in that week or any subsequent week's discussion thread. You may collaborate in this process, building a rich report of the impact of hate speech, to individuals, to our course community, and our broader social lives. I can participate in this work as well. Your time spent on rhetorical looking should be recorded in your weekly labor log, and texts composed count toward your labor agreement category #3 (Community engagement) grade points.

INDEX

CONTRIBUTORS

Kerry Banazek is an Assistant Professor in the English Department at New Mexico State University, where she teaches in the Rhetoric, Digital Media, and Professional Communication programs. Her research deals with impacts that technologies of vision (from microscopes to camera drones) have on rhetorics of sensation, imagination, and education. She is a practicing poet and former web producer; her writing can be found in *Enculturation*, the collection *Geopoetics in Practice*, *Diagram*, and elsewhere.

Katherine T. Bridgman is Associate Professor of English at Texas A&M University-San Antonio, where she directs the Writing Center. Her research focuses on activist use of digital social media with an emphasis on the way protestors work across digital interfaces to garner transnational support. Her scholarship has appeared in venues such as *Kairos*, *South Atlantic Review*, *College English*, and various edited collections.

Eric C. Camarillo currently serves as the director of the Learning Commons at Harrisburg Area Community College, where he oversees testing, the library, user support, and tutoring services for over nineteen thousand students across five campuses. His research agenda is currently focused on writing centers and best practices within these spaces, and he pays particular attention to asynchronous and synchronous online modalities. He has published in *The Peer Review*, *Praxis: A Writing Center Journal*, and *The Journal of Academic Support Programs*. He has also presented his research at numerous conferences, including the International Writing Center Association and the National Conference on Peer Tutoring in Writing.

Joshua L. Daniel (formerly Joshua Daniel-Wariya) is an Associate Professor of Rhetoric and Writing Studies at Oklahoma State University, where he currently serves as Director of Composition after serving as Associate Director from 2014 to 2020. His research areas include writing program administration and game studies. His recent work has appeared in journals such as *Rhetoric Society Quarterly*, *Pedagogy*, and *Games and Culture*.

Lisa Dooley is a PhD Candidate specializing in Rhetoric, Composition, and Technical Communication. Her research interests include intersectional, decolonial, and disability rhetorics and assessments of (un)fitness.

Kristie S. Fleckenstein is a Professor of English and the Director of the Graduate Program in Rhetoric and Composition at Florida State University, where she teaches graduate and undergraduate courses in rhetoric and composition. Her research interests include feminism and race, especially as both intersect with material and visual rhetorics. She is the recipient of the 2005 CCCC Outstanding Book of the Year Award for *Embodied Literacies: Imageword and a Poetics of Teaching* (Southern Illinois University Press, 2003) and the 2009 W. Ross Winterowd Award for Best Book in Composition Theory for *Vision, Rhetoric, and Social Action in the Composition Classroom* (Southern Illinois University Press, 2009). Her current monograph project explores the role of photography in nineteenth-century debates about racial identities.

Scott Gage is an Associate Professor of English and the Director of First-Year Composition at Texas A&M University-San Antonio. His research addresses the intersections of rhetoric, violence, and white supremacy and appears in *College English, Computers and Composition,* and *Present Tense: A Journal of Rhetoric in Society.*

Allison Hargreaves is a settler scholar of Indigenous literatures and Associate Professor in the Department of Critical Studies at the University of British Columbia, Okanagan campus, in unceded Syilx territory. She is the author of *Violence Against Indigenous Women: Literature, Activism, Resistance* (Wilfrid Laurier University Press, 2017). As a composition instructor, she teaches in UBC's Aboriginal Access Program.

Jamila M. Kareem is an Assistant Professor of Writing and Rhetoric at the University of Central Florida. Her current research focuses on racial equity in first-year writing programs and the shift from high school– to college-level writing, influenced by her years of experience teaching at an early-college high school. She is an NCTE Scholar for the Dream and has work published in *Teaching English in the Two-Year College, JAC,* and *Journal of College Literacy and Learning.*

Lynn C. Lewis is an Associate Professor in the English department at Oklahoma State University and currently serves as Director of the Rhetoric and Writing Studies program. She directed the First-Year Composition program from 2015 to 2020. Her research interests include writing pedagogy, visual rhetorics, and digital and new media studies. She has published in *JAC: A Journal of Composition Theory, Pedagogy* (co-author with Joshua Daniel), *Academe,* and several edited book collections. She is the editor of *Strategic Discourse: The Politics of (New) Literacy Crises,* published by CCDP/Utah State Press. She is currently working on a monograph on memes and an edited book on claiming writing studies as a discipline.

Trevor C. Meyer is an Assistant Professor in the Department of Language, Literature, and Writing at Northwest Missouri State University. He teaches courses in rhetorical theory and history, composition, and professional/technical writing. His scholarship focuses on the intersection of writing pedagogy and rhetorical theory, argumentation, and rhetorics of violence. His ongoing project examines how mixed martial arts, specifically the ancient Greek pankration, might provide heuristics and practices in argumentation, in both formal, academic debate and informal quarrels and discussion.

Cathryn Molloy is an Associate Professor in James Madison University's School of Writing, Rhetoric and Technical Communication, where she also serves as director of undergraduate studies. She is the author of the book *Rhetorical Ethos in Health and Medicine: Patient Credibility, Stigma and Misdiagnosis,* coeditor of the volume *Women's Health Advocacy: Rhetorical Ingenuity for the Twenty-First Century,* and coeditor of the *Rhetoric of Health and Medicine* journal.

Elizabeth Chilbert Powers is an Associate Professor of English and the Director of the Writing Center at the University of Maine at Augusta, where she teachers first-year writing, tutoring pedagogy, rhetoric of protest, and digital writing and rhetoric. Her research interests include rhetorics of space and place, digital communication, and writing center studies. Previously, she has published scholarly work in *WLN: A Journal of Writing Center Scholarship, Praxis: A Writing Center Journal,* the *Journal of Florida Studies,* and with Computers and Composition Digital Press.

Krista Speicher Sarraf is a PhD candidate in Composition and Applied Linguistics at Indiana University of Pennsylvania; while writing her contribution to this collection, she served as the graduate assistant director of the Kathleen Jones White Writing Center. Her research focuses on creativity, technical and professional writing, writing centers, digital writing, and trauma, and her poems on the theme of trauma can be found in *The Dandelion Review* and *Rogue Agent*. Krista earned a master's degree in English from James Madison University and a bachelor's degree in English and Art History from Randolph-Macon College.

Kellie Sharp-Hoskins is an Associate Professor in the Department of English at New Mexico State University, where she teaches courses in rhetorical theory and writing studies and is currently working on a book project on rhetorical debt(s). Her work has appeared in *JAC*, *Rhetoric Review*, and *Enculturation*, as well as *Authorship Contested* (Routledge 2015) and *Writing for Engagement* (Lexington 2018); she also coedited *Kenneth Burke + Posthumanism* with Chris Mays and Nathaniel A. Rivers (Penn State University Press 2017).

Ellen Skirvin received a Master of Fine Arts degree in fiction writing from West Virginia University, where she taught a variety of English courses. She also worked as a Teaching Assistant for a course inside a Pennsylvania prison through the Inside-Out Program. She continues to teach college composition, rhetoric, and writing courses. Her fiction appears in *The Baltimore Review* and the *Anthology of Appalachian Writers Volume XI*.

Thomas Sura is an Associate Professor and the Director of College Writing at Hope College. His work focuses on curriculum and faculty development within writing programs including teaching research, service learning, and inclusion. He teaches courses on introductory writing, teaching writing, and rhetoric.

James Zimmerman started out as a reporter, moved into the cable TV industry, and eventually taught technical writing at The Ohio State University while earning his PhD. As a writing instructor, he worked at Case Western Reserve University, Stockton University, and West Virginia University before helping to create the School of Writing, Rhetoric and Technical Communication at James Madison University.